Understanding and Measuring Social Capital

A Multidisciplinary Tool for Practitioners

Christiaan Grootaert and Thierry van Bastelaer

Editors

THE WORLD BANK
Washington, D.C.

© 2002 The International Bank for Reconstruction
and Development/ THE WORLD BANK
1818 H Street, N.W.
Washington, D.C. 20433, USA

Cover photograph from Grameen Bank, copyright Grameen Bank.

ISBN 0-8213-5068-4

Library of Congress Cataloging-in-Publication Data has been applied for.

Contents

Figure

Foreword

The importance of social capital for sustainable development is well recognized by now. Anthropologists, sociologists, political scientists, and economists have in their own ways demonstrated the critical role of institutions, networks, and their supporting norms and values for the success of development interventions. The Social Capital Initiative at the World Bank has endeavored to contribute to this understanding by focusing on how to measure social capital and its impact. The Social Capital Assessment Tool presented in this book is one of the important products of this Initiative.

The value of the tool goes well beyond its role as a measurement device. Building social capital is a core element in the empowerment pillar of the poverty reduction strategy put forth by the *World Development Report 2000/2001*. In this context, the World Bank has begun to support direct investments in social capital in countries in Africa, Eastern Europe, and Latin America. It is critical that we know how to evaluate the outcomes of these efforts. Is sustainable social capital being created, and what project components make the critical contributions to that outcome? This book presents a unique opportunity to have a monitoring and evaluation tool available at the outset of such an investment program.

The Social Capital Assessment Tool draws on a rich, multidisciplinary empirical experience, and its application can provide project managers with valuable baseline and monitoring information about social capital in its different dimensions. I hope that this book will facilitate this application and in that way contribute to improving our knowledge of how to invest effectively in social capital.

Steen Lau Jorgensen
Director
Social Development Department

SOCIAL CAPITAL INITIATIVE

Acknowledgments

We would like to express our thanks to all the researchers who participated in the Social Capital Initiative. Their successful completion of the studies of the Initiative has produced a unique body of evidence on the importance of social capital for economic and social development, and has led to a significantly improved ability to measure social capital and its impacts.

We also thank our colleagues on the Social Capital Team for their many contributions: Susan Assaf, Gracie Ochieng, Gi-Taik Oh, Tine Rossing Feldman, and Casper Sorensen.

We acknowledge gratefully the guidance of the Steering Committee and the leadership of Ian Johnson, Vice-President, Environmentally and Socially Sustainable Development, and Steen Jorgensen, Director, Social Development Department. We would like to pay tribute to Ismail Serageldin, whose vision led to the creation of the Social Capital Initiative. We also honor the memory of Mancur Olson, whose ideas and contributions shaped the early phases of the Initiative.

The Social Capital Initiative received generous funding from the government of Denmark.

Christiaan Grootaert
Thierry van Bastelaer

About the Authors

Christiaan Grootaert is Lead Economist in the Social Development Department at the World Bank and Manager of the Social Capital Initiative. His research centers on the measurement and analysis of poverty, risk, and vulnerability; education and labor markets; child labor; and the role of institutions and social capital in development. He has worked in Africa, Asia, the Middle East, and Eastern Europe. He has published numerous articles and is co-author of *Poverty and Social Assistance in Transition Countries*, *The Policy Analysis of Child Labor: A Comparative Study*, and *World Development Report 2000–01: Attacking Poverty*.

Satu Kähkönen is a Senior Economist at the World Bank. Prior to joining the World Bank, she was Associate Director of the Center for Institutional Reform and the Informal Sector (IRIS) at the University of Maryland. In addition to conducting research on institutional aspects of economic development, she has undertaken fieldwork in a number of developing and transition economies. She is the author and co-editor of *A Not-so-dismal Science: A Broader View of Economies and Societies*, *A New Institutional Approach to Economic Development*, and *Institutions, Incentives and Economic Reforms in India*.

Anirudh Krishna teaches at Duke University in the public policy and political science departments. He holds a Ph.D. in government studies from Cornell University and master's degrees in international development and economics from Cornell University and the Delhi School of Economics. Before taking up an academic career, he served for a number of years in the Indian Administrative Service.

Enrique Pantoja is an urban planner and sociologist. He has worked in several international organizations on development policy and programs in Latin America and South Asia, with special focus on urban development, community-driven development, and social risk management. Mr. Pantoja has carried out research related to social capital, identity politics, collective action, and microfinance. He is currently working at the World Bank as Country Officer for Bangladesh and Bhutan.

Catherine Reid is a consultant with experience in participation methodology, training, agriculture, environment, and women's development issues. She has worked on a wide range of projects for the World Bank, the U.S. Agency for International Development (USAID), and the International Center for Research on Women, and has conducted beneficiary assessments and project evaluations in the health, education, and public infrastructure sectors throughout Africa. She was the team leader of an innovative pilot agricultural extension project for women farmers in the Democratic Republic of Congo. Ms. Reid has an M.S. in development management from the School of International Service of American University.

Lawrence F. Salmen is Lead Social Scientist in the Social Development Department of the World Bank. Mr. Salmen has an MBA and a Ph.D. in urban planning from Columbia University. He is the architect of two participatory research approaches used widely at the Bank, beneficiary assessment and participatory poverty assessment, designed to bring the voices of stakeholders into project management and policy formation, respectively. He is the author of *Listen to the People* and numerous articles. Prior to joining the Bank, Mr. Salmen was Vice President of the Cooperative Housing Foundation and Director of Research and Evaluation at the Inter-American Foundation.

Elizabeth Shrader is an international development consultant specializing in gender violence, civil society strengthening, and reproductive health. She holds a master's degree in public health from the University of California at Los Angeles. Ms. Shrader has lived and worked throughout the Americas.

Thierry van Bastelaer is Director of the Integrated Financial Services Team at the IRIS Center at the University of Maryland, and Study Coordinator for the Social Capital Initiative. After receiving his Ph.D. in economics from the University of Maryland, he worked on private sector policy reform, legal and regulatory reform for microfinance, policy priorities for electronic commerce, small enterprise development, and corruption. His published research has focused on the political economy of commodity pricing, social capital, and microfinance.

1

Social Capital:
From Definition to Measurement

Christiaan Grootaert and Thierry van Bastelaer

Particular villages on the Indonesian island of Java build and maintain complex water delivery systems that require collaboration and coordination, while other villages rely on simple individual wells.

Residents in apparently similar Tanzanian villages enjoy very different levels of income due to differences in their abilities to engage in collective action.

Households in Russia rely on informal networks to gain access to health services, housing, education, and income security.

Some neighborhoods of Dhaka organize for local trash collection, while others allow garbage to accumulate on the streets.

Hutu militias rely on fast networks of information and high levels of mutual trust to carry out a terrifyingly efficient genocide in Rwanda.

Despite their geographical and sectoral diversity, these five examples have something in common: they all testify to the ability of social structures and underlying attitudes to increase the efficiency of collective action.[1] In one form or another, these examples demonstrate the critical role of social interaction, trust, and reciprocity, as elements of social capital, in producing collective outcomes, both beneficial and harmful.

Readers of this book most likely can think of their own personal examples of the impact of social capital on the development activities they engage in or observe. Development practitioners who have witnessed social capital forces at work in their field programs are looking for common lessons from different areas and sectors. Academicians are searching for innovative tools with which to measure and analyze this new socioeconomic element. And governments and donor organizations are hoping to find ways to identify the social settings in which their scarce funds will be used most productively.

Social capital is assuming an increasingly important role in the World Bank's poverty reduction strategy. The *World Development Report*

2000/2001 identifies three pillars to that strategy: promoting opportunity, facilitating empowerment, and enhancing security. Building social capital is at the core of the empowerment agenda, together with promoting pro-poor institutional reform and removing social barriers. However, social capital is also a critical asset for creating opportunities that enhance well-being and for achieving greater security and reduced vulnerability (World Bank 2001).

This book, which is based on the results of the Social Capital Initiative at the World Bank, aims to provide concepts, measurement tools, and literature reviews in a form readily usable by public and private actors interested in the nature and impact of social capital.[2] The book discusses the respective value of quantitative and qualitative approaches to the analysis of social capital and provides specific examples of research based on these two approaches. It presents new field-tested tools designed to measure social capital in urban and rural settings, along with the questionnaires and interview guides to apply these instruments. Finally, it reviews how the concept of social capital has been used in important areas of economic development.

The Search for a Definition of Social Capital

Research on social capital is relatively recent. Although the concept in its current form can be traced to the first half of the 20th century, and early applications to the 19th century, only in the last 20 years has it captured the attention of practitioners and academicians from different backgrounds.[3]

Not surprisingly, the lack of an agreed-upon and established definition of social capital, combined with its multidisciplinary appeal, has led to the spontaneous growth of different interpretations of the concept. The resulting definitions, which fortunately are more often complementary than contradictory, have been used in a growing number of research projects and field activities to try to capture the essence and development potential of the concept. It is perhaps a testimony to the seriousness of these activities that the lack of agreement on a precise definition of social capital has not inhibited empirical and applied work. By clearly delineating the concept they are using and developing methodologies adapted to it, most researchers have shown that solid and replicable results regarding the impact of social capital on development can be produced without a prerequisite fieldwide agreement on a specific definition.

This lack of agreement, and the reluctance to impose a narrow definition on a still-evolving conceptual debate, has led us to define social capital broadly as the *institutions, relationships, attitudes, and values that govern interactions among people and contribute to economic and social development.*[4]

The Forms and Scope of Social Capital

The broad general definition implicitly distinguishes two elements, or forms, of social capital. The first, which Uphoff (2000) called "structural social capital," refers to relatively objective and externally observable social structures, such as networks, associations, and institutions, and the rules and procedures they embody. Athletic and musical groups, water user committees, and neighborhood associations are all examples of this form of social capital. The second form, known as "cognitive social capital," comprises more subjective and intangible elements such as generally accepted attitudes and norms of behavior, shared values, reciprocity, and trust.

Although these two forms of social capital are mutually reinforcing, one can exist without the other. Government-mandated organizations represent structural social capital in which the cognitive element is not necessarily present. Similarly, many relations of mutual trust persist without being formalized in organizations. This description of social capital according to its forms has proven quite useful as a basis for empirical analysis.[5]

A second distinction that allows researchers to isolate the elements of social capital is based on its scope, or the breadth of its unit of observation. Social capital can be observed at the micro level, in the form of horizontal networks of individuals and households and the associated norms and values that underlie these networks. The choral groups highlighted by Robert Putnam in his 1993 study of civic associations in Italy are rapidly becoming a favorite example of this unit of observation, in large part due to the impact of Putnam's study.

The meso level of observation, which captures horizontal and vertical relations among groups (in other words, at a level situated between individuals and society as a whole) has been illustrated by regional groupings of local associations, such as the Andean poor people's organizations described by Bebbington and Carroll (2000).

Finally, in the broader use of the concept, social capital can be observed at the macro level, in the form of the institutional and political environment that serves as a backdrop for all economic and social activity, and the quality of the governance arrangements. These elements, which were the focus of inquiries by Olson (1982) and North (1990) into the sources of development and growth, put the concept of social capital within the realm of institutional economics, which posits that the quality of incentives and institutions (such as the rule of law, the judicial system, or the quality of contract enforcement) is a major determinant of economic growth.

The discussion of social capital according to its forms and scope is illustrated in figure 1.1, where specific concepts of structural and cognitive social capital are presented along a continuum from the micro to the macro dimensions. The breadth of the concept of social capital, as illustrated by figure 1.1, has been seen as a sign of both strength and weakness of the conceptual debate so far.

The strength of such a broad concept is that the inclusion of micro, meso, and macro levels of social capital allows for important effects of complementarity and substitution between the three levels. These various levels of social capital can complement each other, as when national institutions provide an enabling environment in which local associations can develop. However, local forms of social capital can develop as a result of both "good" and "bad" government. Tendler's 1997 study of decentralization in Brazil, for example, shows how well-functioning government at the central level affects the success of local programs. Similarly, Skocpol (1995) shows that over time in the United States, local groups have benefited from the strength of state institutions. Conversely, informal networks can be created to respond to a dysfunctional state, as happened in Russia (Rose 1998). In turn, micro- and meso-level social capital can contribute to either improved or weakened functioning of the state. On the positive side, local associations can sustain regional and national institutions and enhance their legitimacy and stability. On the negative side, excessive ethnic identification in local associations can impede successful policies or even lead to violence (Bates 1999, Colletta and Cullen 2000).

Figure 1.1 The Forms and Scope of Social Capital

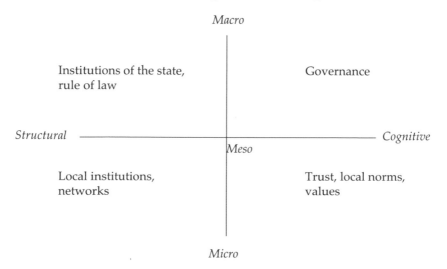

A certain level of substitution is also present among the levels of social capital. For example, communities in developing countries often rely on social pressure and reputation to enforce agreements between individuals or groups. When institutional development strengthens the rule of law and the court system, local informal arrangements for dispute resolution become less relevant and may lead to the weakening of the social ties that supported them. An exclusively micro-level focus on this transformation may exaggerate its impact on social capital by ignoring the positive effects of a stronger rule of law on society as a whole. As expressed by Stiglitz (2000, p. 65), "[a]s the modern capitalist state matures, representative forms of governance with a clear hierarchical structure and a system of laws, rules, and regulations enforced by traditions replace the 'community' as the guardian of social, business, and personal contracts." Hence a concept of social capital that encompasses the micro, meso, and macro dimensions will be better able to capture the counterbalancing effects of structures and attitudes at all levels of society.

The potential weakness of using such a comprehensive concept of social capital in research and development programs is that it may be too broad to draw specific conclusions about the role of attitudes, behaviors, or structures. In other words, by trying to be a catch-all concept, social capital may end up capturing nothing. Our experience with the Social Capital Initiative suggests, however, that when cautious researchers develop methodologies and indicators that match the specific concept that they choose, they can produce solid and verifiable results. Although the empirical studies of the Social Capital Initiative examine different forms and levels of social capital, covering all quadrants of figure 1.1, their choice of rigorous research methodologies—whether quantitative or qualitative—has helped ensure relevant and analytically focused results.[6]

Interdisciplinary Concepts

The definition and classification of social capital given above parallels other conceptual attempts from a variety of disciplines of social sciences. For example, as synthesized by Woolcock and Narayan (2000), the sociological literature on social capital has produced a different but compatible categorization of social capital.[7] This approach includes four categories, which largely overlap those in figure 1.1.

The *communitarian* perspective describes social capital in terms of local organizations and groups, such as those that make up the micro/structural quadrant of figure 1.1, with a focus on productive social capital. Although this approach has helped focus the attention of development practitioners on the role of social relations in the fight against poverty, it is not designed to capture the detrimental aspects of social capital (such as sectarian interest groups, crime syndicates, or ethnic mobs). It also ignores the fact that a large number of local organizations, in itself, can be of little use for development if the groups lack external links and influence or if these structures are not complemented with strong cognitive elements, such as common values, norms, and mutual trust.

The *networks* view encompasses relationships between and within horizontal and vertical associations, and as such injects a meso element in this largely structural category. This view has led to the "bridging/bonding" dichotomy, which distinguishes intercommunity from intracommunity ties.[8] This perspective also takes into account productive consequences as well as detrimental consequences of social capital. In particular, it draws attention to the benefits that social capital can provide to members of a community, as well as to the costs of nonconformist behavior. Similarly, this approach recognizes that while social capital can unite the members of a community, it often does so at the cost of excluding nonmembers, as is, for example, the case with sects.

The *institutional* view posits that the political, legal, and institutional environments are the main determinants of the strength of community networks. This approach reflects the influence of works by Olson (1982) and North (1990), in that it suggests that the ability of social groups to act in their collective interest is affected by the quality of overarching formal institutions. Reliable, transparent, and predictable operations of the state, low levels of corruption, an independent judiciary, and strongly enforced property rights are but a few of the attributes of societies in which individual and collective initiatives can be successful. As such, this approach closely echoes the macro scope of social capital illustrated in the top half of figure 1.1.

Finally, the *synergy* view aims to integrate the micro, meso, and macro concerns of the networks and institutional approaches, in effect covering all four quadrants of figure 1.1. Based on the assumption that none of the development actors (states, businesses, and communities) have access on their own to the resources necessary to create sustainable and equitable growth, this approach focuses on the relationships between and within governments and civil society.[9]

The similarities and overlaps between the two sets of definitions in the above discussion underscore the unique multidisciplinary aspects of social capital research. Although the relative novelty of the concept manifests itself through a healthy proliferation of definitions, most of them fall within the boundaries described above.[10]

Rigorous Economic Terminology or Value as an Interdisciplinary Tool?

Because noneconomists are usually credited with coining the term *social capital*, it should probably not come as a surprise that many economists feel that the use of the word *capital* to describe the concepts discussed here is not consistent with the use of the term in traditional economic theory.

Social capital shares a number of features with the more traditional forms of capital. For example, social capital, like physical capital, accumulates as a stock that produces a stream of benefits (in the form of information sharing, and collective decisionmaking and action, as described below). Like physical capital, this stock requires an initial investment and regular maintenance, in the form of repeated social interaction or trust-building behavior. Social capital can take years to build and is more easily destroyed than built or rebuilt.

Social capital also exhibits several features that set it apart from physical and human capital. First, and by definition, social capital, unlike human capital, cannot be built individually. Second, unlike physical capital (but like human capital), the stock of social capital does not decrease—and can actually increase—as a result of its use. As Ostrom (2000, p. 179) points out, "social capital does not wear out with use but rather with disuse."

On the basis of these and other similar concerns, respected economists have expressed serious misgivings about the use of the term *capital* to describe the concepts discussed in these pages, although they do not question their importance for development. Arrow (2000, p. 4), for example, has indeed urged the abandonment of the concept of social capital, largely on the grounds that it does not meet the definition of capital used by economists, in particular the aspect of "deliberate sacrifice in the present for future benefit." For his part, Solow (2000, p. 7) suggests that the difficulties in the measurement of this capital as "a cumulation of past flows of investment, with past flows of depreciation netted out" fundamentally invalidates the underlying concept. As economists, we are sympathetic to the concern for terminological rigor that undergirds these arguments. We are also aware, however, of the unique opportunities for interdisciplinary research and development activities that are opened by the use of a common—if maybe incompletely focused—term by sociologists, economists, anthropologists, practitioners, and others. As Woolcock (2001, p. 15) puts it, "one of the primary benefits of the idea of social capital is that it is allowing scholars, policy makers and practitioners from different disciplines to enjoy an unprecedented level of cooperation and dialogue." In short, the unique horizons opened by this interdisciplinary collaboration may well outweigh, for now, the benefits of a more rigorous economic definition.

How Does Social Capital Affect Economic Development?

Since it first entered conceptual and empirical debates, social capital has captured the imagination of development researchers and practitioners as a particularly promising tool for alleviating poverty. Indeed, because social capital is often the only asset that the poor have access to, development programs that build on it have rapidly become a priority for donors and governments.

Social capital affects economic development mainly by facilitating transactions among individuals, households, and groups in developing countries. This effect can take three forms. First, participation by individuals in social networks increases the availability of information and lowers its cost. This information, especially if it relates to such matters as crop prices, location of new markets, sources of credit, or treatments for livestock disease, can play a critical role in increasing the returns from agriculture and trading. For example, research under the Social Capital Initiative shows that better-connected Malagasy traders have access to more accurate information on prices and credibility of clients, resulting in higher profit margins (Fafchamps and Minten 1999). Lack of access to credit by the poor in developing countries is largely a consequence of limited information about potential borrowers' credit risk, loan use, and truthfulness in reporting repayment ability. Several informal arrangements, drawing on social capital between participants and within their communities, have been developed to address these information imperfections. These arrangements, which include rotating credit and savings associations, money lenders, trade credit, and microfinance, are described in annex 2.

Second, participation in local networks and attitudes of mutual trust make it easier for any group to reach collective decisions and implement collective action. Since property rights are often imperfectly developed and applied in developing countries, collective decisions on how to manage common resources are critical to maximizing their use and yield. Krishna and Uphoff (1999) describe how farmer groups in the Indian state of Rajasthan use local structural and cognitive social capital to build consensus on the use of watershed land, resulting in more productive use of these lands, as well as improved outcomes for broader development goals. Managing collective action is also central to securing access to water and sanitation services, such as irrigation, drinking water, and urban waste disposal. Annex 3 discusses the literature that describes how social capital can help in the provision and maintenance of these essential services.

Finally, networks and attitudes reduce opportunistic behavior by community members. In settings where a certain behavior is expected from individuals for the benefit of the group, social pressures and fear of exclusion can induce these individuals to provide the expected behavior. For example, farmers have resorted to these networks and attitudes and exerted mutual pressures to prevent individual diversion of irrigation water. This issue is also discussed at length in annex 3.

Approaches to Measuring Social Capital

The main goal of this volume is to discuss the merits of various approaches to measuring and analyzing the nature and amount of social capital at the micro and meso levels and to provide field-tested measurement tools to do so. Growing empirical evidence indicates that social capital is best measured using a variety of qualitative and quantitative instruments. Indeed, the concept cannot be comprehended strictly within the economic paradigm, using quantitative methods. Neither can it be investigated solely through anthropological or sociological case studies. A combination of both methods can be successful at isolating the role of social capital in increasing incomes and facilitating access to services.[11]

The Social Capital Assessment Tool (SOCAT), described and made available in this book, integrates quantitative and qualitative instruments. SOCAT's community and organizational profiles each contain a quantitative and a qualitative component, while the household survey is a quantitative instrument. For collecting the data, structured questionnaires are used along with open-ended participatory methods. As a result, the SOCAT data can support a wide range of quantitative and qualitative analyses. This book provides examples of each type of analysis.

Ideally the measurement of social capital should capture all four quadrants of figure 1.1, but in practice most experience has been gained with measurement at the micro and meso levels. The SOCAT is geared toward measuring social capital at these levels. Three units of data collection and analysis are considered: the household, the community, and the organization. Thus, the SOCAT instruments consist of a household survey, a community questionnaire and interview guide, and an organizational interview guide and scoresheet. Each of these instruments attempts to capture the relevant structural and cognitive dimensions of social capital. The importance of obtaining information on both these dimensions has been well established in the empirical literature and is discussed at length in chapter 2. In terms of the conceptual framework represented in figure 1.1, the Social Capital Assessment Tool covers the entire lower half of the diagram.

The data derived from the SOCAT can be analyzed on their own, when the objective is to inventory existing social capital, to map the distribution of social capital across areas or socioeconomic groups, or to gain a better understanding of the functioning of key organizations. More often than not, the objective will also be to relate social capital to outcome variables such as household or community welfare, access to services, or general development indicators. In such cases, the SOCAT questionnaires need to be combined with other survey modules capturing income or expenditures and use of services. Indeed, most of the analytic examples in this book come from studies that combined a social capital measurement instrument with other surveys. Most countries have experience with surveys that capture income and expenditures data, labor market participation, or integrated socioeconomic information. The World Bank has several prototype surveys available, such as the Living Standards Measurement Surveys (Grosh and Glewwe 2000) and the Social Dimensions of Adjustment Integrated Surveys (Delaine and others 1991), which have been used extensively in many countries. The Local Level Institutions Study, from which several examples in chapter 3 are drawn, combined a social capital instrument with a household expenditure module (World Bank 1998).

The SOCAT is a flexible instrument that can be implemented at the national level and at the project level. At the national level, an application in conjunction with a Living Standards Measurement Survey or household income or expenditure survey would yield a data base suitable for studying the relation between social capital and poverty or for analyzing the impact of policy reform on social capital. At the project level, an early application of the SOCAT can provide baseline information on the different dimensions of social capital while the project is still in the development stage. This is valuable both for projects that aim to stimulate social capital directly and for sectoral interventions (agriculture, education, water and sanitation, infrastructure, and the like) that need to draw on local social capital resources for successful implementation. Repeat application throughout the project cycle can be used for monitoring and evaluating the effect of the project on social capital.

Structure of the Book

In chapter 2, Anirudh Krishna and Elizabeth Shrader explore the relative advantages of different approaches to measuring social capital, argue the importance of locally and contextually relevant measurement tools, and discuss how to integrate qualitative and quantitative methodologies in developing these tools. This is followed by a detailed description of the Social Capital Assessment Tool. The community profile integrates participatory qualitative methods with a structured community survey to identify features associated with social capital within a specific community. The household survey explores participation in local organizations and attitudes of trust and cooperation among individuals and households. Finally, the organizational profile examines the relationships and networks that exist among formal and informal organizations in the community. Together, these three instruments constitute a tool for multisectoral and multidisciplinary application in diverse communities and countries. The tool was developed on the basis of a large set of existing research instruments and has been successfully pilot-tested in Panama and India.

In chapter 3, Christiaan Grootaert discusses basic quantitative methods for analyzing the data collected by the SOCAT and similar measurement instruments. Three types of proxy indicators for social capital are recommended: membership in local associations and networks (structural social capital), indicators of trust and adherence to norms (cognitive social capital), and indicators of collective action (an output measure). Each of these indicators can be cross-tabulated with relevant socioeconomic data to provide a picture of the distribution of social capital. Various methods are discussed to aggregate the data through suitable rescaling and factor analysis. Multivariate models can be estimated to assess the contribution made by social capital to household welfare (including its monetary and nonmonetary dimensions) and the management of risk by households through better access to credit. The link between social capital and poverty receives special attention, especially the question of whether the investment that poor households make in social capital provides an adequate return and helps them escape from poverty. Finally, the chapter draws attention to critical methodological issues, such as the possible endogeneity of social capital in multivariate analysis, and suggests various solutions.

Shifting focus to the qualitative measurement of social capital, the second part of the book suggests that this approach to measurement is best implemented through case studies. Two specific examples are presented: an agricultural sector case study from Africa, and an industrial sector case study from Asia.

The case study presented in chapter 4 by Catherine Reid and Lawrence Salmen posits that trust is a key determinant of the success of agricultural extension in Mali. The study identifies three equally important aspects of trust: trust among farmers, trust between farmers and extension workers, and the relationship between extension workers and their national organizations. Using the beneficiary assessment methodology, which capitalizes on the establishment of trust for deriving insights, the study documents the importance of preexisting social cohesion. In that context, women and their associations are found to be consistent diffusers of information and technology, able to tap into and generate social capital. The most important practical finding of the case study is that extension workers and development agencies in general need to gain an operationally relevant understanding of the social and institutional fabric in places where they work.

In chapter 5, Enrique Pantoja describes a qualitative case study that explores the role of social capital in the rehabilitation of coal mining areas in the Indian state of Orissa. Through the use of interviews and focus groups, the author finds that different forms of social capital (family and kinship, intracommunity, and intercommunity) interact to produce a mixture of positive and negative results for the rehabilitation process. The same strong ties that help members of a group work together can also be used to exclude other community members from the benefits of collective action. Although mutual trust exists in abundance around the mining sites, it is highly fragmented by gender, caste, and class, and results in closed groups with high entry costs and a considerable lack of horizontal links. The practical conclusion of the chapter is that lack of social cohesion at the village level can be a major impediment to community involvement in the rehabilitation process and to community-based development in general.

The full text of the SOCAT—the community profile interview guide and questionnaire, the household survey questionnaire, and the organizational profile interview guides and scoresheet—is reproduced in annex 1 as well as on the CD-ROM enclosed with this book. As mentioned above, annexes 2 and 3 discuss how social capital facilitates the delivery of services such as credit, and water and sanitation.

Notes

1.   These examples are excerpted from the following papers, respectively: Isham and Kähkönen (1999); Narayan and Pritchett (1999); Rose (1999); Pargal, Huq, and Gilligan (1999); and Colletta and Cullen (2000).

2.   The Social Capital Initiative, a large-scale research project funded by the government of Denmark, produced an extensive body of original data on social capital. It drew on these data to provide strong empirical evidence of the pervasive role of social capital in a wide variety of development processes and projects. For a description of the Initiative and its main findings, see Grootaert and van Bastelaer (2001).

3.   Woolcock (1998) identifies Lyda J. Hanifan, superintendent of schools in West Virginia in 1916, as the first promoter of the concept of social capital, a concept that was resurrected in the 1950s and 1960s. The concept gained new attention in the early 1990s (Putnam 1993). Woolcock also describes the conditions that led to the

"first deliberate attempt to establish financial institutions with the poor in developing economies on the basis of their social, rather than their material, resources" (p. 95), referring to the "People's Banks," as the credit cooperatives that Frederick Raiffeisen created in mid-19th-century Germany were collectively called.

4. Grootaert and van Bastelaer (2001, p. 4). The last elements of this definition can be interpreted broadly to allow for the existence of damaging or harmful social capital.

5. See Krishna and Uphoff (1999) for a particularly persuasive empirical use of this classification.

6. See Grootaert and van Bastelaer (2002) for a selection of these studies.

7. For an authoritative review and discussion of the sociological and development literature on social capital, see Woolcock (1998).

8. Although the relevance of the bridging/bonding distinction is somewhat limited by the malleable and dynamic nature of the concept of community (at what point does successful bridging social capital turn into bonding social capital?), it has been a useful basis for the discussion of sectarian interest groups and exclusion mechanisms.

9. Isham and Kähkönen (1999) present an empirical study of the importance of "coproduction" between local authorities and communities in designing and maintaining water delivery systems on the island of Java.

10. A small number of definitions of social capital differ from the general approach described here by focusing on a subset of the elements discussed above. For example, Robison, Schmid, and Siles (forthcoming) define social capital as "a person's or group's sympathy toward another person or group that may produce a potential benefit, advantage, and preferential treatment for another person or group of persons beyond that expected in an exchange relationship." Accordingly, their definition roughly corresponds to the micro/cognitive quadrant of figure 1.1, with an added unilateral feature.

11. See Grootaert and van Bastelaer (2002) for a collection of empirical studies that draw on both quantitative and qualitative analytical methods.

References

Arrow, Kenneth. 2000. "Observations on Social Capital." In Partha Dasgupta and Ismail Serageldin, eds., Social Capital: A Multifaceted Perspective. Washington, D.C.: World Bank.

Bates, Robert. 1999. "Ethnicity, Capital Formation, and Conflict." Social Capital Initiative Working Paper 12. World Bank, Social Development Department, Washington, D.C.

Bebbington, Anthony J., and Thomas F. Carroll. 2000. "Induced Social Capital and Federations of the Rural Poor." Social Capital Initiative

Working Paper 19. World Bank, Social Development Department, Washington, D.C.

Colletta, Nat J., and Michelle L. Cullen. 2000. "The Nexus between Violent Conflict, Social Capital, and Social Cohesion: Case Studies from Cambodia and Rwanda." Social Capital Initiative Working Paper 23. World Bank, Social Development Department, Washington, D.C.

Delaine, Ghislaine, Lionel Demery, Jean-Luc Dubois, Branko Grdjic, Christiaan Grootaert, Christopher Hill, Timothy Marchant, Andrew McKay, Jeffrey Round, and Christopher Scott. 1991. "The Social Dimensions of Adjustment Integrated Survey: A Survey to Measure Poverty and Understand the Effects of Policy Change on Households." Social Dimensions of Adjustment in Sub-Saharan Africa Working Paper 14. World Bank, Africa Region, Washington, D.C.

Fafchamps, Marcel, and Bart Minten. 1999. "Social Capital and the Firm: Evidence from Agricultural Trade." Social Capital Initiative Working Paper 17. World Bank, Social Development Department, Washington, D.C.

Grootaert, Christiaan, and Thierry van Bastelaer. 2001. "Understanding and Measuring Social Capital: A Synthesis and Findings from the Social Capital Initiative." Social Capital Initiative Working Paper 24. World Bank, Social Development Department, Washington, D.C.

————, eds. 2002. The Role of Social Capital in Development: An Empirical Assessment. Cambridge, U.K.: Cambridge University Press.

Grosh, Margaret, and Paul Glewwe, eds. 2000. Designing Household Survey Questionnaires for Developing Countries—Lessons from 15 Years of the Living Standards Measurement Study. Washington, D.C.: World Bank.

Isham, Jonathan, and Satu Kähkönen. 1999. "What Determines the Effectiveness of Community-Based Water Projects? Evidence from Central Java, Indonesia, on Demand Responsiveness, Service Rules, and Social Capital." Social Capital Initiative Working Paper 14. World Bank, Social Development Department, Washington, D.C.

Krishna, Anirudh, and Norman Uphoff. 1999. "Mapping and Measuring Social Capital: A Conceptual and Empirical Study of Collective Action

for Conserving and Developing Watersheds in Rajasthan, India."
Social Capital Initiative Working Paper 13. World Bank, Social
Development Department, Washington, D.C.

Narayan, Deepa, and Lant Pritchett. 1999. "Cents and Sociability:
Household Income and Social Capital in Rural Tanzania." *Economic
Development and Cultural Change* 47 (4): 871–97.

North, Douglass C. 1990. *Institutions, Institutional Change, and Economic
Performance.* New York: Cambridge University Press.

Olson, Mancur. 1982. *The Rise and Decline of Nations: Economic Growth,
Stagflation, and Social Rigidities.* New Haven, Conn.: Yale University
Press.

Ostrom, Elinor. 2000. "Social Capital: A Fad or a Fundamental Concept?"
In Partha Dasgupta and Ismail Serageldin, eds., *Social Capital: A
Multifaceted Perspective.* Washington, D.C.: World Bank.

Pargal, Sheoli, Mainul Huq, and Daniel Gilligan. 1999. "Social Capital in
Solid Waste Management: Evidence from Dhaka, Bangladesh." Social
Capital Initiative Working Paper 16. World Bank, Social Development
Department, Washington, D.C.

Putnam, Robert D., with Robert Leonardi and Raffaela Nanetti. 1993.
Making Democracy Work: Civic Traditions in Modern Italy. Princeton, N.J.:
Princeton University Press.

Robison, Lindon, Allan Schmid, and Marcelo Siles. Forthcoming. "Is
Social Capital Really Capital?" *Review of Social Economy.*

Rose, Richard. 1998. "Getting Things Done in an Anti-Modern Society:
Social Capital Networks in Russia." Social Capital Initiative Working
Paper 6. World Bank, Social Development Department, Washington, D.C.

————. 1999. "What Does Social Capital Add to Individual Welfare?"
Social Capital Initiative Working Paper 15. World Bank, Social
Development Department, Washington, D.C.

Skocpol, Theda. 1995. *Protecting Soldiers and Mothers: The Political Origins
of Social Policy in the United States.* Cambridge, Mass.: Harvard
University Press.

Solow, Robert. 2000. "Notes on Social Capital and Economic Performance." In Partha Dasgupta and Ismail Serageldin, eds., *Social Capital: A Multifaceted Perspective*. Washington, D.C.: World Bank.

Stiglitz, Joseph E. 2000. "Formal and Informal Institutions." In Partha Dasgupta and Ismail Serageldin, eds., *Social Capital: A Multifaceted Perspective*. Washington, D.C.: World Bank.

Tendler, Judith. 1997. *Good Government in the Tropics*. Baltimore, Md.: Johns Hopkins University Press.

Uphoff, Norman. 2000. "Understanding Social Capital: Learning from the Analysis and Experience of Participation." In Partha Dasgupta and Ismail Serageldin, eds., *Social Capital: A Multifaceted Perspective*. Washington, D.C.: World Bank.

Woolcock, Michael. 1998. "Social Capital and Economic Development: Toward a Theoretical Synthesis and Policy Framework." *Theory and Society* 27 (2): 151–208.

———. 2001. "The Place of Social Capital in Understanding Social and Economic Outcomes." *Isuma* 2 (1): 11–17.

Woolcock, Michael, and Deepa Narayan. 2000. "Social Capital: Implications for Development Theory, Research and Policy." *World Bank Research Observer* 15 (2): 225–49.

World Bank. 1998. "The Local Level Institutions Study: Program Description and Prototype Questionnaires." Local Level Institutions Working Paper 2. World Bank, Social Development Department, Washington, D.C.

———. 2001. *World Development Report 2000/2001: Attacking Poverty*. New York: Oxford University Press.

2

The Social Capital Assessment Tool: Design and Implementation

Anirudh Krishna and Elizabeth Shrader

As the concept of social capital has traveled beyond its seminal application in Italy and analysts have extended it to other countries and regions, new and different measurement tools have emerged. These tools differ substantially from those originally developed by Putnam (1993). This raises a key question: Must the measurement of social capital necessarily vary by national, regional, or ethnic setting? Can some common method of measurement be developed that can be applied uniformly across different countries, regions, and cultures of the world?

To some extent, the existence of different measurement concepts is justified because empirical correlates of social capital vary from one context to another. Recognizing that context matters, however, does not imply the need to have countless measurement tools unrelated to each other by a unifying concept. The number of useful categories for examining social capital may well remain fairly constant, even as inquiry shifts from one context to another. It would be desirable, therefore, to have a toolkit for measuring social capital that subscribes to a commonly agreed definition of social capital but that is broad enough and flexible enough to be applied in diverse cultural contexts.

As discussed in chapter 1, the broad definition of social capital used in this volume embraces micro (individual), meso (community), and macro (national) phenomena. Examples of social capital at work have been documented at all three levels. The tool proposed in this chapter focuses mainly on social capital at the micro and meso levels.

As defined in this book, the social capital of a society consists of the institutions, relationships, attitudes, and values that govern interactions among people and contribute to economic and social development. Two sets of empirical questions emerge from this definition:

- What types of networks are most commonly associated with social trust and with norms that promote coordination and cooperation for mutual benefit? Do all networks or only some types of networks need to be aggregated into a measure of social capital? Should the same network types be considered in all settings, or should there be some variation across cultural contexts?

- Can norms and trust be assessed directly? Can they be graded in terms of their effectiveness for facilitating mutually beneficial collective action? What instruments enable a researcher to identify and assess these measures across diverse cultural contexts?

Empirical studies of social capital differ in the manner in which they have addressed these issues. While some studies have assessed social capital solely in terms of network density, others have relied purely on a measure of trust. Yet other studies combine a measure of network density with some proxies for evaluating the strength of the relevant norms. We argue that neither an exclusively networks-based nor an entirely norms-dependent measure suffices for scaling social capital.

Sociologists generally agree that the shape of any network—horizontal or vertical, homogeneous or heterogeneous, formal or informal—does not by itself indicate much about the nature of human relationships within that network. What sorts of norms are related to which type of networks cannot be assumed a priori but must be investigated independently for each context. Granovetter (1985, p. 487) offers an oft-quoted view:

> Actors do not behave or decide as atoms outside a social context, nor do they adhere slavishly to a script written for them by the particular intersection of social categories that they happen to occupy. . . . While social relations may indeed often be a necessary condition for trust and trustworthiness, they are not sufficient to guarantee these and may even provide occasion and means for malfeasance and conflict on a scale larger than in their absence.

Social capital in one context can be unsocial capital in another. Organized religion that supports peace in one context becomes a forum for armed militancy in another. Unions that may promote coordination and cooperation with the state in a corporatist context can wage bitter confrontation in another context. It is hardly surprising, therefore, that analysts studying social capital in different contexts have found different network forms to be associated with social capital formation. The horizontal or vertical nature of an organization may matter a lot in Italy but little in Panama or rural north India. Heterogeneous organization may be more valuable in some countries and less so in others. Context matters, because norms of behavior associated with different network types are not constant across cultures. Different types of networks are associated with cooperative norms in different cultural contexts.

Minimum Requirements for an Acceptable Measurement Tool

A tool for measuring social capital must recognize and be sensitive to cultural variation, but it must also provide a common conceptual framework that helps unify the different dimensions of social capital. Flexibility is essential, but it must be contained within what Peters and Waterman (1982) have referred to in a different context as a "loose-tight" framework: loose, or flexible, in the details but tight on the essential concepts. The types of organizations to be included in the measure of social capital can be determined through careful examination of the existing local structure of organizations, suggesting that organizational-level analysis should accompany assessments of social capital among communities and households. (The organizational profile presented later in this chapter is helpful in this regard.)

Incorporating Different Dimensions of Social Capital

Social capital was originally defined and measured in terms that related entirely to the density of horizontally organized social networks. Subsequent investigations have increased the complexity of the concept by adding a number of dimensions.

STRUCTURAL VERSUS COGNITIVE SOCIAL CAPITAL. The structural elements of social capital (relating to networks, roles, rules, and precedents) must be assessed separately from cognitive elements (relating to norms, values, attitudes, and beliefs). While cognitive elements predispose people toward mutually beneficial collective action, structural elements of social capital facilitate such action (Krishna 2000, Uphoff 1999). Both structural and cognitive dimensions matter; they must be combined to represent the aggregate potential for mutually beneficial collective action that exists within a community.

As Hechter (1987) has trenchantly argued, group solidarity is difficult to verify with reference to norms alone. By the same token, the type of network is not a reliable indicator of the type of human interaction occurring within a group: network types that support cooperation and coordination in one context may promote competition and conflict in another. Ethnographic examination by Eastis (1998) of two otherwise similar choir groups concludes that mere membership in one or another category of voluntary association is too crude a measure to capture empirically the complex experience of membership. Members of both choir groups reported very extensive participation, yet came away from the experience with a rather different mix of human, cultural, or social capital. Such variation owes much to the characteristics of the groups and the structure of relations between their members—not to participation per se nor to the types of groups per se. From his study of groups and associations in contemporary Russia, Rose (1998) concludes that trust is not associated with all types of networks, even those that are horizontally organized or that have a heterogeneous group of members. In the Russian context, some (but not all) informal networks are associated with trust and trustworthy behavior.

To understand the separate importance of norms and networks, consider the following example. Someone's house or barn burns down at night. Neighbors come together the next day to help the family rebuild the structure. This kind of collective action can be found not just in developing country villages, but also among diverse social groups in all parts of the world. What is interesting to examine are the factors that lead people to behave in this way.

Two alternative scenarios can be envisioned. It is possible that there is well-recognized leadership within the neighborhood. Receiving information about the unfortunate event, community leaders direct villagers to collect at the site, bringing along whatever tools and building material they may possess. Alternatively, no clear roles for organizing such action exist in the community. Motivated instead by norms of what is appropriate behavior, people collect spontaneously to assist with the rebuilding.[1] Thus the same cooperative outcome can come about in two different ways. In the first case, the structural dimensions of social capital (roles, rules, networks) facilitate cooperation and coordinated action. In the second case, collective action is based on norms and beliefs—that is, it has a cognitive, not a structural, basis. Considering only networks neglects mutually beneficial collective action that has a cognitive basis. Considering only norms underestimates social capital by ignoring its structural dimensions. To be valid and accurate, a tool for measuring social capital must account for both its structural and its cognitive dimensions. Both norms and networks must be assessed, and the measure of social capital must represent the aggregate potential for mutually beneficial collective action.

Specific dimensions have also been added to the concept of structural social capital, in the form of the following distinctions among types of organizations:

HORIZONTAL VERSUS VERTICAL ORGANIZATIONS. In his seminal 1993 work, Putnam argues that horizontally organized networks contribute to social capital formation, while vertical relationships inhibit it. Later analysts of social capital have challenged Putnam's preference for horizontal over vertical and hierarchical organizations. The Boy Scouts (Berman 1997, p. 567), for example, are a hierarchically organized group, yet they seem to be favorably regarded by most social capital analysts. Empirical investigations carried out in a variety of countries indicate that horizontal networks do not necessarily reveal the presence of greater social capital. Studying variations in economic growth in 29 countries, Knack and Keefer (1997) conclude that trust and civic cooperation are associated with stronger economic performance but that associational activity is unrelated to trust.

HETEROGENEOUS VERSUS HOMOGENEOUS ORGANIZATIONS. That the internal heterogeneity of groups matters for both social capital and economic welfare has been independently verified by Narayan and Pritchett's 1999 study of Tanzanian villages and Grootaert's 1999 study of Indonesian villages. In each case, a household-level index of social capital—combining the number of association memberships, the internal heterogeneity of associations, and the span of activities—was found to be positively and consistently related to household economic welfare. Another group of scholars derives the opposite conclusions. Drawing on data gathered from five U.S. cities, Portney and Berry (1997) conclude that compared with social, service, self-help, and issue-based organizations, "participation in neighborhood associations is more strongly associated with a high sense of community" and civic engagement. All else equal, more homogeneous neighborhoods are more likely to have more effective neighborhood associations. What is a researcher to make of these seemingly conflicting views? Stolle (1998) concludes that the type of group matters more in some contexts than in others, suggesting that selecting an appropriate network measure for social capital depends on the country or culture being studied.

FORMAL VERSUS INFORMAL ORGANIZATIONS. Several other issues are also related to selecting appropriate types of organizations. Should one include only formally organized groups, as Putnam does? Or should informal groups also be considered, especially since, as Newton (1992, p. 582) suggests, "the socialization role of creating 'habits of the heart' is more likely to be played . . . by informal groups"? Should only small face-to-face groups be considered, or are large multiregional and multinational organizations also instrumental in promoting coordination and cooperation for mutual benefit (Minkoff 1997, Oliver and Marwell 1988)? Are strong associational ties better than weak ones, or vice versa?

Observing the Appropriate Collective Activities

Social capital exists "in the *relations* among persons" (Coleman 1988, pp. S100–S101); thus only activities that residents in a community carry out collectively rather than individually should be considered for assessing social capital. What these activities are varies from one context to another.

Crop diseases, but not crop harvesting, are usually dealt with collectively in rural north India. House construction is an individual enterprise in Indian villages and a collective one in Somalia (Farah 1992). Investigators comparing social capital among Somali communities should therefore look at networks that build houses. In rural India, however, they must look at social behavior for dealing with crop disease.

Past practice and future expectations of community action are likely to vary considerably across communities. Members of communities that have acted collectively in the past expect that the community will continue to cooperate regularly. These variations in the observance of shared collective norms and practices provide the locus for measuring social capital within any given cultural space.

A tool for measuring social capital must build primarily on those activities that community members consider appropriate for collective execution. What these activities are in any given region can be determined only through on-the-ground investigation of community organization (the community profile presented later is helpful for this purpose).

Integrating Quantitative and Qualitative Methodologies

Increasingly, social science research, including economic research, integrates both quantitative and qualitative methods.[2] Integrating complementary methodologies allows researchers to confirm and corroborate results, elaborate or develop analysis, provide richer detail, and initiate new lines of thinking by studying surprising results or paradoxes (Rossman and Wilson 1985, 1994). Integrating complementary data collection techniques is especially important when trying to analyze a complex and innovative concept such as social capital.

A tool for measuring social capital that integrates both quantitative and qualitative methods is likely to be more useful and reliable than measures based on only one type of research methodology. Coupled with results from validated survey data presented in the form of scaled items, qualitative indicators can provide a deeper understanding of what individuals, households, and communities regard as social capital. Survey data generate a broad overview of the institutional framework in a particular community. Institutional mapping, focus groups, and other qualitative techniques provide a more nuanced understanding of institutional characteristics. Applied together, qualitative and quantitative techniques can provide a more complete and convincing rendering of the local institutional landscape.

Designing the Social Capital Assessment Tool (SOCAT)

The preceding discussion makes clear that a tool for measuring social capital must fulfill the following minimum criteria:

1. It must recognize and be sensitive to cultural variation while at the same time provide a unifying conceptual framework.
2. It must take account of the structural as well as the cognitive dimensions of social capital. Both networks and norms must be assessed to obtain a valid estimate of the aggregate potential for mutually beneficial collective action.
3. It must build primarily on those activities local people consider appropriate for collective execution.
4. It should be constructed using both qualitative and quantitative methods.

These four criteria are not only theoretically valid, they are also helpful in practice for resolving measurement issues. Whether to include only horizontal organizations or both vertical and horizontal organizations can be resolved in terms of the third criterion, for instance. How are mutually beneficial collective activities commonly undertaken in the context being studied? What types of organizations do people use to carry out undertakings valued by the community? Horizontal organizations may be the common carriers of collective action in some settings, but vertical ones may be more appropriate in others. Similarly, heterogeneous organizations may serve valued collective purposes in some cultural contexts, but more homogeneous membership patterns may be associated with cooperative norms in other cultural settings.

The design and field testing of the Social Capital Assessment Tool represents a first step toward the development of a uniform measure of social capital. The tool—described in detail below—accounts for cognitive and structural social capital, integrates qualitative and quantitative measures developed concurrently and iteratively, and is valid and reliable across a wide range of community, household, and institutional contexts. It is applicable at all levels of project design. In the earliest exploratory phase, an abbreviated version of the SOCAT can be used to assess quickly levels of social capital as well as community needs and assets. In the preparation phase, the SOCAT can be used to collect baseline data on norms and networks to determine the extent and types of social capital present in the project area. The flexibility and rapid application of the SOCAT allows for the collection of monitoring data throughout the project cycle, providing quantitative and qualitative supervision benchmarks. Project evaluation will benefit enormously from a full SOCAT conducted upon project completion, ideally comparing the results with data from control communities that did not participate in the project. This information can provide insight regarding project sustainability and the role of social capital in future development interventions.

A key objective of the SOCAT is to contribute to the understanding of how community-, household-, and organization-level measures of social capital interact with other development indicators and thus to assess whether social capital contributes to or erodes economic and social development. Pertinent development indicators—including measures of poverty, education, health, infrastructure, crime and violence, public sector reform, and labor—can be incorporated at all levels of project intervention, including initial preparation, implementation, and evaluation. Associating these development indicators with measures of social capital may begin to explain important, perhaps previously overlooked, aspects of successful and replicable community development.

Structure and Implementation of the SOCAT

The Social Capital Assessment Tool consists of three instruments: the community profile, the household survey, and the organizational profile. These instruments were developed after studying a large set of research instruments applied in more than 25 studies conducted in 15 different countries. The SOCAT was pilot-tested among urban, rural, and indigenous populations in Panama and India, and refined based on the results.[3]

Community Profile

A SOCAT exercise should begin with the administration of the community profile, for several reasons. First, meeting with community members in groups enables the research team to familiarize itself quickly with important community characteristics, which should be known before the other instruments can be applied. Group interviews help establish boundaries for the "community" within which the research will take place. This understanding of community boundaries will be used throughout the exercise for selecting household members to be interviewed and for identifying organizations that will be studied with the help of the organizational profile.

Second, social capital needs to be investigated with reference to activities that are commonly undertaken collectively within the cultural setting being studied. The nature of such activities varies from one culture to another. Group discussions help identify activities that are commonly executed collectively in the community in question.

Third, and perhaps most important, are the intangible benefits that arise as the investigating team and members of the local community come to know each other better in the course of these open discussion sessions. Misgivings are dispelled as community members become familiar with the purposes and proposed activities of the research team. Everyone is welcome to participate at these sessions, which are publicized widely in advance. A diversity of views is represented, and the research team gleans a preliminary sense of the various characteristics of interaction salient for assessing social capital in the community. The community maps, diagrams, and field notes generated from this exercise serve as primary sources of information on organizations and relationships within the community.

Researchers begin the community profiling exercise with an initial open-ended discussion with the community, based on a participatory interview guide. They then administer a standardized structured questionnaire, which will help to compare responses across communities. This questionnaire inventories basic community infrastructure and identifies available resources and development needs and priorities.

OPEN-ENDED COMMUNITY DISCUSSIONS. Before convening a community meeting and administering this instrument, the research team should spend several hours to one full day walking through the community to gain a sense of the special characteristics that might influence fieldwork interactions and logistical planning. Ideally, this community "transect walk" should be guided by a community leader who acts as a kind of gatekeeper of knowledge to facilitate the researchers' access to community-level information. Initial contacts made during this transect walk can serve to identify key informants, establish convenient times and venues for community meetings, and facilitate interactions between community members and researchers.

A convenient public space should be selected as the venue for each group meeting, which may be either spontaneous or planned. Planned meetings involve inviting key informants (or having a key informant invite other key informants). These informants are particularly useful when the viewpoint of a certain demographic group—youth, women, laborers—is of interest. In societies in which divisions based on gender, ethnicity, or some other factor are likely to be important, it is often useful to conduct separate meetings with different subgroups. Two to eight group interviews can be conducted in each community, with a larger number of interviews required in communities that appear to be more deeply divided. Generally, however, at least two group interviews should be carried out with women and men separately. Mixed groups can also be interviewed to assess levels of consensus, but these interviews should be in addition to the gender-based group interviews. Spontaneous interviews take place at any given moment in a public place. These interviews should be in addition to the planned meetings, which should be announced and publicized widely in advance and held at times convenient for large numbers of community members.

Each group interview should have a moderator and two observers. The moderator's role is to facilitate discussion, probe key issues, elicit comments from all participants, and focus the discussion on issues of interest without seeming to interrupt group dynamics. The observers' role is to take notes on the content of the discussion, the group dynamic process, and the composition of the group. Most important, the observers record the substance of the discussion that takes place while the community develops its maps, Venn diagrams, and institutional flowcharts.

Materials needed for each community interview include a copy of the interview guide (on paper or summarized on index cards), pads of notepaper for recording field notes, pens, pencils and pencil sharpeners, flip-chart paper, markers (several colors), colored paper, masking tape, and scissors.

The participatory interview guide, presented in annex 1A, assists the flow of discussion at these group meetings. The guide has six sections:

1. *Definition of community boundaries and identification of community assets.* The group interview begins with a mapping exercise. Setting out large sheets of paper and distributing markers, the facilitator asks the group to draw the geographic boundaries of the community. The assembled group also identifies the community's principal assets, resources, and important local landmarks on the map.[4] This mapping exercise usually generates open discussions, with participants speaking freely about items such as the location of drinking water supplies, roads, and school buildings, and residential patterns. This exercise also opens the way to discussion of other issues.

2. *Discussion of case study of community collective action.* We have found it useful to focus discussions of collective action and solidarity on a specific case in which the community worked collectively to resolve an issue, whether or not the outcome was positive. The facilitator probes a specific instance of collective action undertaken at some time within the past three years.

3. *Discussion of community governance and decisionmaking process.* The community informants identify leaders within the community and describe the processes of leadership selection and community deci-

sionmaking. Facilitators probe specific instances that illustrate these features of community-level social capital.

4. *Identification of local organizations.* Both formal and informal organizations are assessed in terms of accessibility by different community members, involvement of different groups in the community, and extent of inclusion and exclusion. A brief history of each organization is recorded. For the most important organizations, this information will be supplemented later with data collected for the organizational profiles.

5. *Assessment of the relationships between organizations and the community.* This assessment is done by means of a Venn diagram exercise. Organizations are assessed in terms of their contribution to different community purposes and their accessibility by different community members. This Venn diagram exercise is simple to conduct, and it has an immediate visual appeal. The exercise sparked a great deal of interest and lively debate in Panama and India.

6. *Institutional networks.* Another visual exercise, institutional mapping, also serves to spark animated discussions. Functional relationships between pairs of organizations are mapped using a flowchart. All sorts of organizations working within the community are considered, including local government departments, nongovernmental organizations (NGOs), community groups, and other civil society actors.

At first sight, the participatory interview guide may appear to involve long and complex discussions between researchers and community members. In practice, however, during the pilot tests in India and Panama these interviews were usually completed within one to three hours. They generated a great deal of useful information and helped the research teams gain a clearer understanding of the community and its component parts.

Upon completion of each group interview, observers write up detailed field notes, allowing about as much time for the write-up as for the interview itself. When all group interviews for a single community are completed, the team writes up a summary assessment of the community profile. The focus should be on issues salient to the measurement of social capital, such as the collective activities and identified organizations. Issues related to social and economic development in the community are also noted, but these will be covered in greater detail in the second and more structured part of the community profile. The team also writes up at least one case study in which some community-level effort was undertaken in the past three years.

The following outputs are obtained from this process of open-ended community interviews:

- Community maps indicating the location of community assets and services.
- Observation notes of group process and summary of issues discussed.
- List of existing (and desired) community assets and services.
- List of all formal and informal community organizations.
- Case study of previous collective action.
- Venn diagram indicating the accessibility of different local organizations.
- Institutional (web) diagram of relationships among local organizations and service providers.

These community exercises constitute a set of qualitative data about the extent and nature of social capital in the community. These data are complemented with the more quantitative information collected with the help of the structured community interviews and the household profile.

STRUCTURED COMMUNITY INTERVIEWS. The community questionnaire (annex 1B) inventories basic community characteristics and provides an initial identification of community needs and assets. A subset of questionnaire items (questions 1.16 through 1.19 and section 8) are directly related to measures of social capital. The remaining items record sector-specific information, useful for identifying local needs and formulating programs and projects with a social capital component.

Annex 1B focuses on several different types of community assets and services:

1. *General community characteristics.* These includes age, size, main economic activities, geographic boundaries, and means of reaching and making contact with the outside world. This information can be used to assess the community's capacity to create and maintain networks within and beyond its boundaries. This section also includes measures of cognitive social capital—perceptions of trust, solidarity, and quality of life—comparable to items included in the household survey.
2. *Principal services.* The availability and quality of services are assessed: electricity, public lighting, potable water, communication services, waste disposal, public markets, transportation, recreation, and public safety and security. This information can be used for assessing levels of infrastructure development and identifying community needs for projects to improve access to services. The effective provision of many of these services requires some form of collective action by the community. Communication services are indicative of the community's ability to maintain social networks. Taken over time, these data may

allow for an analysis of the relationship between levels of physical capital and social capital.

3. *Labor migration.* Assessing levels of migration both into and out of the community allows greater understanding of the extent to which community boundaries are fixed or flexible and how receptive a community may be to new ideas and relationships.

4. *Education.* This module describes available school facilities, teaching staff, and community access to these resources through school attendance. These data may allow for an analysis of the relationship between levels of human capital and social capital.

5. *Health.* This section assesses principal health problems affecting men, women, and children; available health facilities; and level of service.

6. *Environmental issues.* This unit covers the presence of environmental hazards and perceptions of overall environmental quality and deterioration. These data may be useful in evaluating the relationship between levels of natural resource capital and social capital.

7. *Community support.* This module identifies grassroots groups, NGOs, and government organizations that enable community members to deal with their common problems. Questions are included to assess patterns of community decisionmaking and perceived levels of risk and vulnerability. This information indicates the extent to which common solutions to common problems are found within a community, and it inventories types of organizations that may be studied with the help of the organizational profile.

The community questionnaire collects basic information known to most adult members of the community and is therefore designed for application in a group setting. The group interview should be conducted with between 4 and 10 adult community members and their responses should be coded directly on the instrument. The interview time generally does not exceed one hour. Not all sections may be relevant for every investigation. The team conducting the field investigation should select those parts that are likely to be most useful for preparing projects in the given setting. Sections can also be modified, and additional sections added, to reflect the economic or social context relevant to the research.

Household Survey

Once both parts of the community profile have been completed, work should begin on the second SOCAT instrument, the household survey. This survey should be administered to a random sample of households in the community. It is therefore necessary to obtain or develop a list of all households in the community and then to draw a random sample from that list. Sometimes a list of households may be available in advance (from voter registration records or previous surveys, for example). If a list is not available, the investigation team must compile one.[5]

The household survey (annex 1C) is the primary instrument used for generating quantified indicators of social capital. It has five main sections.

1. *Introduction.* This section identifies the selected household, registers the time and date of the interview, and lists the names of the interviewer and field supervisor.
2. *Household characteristics.* This section contains a roster of all household members and their demographic and socioeconomic information (age, gender, marital status, occupation, education). The module also collects basic information about the housing unit (type, construction material) and the available amenities (water, electricity, sanitation).
3. *Genogram.* This module involves the participatory development of a genogram, or family tree, which shows at a glance the relationships both within the household and between household members and the larger community. At a minimum, the genogram systematically identifies the respondent's siblings, parents, children, cousins, aunts, uncles, nieces, and nephews. It distinguishes between family members living within and outside the research community, a potentially important link for the construction of social networks outside one's immediate sphere. Membership in local institutions is also recorded for each member of the household. Annex 1C includes an example of a genogram.
4. *Structural dimensions of social capital.* The structural dimensions of social capital relate to the networks and organizations to which the household belongs. Structural social capital is further investigated with the help of questions about past experience, present practice, and future expectations regarding collective action and mutual support. Triangulating information in this manner enables the investigating team to derive more reliable assessments of the structural aspects of social capital. This section of the household profile has four subsections:
   - *Organizational density and characteristics.* Questions in this subsection are intended to elicit information about the household's current membership in different types of local organizations. A typology of organizations is provided (see code box at the bottom of question 4A.1), and respondents are asked whether they or any other household members participate in the activities of any of these organizations. The quality of participation is assessed by asking whether the household member is a leader, an active member, or merely an occa-

sional member with irregular participation. The relative importance to the household of groups and organizations attended by household members is also assessed. The internal characteristics of the organizations are judged by asking questions about membership characteristics (homogeneous versus heterogeneous membership), decisionmaking processes and leadership patterns (inclusive versus exclusive), and the opportunities provided by organization membership for learning new skills and acquiring valuable information. The idea is to obtain information about organizational density, the quality of participation, and the intensity of members' involvement in order to assess the functioning of social networks more accurately (Narayan and Pritchett 1999, Grootaert 1999).

- *Expectations regarding networks and mutual support.* This section presents a series of hypothetical questions intended to gauge respondents' expectations about how community members would act in situations such as crop failure, urban violence, or a teacher's long-term absence from the classroom, where resolution of the problem would require collective action. Different types of activities can be included within this subsection; the selection of activities depends on the specific context. Asking respondents to think through these situations helps researchers understand expectations with respect to collective action and solidarity in the future. If social capital is high, it will be reflected not only in high participation in organizations at the present time but also in people's positive expectations about others' behavior in future.

- *Exclusion.* Questions in this section are intended to find out who in the community feels excluded from collective action or access to services, and to identify the perceived grounds for such exclusion. Respondents are asked questions about the community generally ("Who in this community is excluded?") as well as about their own specific situation ("Are you and your family excluded?"). Understanding who is excluded helps researchers identify the appropriate unit of collective action and whether social capital should be assessed for the entire community or for particular subgroups.

- *Previous collective action.* Information about present organization membership and future expectations is supplemented by asking respondents about their participation in collective activities undertaken in the past. Social capital has been found to be high in communities in which large numbers of people have participated in previous collective activities (Hirschman 1984). Both current membership in organizations and expectations of future collective action should be high in these communities. Answers to the different modules on structural social capital thus complement one another, and the measure of social capital is approached from different angles. This provides a more complete picture about how the community behaves as a collective entity and how well a particular household is integrated in community efforts.[6]

5. *Cognitive dimensions of social capital.* The cognitive dimension of social capital assesses norms, values, attitudes, and beliefs related to solidarity, trust, and reciprocity. Because these dimensions cannot be observed directly—people carry them inside their heads—researchers probe indirectly, asking questions about hypothetical situations that people in a community might typically face. The specific situations addressed in these questions will vary from context to context; the questions included in the annex are illustrative situations that we believe may apply widely, in both agrarian and urban contexts. We encourage researchers to fine-tune these questions to relate them more closely to the communities they study.

This section of the household survey is divided into three subsections:

- *Solidarity.* The hypothetical situations depicted in this part of the questionnaire relate to situations, such as the death of a parent or the failure of a crop, in which members of a community might need assistance from others. Do members of this community typically assist one another in times of need, or do individuals in need usually fend for themselves? Do people expect that they will be assisted by others and, reciprocally, have the expectation that they will render assistance to others? How widespread is the network of mutual assistance? Do only neighbors or family members assist each other, or can the entire community be relied upon to assist any of its members when they are in trouble? Communities with high scores on other dimensions of social capital tend to report greater solidarity.
- *Trust and cooperation.* We found that a question commonly used to investigate trust—"Do you think most people can be trusted?"—is flawed in that respondents do not usually know which people are being referred to by the investigator.[7] If different people consider different reference groups in answering this question, their responses are not comparable. Consequently, we decided to focus the trust questions on specific types of individuals ("people in your village") or on transactions requiring trust ("matters of lending and borrowing"). These trust items were found to be consistently useful and valid during the pilot tests conducted across different parts of India and Panama. People in both settings could readily relate these situations to their own notions of how trust functions in their commu-

nity. In addition, the trust questions are complemented by questions on people's beliefs about cooperation and reciprocity in their communities.

- *Conflict and conflict resolution.* An important aspect of social capital relates to the dynamics that create conflict and the mechanisms available for resolving conflicts among community members. Where a large number of interpersonal or intergroup conflicts exists or where communities are unable to resolve such conflicts peacefully and efficiently, social capital may be adversely affected. Trust among community members may suffer, and bonds of reciprocity may be weakened. Mechanisms for resolving conflict and its effects—assessed in terms of harmonious relationships within the community—are addressed within this subsection.[8]

Organizational Profile

The organizational profile (annex 1D) seeks to assess the internal characteristics of specific local organizations and to delineate the relationships and networks they have with other organizations. Both formal and informal organizations can be studied using this instrument.

The organizational profile uses data collected in a series of semistructured interviews with organization leaders, members, and nonmembers. Key information sets relate to the organization's origins and history; quality of membership (why people join, exclusion and inclusion of particular subgroups); institutional capacity (quality of leadership, participation, organizational culture, and organizational capacity); and institutional linkages (extent and nature of exchange with other governmental and nongovernmental agencies). Separate interviews with leaders, members, and nonmembers are recorded as field notes. Characteristics of organizations that are amenable to quantification can be scored using the score sheet (annex 1E), and a comparative index of organizational scores can be generated. Three to six organizations per community are usually profiled, depending on the size of the community. The organizations are identified through the community profile, the household survey, or both.

It helps to make appointments with key informants, especially with the leaders of these organizations. Individual interviews can be conducted with up to three leaders per organization. Key informants include the executive director (or functional equivalent), a member or members of the board of directors or other recognized leaders, and senior staff. These interviews should preferably be conducted face-to-face, but a self-administered written questionnaire may be substituted. Interviews generally last 45 minutes to an hour. One or two members of the research team can be trained to conduct these interviews. It is useful to use a two-member team, with one person acting as interviewer and the other as note taker.

Focus group interviews are carried out separately with members and nonmembers. Obtaining information from leaders, members, and nonmembers separately enables the team to assemble a more reliable assessment of the organization and its capacity. Depending on the size and diversity of the organization's membership, one to four focus groups should be conducted. Effort should be made to conduct at least two separate focus groups among nonmembers, one for nonmembers who wish to become members and another for nonmembers who have no interest in becoming members. These focus group interviews generally take about 15 to 30 minutes and include 5 to 12 participants per group.

Each focus group should have a moderator and one or two observers. The moderator's role is to facilitate the discussion, probe key issues, elicit comments from all participants, and focus the discussion on issues of interest. The observers' role is to take notes on the content of the discussion and the process of group decisionmaking. Upon completing the focus group interview, the moderator and observers should meet to refine the interview notes and discuss preliminary findings.

When the series of interviews required to profile any particular organization is completed, the research team should draft a summary memo of the key characteristics of the organization, its strengths and weaknesses, and its relationship with the broader community and with other local-level institutions. This summary serves as an initial analysis of the organization. The research team should complete the organizational scoresheets using all the information at hand. In order to ensure consistency in scoring, we recommend that two or more interviewers work together for assigning numerical scores.

Lessons Learned from the Pilot Tests in Panama and India

The SOCAT instruments were pilot-tested in 1999 in 14 communities in Panama (including 3 urban, 6 rural nonindigenous, and 5 rural indigenous communities) and in 9 communities in Rajasthan, India (6 rural and 3 urban). The instruments were translated into the relevant dominant language (Spanish or Hindi) and, as needed, bilingual researchers orally translated the interview questions into local languages. The objective of this exercise was not simply to translate the SOCAT from the English version but also to contextualize the inquiry and to situate it within the specific social context being examined. In making this adaptation, it is important to keep the questions as simple as possible for investigators to administer and as easy as possible for respondents to follow. Any questions in which respondents might feel under some kind of social pressure to provide the "right" response should be reworded or omitted. Translated instruments were first applied in Panama, and further modifications were made before the instruments were applied in the field in India.

STAFF TRAINING. In each country, a team of local investigators was selected and trained to administer the SOCAT. We found that engaging very experienced or highly educated persons to administer the SOCAT instruments is unnecessary; a middle school education is sufficient. The household survey requires the largest commitment of time from the investigating team, as many households need to be interviewed. However, the household profile is also the simplest of the three SOCAT instruments to administer. The community profile and especially the organizational profile require more sophisticated skills to administer and record; it is preferable that at least one member of each team is a college graduate (see annex 1F for selection criteria and terms of reference for interviewers).

Training is critical. Originally planned for two days, the training for the Panamanian team was expanded to four days. The training focused on the definition and concepts of social capital, a review of the study objectives, the development of qualitative and quantitative interview techniques, a review of the research instruments and their application, and field exercises for practicing the techniques involved. (See annex 1G for the detailed lesson plan used for training.) In India, the training lasted five days.

A full set of revised instruments had been circulated ahead of time among all investigators and supervisors so that they could study and familiarize themselves with the instruments before coming to the training session. Team members were expected to study these instruments carefully and to identify items that appeared difficult or complicated to administer. Each of the three SOCAT instruments was discussed fully during training, with special attention given to questions that the investigators had identified as being difficult or complex. Team members were provided with an opportunity to administer these instruments in practice sessions organized among both rural and urban inhabitants and, in the case of the organizational profiles, with a community organization. Training staff had a chance to see how the process was going and to incorporate final refinements before field testing commenced.

FIELDWORK. After training, the investigators were divided into teams, which were sent into different communities. Each team was jointly responsible for administering the entire set of SOCAT instruments in a particular community. The field staff in Panama was divided into four gender-balanced teams, each made up of a supervisor and three interviewers. In India, each field team consisted of three female and three male interviewers, along with one male and one female supervisor. Interviewers had primary responsibility for administering the household questionnaires, while supervisors were responsible mainly for the community and organizational profiles.

Depending upon the size of the community, a research team spent two to five days in a community, to conduct the community interviews, the household survey, and the organizational interviews. Sufficient time was allotted during the process for writing up and transcribing field notes and coordinating field activities.

Administering the community profile was the first exercise upon entering a town or village. It provided the community with a useful introduction to the purposes, and it helped team members form general impressions about collective action and social organization in the community. Community interviews were usually organized early in the morning or late at night, times that were most convenient for community members. In Panama, the pilot test took place during the highly politicized weeks preceding national elections, which required the research teams to be especially sensitive to respondents' suspicions and lack of trust. In India, the pilot test was organized during a relatively quiet period in the agricultural cycle, when rural residents were not especially busy with activities on the farm.

Participants in both countries showed considerable interest in the profile process, particularly while drawing village maps and constructing Venn diagrams and flowcharts. Community members participated actively in these visually appealing exercises. Venn diagrams and flowcharts also helped focus respondents' thoughts and helped researchers understand the importance of local organizations, the psychological distance that people in the community experience with respect to different local organizations, and the nature of interorganizational linkages. Useful information was derived about collective efforts undertaken in the past by the community and about the extent to which these actions had succeeded or failed. Researchers compiled a list of organizations active in the community that could be studied further with the help of the organizational profile.

The household survey was administered after completing the community profile. In Panama, household surveys took between 15 and 90 minutes to complete; in households where no members belonged to a community organization, interview time did not exceed 15 minutes. In India, household questionnaires took between one-and-a-half and two hours to complete. Because some respondents will not agree to be interviewed, the random sample must contain a reserve list of households that can be drawn on. Fewer than 2 percent of respondents in India and Panama refused to be interviewed, however, so very few replacements were required.

No difficulty was encountered in administering any questionnaire item, even among less-educated respondents. In India, however, the questionnaire was found to be too lengthy. Ideally, the household survey should take no more than one hour to administer, since respondents tend to lose interest if the interview drags on too long. Some survey questions might need to be omitted in order to reduce the length of the interview.

Survey items are precoded, so data entry is a straightforward task that can be completed relatively rapidly. It is useful to verify 5–10 percent of the completed questionnaires through repeat interviews before the data are entered, so that errors arising from lack of understanding can be detected and rectified at an early stage.

The organizational profiles took the field teams three to four hours to administer and another three to four hours to write up. Several different formal and informal organizations were studied. The scoring index provided a standardized summary assessment of organizational characteristics useful for baseline, monitoring, and evaluation activities.

Notes

1. This hypothetical example is discussed along with other real-world cases in Krishna (2000).

2. For lack of more precise terminology, *quantitative* methods refers here to methods that maximize representativity and generalizability to the larger study population, such as surveys based on random sampling, structured individual interviews, and the statistical analyses generated thereby. *Qualitative* methods refers to a wide range of data collection and analysis techniques whose nonrandom sampling criterion of "saturation of information" allows for in-depth analysis of social phenomena.

3. The list of these research instruments can be found in Krishna and Shrader (2000), which also contains detailed information on the pilot tests.

4. We found it useful to begin the SOCAT community profile exercise by focusing on what communities have (assets) rather than on what they do not have (needs). This approach avoids creating the impression that the research team has come to the community to distribute tangible benefits.

5. Even if a list is available, it is advisable to verify with community leaders and/or in a meeting with community members that the list is comprehensive and current.

6. In some research settings, it will be useful to supplement this module with questions about participation in sector-specific collective action (irrigation, road maintenance, education, and so forth). This information can be used in conjunction with the sector-specific data from the community profile in the design of projects.

7. We had included this question in our original questionnaire, and as an exercise, we followed up this question by asking 42 respondents in one Indian village who (that is, which "people") they were thinking about in answering this question. Fifteen respondents said they had been thinking of people in their village, another 13 said they had thought of people in a group of villages (their own village and adjoining villages), 8 said they had thought of people in general, and 4 said they had been thinking of people with whom they had business dealings.

8. Although conflict is often the result of a failure of trust (that is, a cognitive social capital issue), the mechanisms for conflict resolution, such as courts or councils of elders, are often part of structural social capital. Thus, the theme of conflict and conflict resolution combines issues of structural and cognitive social capital.

References

Berman, Sheri. 1997. "Civil Society and Political Institutionalization." *American Behavioral Scientist* 40 (5): 562–74.

Coleman, James. 1988. "Social Capital in the Creation of Human Capital." *American Journal of Sociology* 94 (Supplement): S95–S120.

Eastis, Carla M. 1998. "Organizational Diversity and the Production of Social Capital." *American Behavioral Scientist* 42 (1): 66–77.

Farah, Nuruddin. 1992. *Close Sesame*. Saint Paul, Minn.: Graywolf Press.

Granovetter, Marc. 1985. "Social Structures and Economic Action: The Problem of Embeddedness." *American Journal of Sociology* 91 (3): 481–510.

Grootaert, Christiaan. 1999. "Social Capital, Household Welfare, and Poverty in Indonesia." Local Level Institutions Working Paper 6. World Bank, Social Development Department, Washington, D.C.

Hechter, Michael. 1987. *Principles of Group Solidarity*. Berkeley: University of California Press.

Hirschman, Albert. 1984. *Getting Ahead Collectively: Grassroots Experiences in Latin America*. New York: Pergamon Press.

Knack, Stephen, and Philip Keefer. 1997. "Does Social Capital Have an Economic Payoff? A Cross-Country Investigation." *Quarterly Journal of Economics* 52 (4): 1251–87.

Krishna, Anirudh. 2000. "Creating and Harnessing Social Capital." In Partha Dasgupta and Ismail Serageldin, eds., *Social Capital: A Multifaceted Perspective*. Washington, D.C.: World Bank.

Krishna, Anirudh, and Elizabeth Shrader. 2000. "Cross-Cultural Measures of Social Capital: A Tool and Results from India and Panama." Social Capital Initiative Working Paper 21. World Bank, Social Development Department, Washington, D.C.

Minkoff, Debra. 1997. "Producing Social Capital: National Social Movements and Civil Society." *American Behavioral Scientist* 40 (5): 606–19.

Narayan, Deepa, and Lant Pritchett. 1999. "Cents and Sociability: Household Income and Social Capital in Rural Tanzania." *Economic Development and Cultural Change* 47 (4): 871–97.

Newton, Kenneth. 1997. "Social Capital and Democracy." *American Behavioral Scientist* 40 (5): 575–86.

Oliver, Pamela E., and Gerard Marwell. 1988. "The Paradox of Group Size in Collective Action: A Theory of the Critical Mass, II." *American Sociological Review* 53 (1): 1–8.

Peters, Thomas J., and Robert H. Waterman. 1982. *In Search of Excellence: Lessons from America's Best Run Companies*. New York: Warner Books.

Portney, Kent E., and Jeffrey M. Berry. 1997. "Mobilizing Minority Communities: Social Capital and Participation in Urban Neighborhoods." *American Behavioral Scientist* 40 (5): 632–44.

Putnam, Robert D., with Robert Leonardi and Raffaela Nanetti. 1993. *Making Democracy Work: Civic Traditions in Modern Italy*. Princeton, N.J.: Princeton University Press.

Rose, Richard. 1998. "Getting Things Done in an Anti–Modern Society: Social Capital and Networks in Russia." Social Capital Initiative

Working Paper 6. World Bank, Social Development Department, Washington, D.C.

Rossman, Gretchen B., and Bruce L. Wilson. 1985. "Numbers and Words: Combining Quantitative and Qualitative Methods in a Single Large-Scale Evaluation Study." *Evaluation Review* 9 (5): 627–43

———. 1994. "Numbers and Words Revisited: Being 'Shamelessly Eclectic.'" *Quality and Quantity* 28: 315–27.

Stolle, Dietlind. 1998. "Making Associations Work: Group Characteristics, Membership, and Generalized Trust." Paper presented at the annual meeting of the American Political Science Association, September 3–6, Boston.

Uphoff, Norman. 1999. "Understanding Social Capital: Learning from the Analysis and Experience of Participation." In Partha Dasgupta and Ismail Serageldin, eds., *Social Capital: A Multifaceted Perspective.* Washington D.C.: World Bank.

3

Quantitative Analysis of Social Capital Data

Christiaan Grootaert

As explained in the previous chapter, the Social Capital Assessment Tool (SOCAT) is a multifaceted instrument designed to collect social capital data at the household, community, and institutional levels. Structured questionnaires are used as well as open-ended participatory methods. As a result, a wide range of quantitative and qualitative analyses are possible using multiple units of analysis (table 3.1). It is beyond the scope of this book to cover all possible uses of the data collected with the SOCAT. The most novel feature is probably the detailed information about structural and cognitive social capital at the level of the household, and this chapter focuses on the analysis of these data. Since these data are obtained through a household survey, the analysis is predominantly quantitative. As a complement, the next two chapters illustrate qualitative analysis of social capital data, with a focus on the community as the unit of analysis.

The first section of this chapter presents a tabular analysis of social capital data, centered on three basic sets of indicators of social capital: membership in associations and networks (structural social capital), trust and adherence to norms (cognitive social capital), and collective action (an output measure). Tabular analysis is a simple and convenient way to organize data and to extract the basic messages that the data contain. The basic messages of the SOCAT household survey pertain to the extent social capital is observed across different types of households and the main characteristics or dimensions of this social capital. As explained in chapter 1, the typology used here is anchored in the distinction between structural and cognitive social capital. The household information can also be aggregated at the level of the community and cross-tabulated by different characteristics of the community. The main limitation of tabular analysis is that only a few variables can be tabulated at once, making it difficult to discern social capital's contribution to the welfare of the household.

The second section of this chapter therefore turns to econometric analysis, in particular the estimation of multivariate models of household

Table 3.1 The Social Capital Assessment Tool

Instrument	Data collection method	Unit of analysis	Type of analysis
Community profile interview guide	Focus groups, community mapping, institutional diagram	Community, institution	Qualitative
Community characteristics and services questionnaire	Key respondent interviews, focus groups	Community	Quantitative
Household questionnaire	Household survey	Household, individual	Quantitative
Organizational profile interview guide	Interviews with leaders, focus groups with members and non-members	Institution	Qualitative
Organizational profile score sheet	Scoring by field team	Institution	Quantitative

welfare. Such models aim to identify the contribution of social capital to monetary and nonmonetary aspects of household welfare (consumption of goods, health, and education) in relation to other household assets (land, human and physical capital). A key question in this context is the direction of causality: is it social capital that makes higher household welfare possible, or is it existing higher household welfare that allows the acquisition of more social capital? Several ways are proposed for dealing with this problem of "endogeneity" of social capital, as it is generally called. This section also discusses how to analyze the links between social capital and poverty reduction, that is, whether social capital is of special importance to the poor, considering that poor households typically are unable to accumulate other forms of capital. Finally, the section addresses whether it is possible to estimate models of the determinants of social capital, that is, models that can explain why some households or communities have more social capital than others.

By necessity, the section dealing with the econometric analysis of social capital data is technically more complex than the rest of this book. It is geared toward readers with an interest in and a working knowledge of econometric analysis. However, the section can be skipped without loss of continuity.

Throughout the chapter, examples illustrate the proposed analysis. Most of these are taken from the studies undertaken in the context of the World Bank's Social Capital Initiative and Local Level Institutions Study, since this book aims to disseminate the results of that work.[1] There are, of course, many other empirical studies on social capital in the literature, and chapter 1 and the literature reviews in annexes 2 and 3 of this book contain a wide range of citations.[2]

Tabulations of Indicators of Social Capital

Recent experience in measuring social capital and its impact, including the studies that constitute the Social Capital Initiative, has shown quite clearly that empirical analysis must look at both structural and cognitive social capital (Grootaert and van Bastelaer 2001). Whether and how networks and associations function depends on trust and adherence to norms. Likewise, the potential benefits of trust are often fully realized only when interactions are leveraged through networks or associations. Thus, a basic set of indicators of social capital must include those reflecting structural social capital as well as those reflecting cognitive social capital.

Some skepticism has been voiced about the measurement of social capital on the grounds that social capital really refers to an underlying social force that eludes measurement and that proposed indicators are at best imperfect proxies. There is some validity to this point of view. Indeed, one must be careful not to equate the measurement variables with the underlying social capital. Not every association or collective action reflects the presence of social capital; take, for example, associations or collective actions that are the result of government force. However, the fact that proxy indicators are being used to measure social capital does not, in our view, detract from the validity of the exercise. Human capital provides a useful analogy. This theory, developed some 40 years ago, claims that human capital embodied in individuals increases their ability to earn income over their lifetimes. Two convenient proxies were proposed to measure this ability: years of schooling and years of work experience. No one confused these proxy indicators with human capital per se. Rather, the proxies are input measures that capture the two most important ways in which human capital is acquired. Even 40 years after the development of the human capital model, measuring human capital directly (through performance or aptitude tests) remains very difficult. But this difficulty has not prevented the empirical literature on human capital from blossoming and leading to many extremely useful results for developing and implementing education policy. The social capital model may currently be at the same early stage that human capital theory was 30 to 40 years ago.

Based on extensive empirical work, several useful proxies have been identified for measuring social capital in a policy-relevant manner (Grootaert and van Bastelaer 2001). Specifically, we propose three types of proxy indicators: memberships in local associations and networks, indicators of trust and adherence to norms, and indicators of collective action:

- *Memberships in local associations and networks.* This indicator of structural social capital is based on the density of associations and the incidence of household memberships. Various aspects of membership (such as internal diversity) and institutional functioning (such as the extent of democratic decisionmaking) are also relevant indicators. Which associations to include in the indicators is culture-specific: agrarian syndicates could be relevant in one country, rotating credit and savings associations in another, parent-teacher associations in yet another. In the case of networks, which are less formal, the key information is the scope of the network and the internal diversity of membership.
- *Indicators of trust and adherence to norms.* Measuring trust and adherence to norms (cognitive social capital) requires asking respondents about their expectations about and experiences with behavior requiring trust. Key questions relate to the extent to which households received or would receive assistance from members of their community or network in case of various emergencies (loss of income, illness).
- *Indicators of collective action.* The provision of many services requires collective action by a group of individuals. The extent to which this collective action occurs can be measured and is an indicator of underlying social capital (at least to the extent that the cooperation is not imposed by an external force, such as the government).

As proxies, these three types of indicators measure social capital from different vantage points. Membership in local associations and networks is clearly an input indicator, since the associations and networks are the vehicles through which social capital can be accumulated. This indicator resembles perhaps most closely the use of years of schooling as a proxy for human capital. Trust can be seen as an input or output indicator or even as a direct measure of social capital, depending on one's conceptual approach. Collective action is an output indicator. Because of their different perspectives, we suggest that these three types of indicators be tabulated and analyzed together, in order to provide a fuller picture of social capital and its impacts.

Structural Social Capital

As explained in chapter 1, social capital helps to disseminate information, reduces opportunistic behavior, and facilitates collective decisionmaking. The effectiveness with which structural social capital, in the form of associations and networks, fulfills this role depends upon many aspects of these groups, reflecting their structure, their membership, and the way they function. The SOCAT questionnaire (questions 4A.1 to 4A.13) makes it possible to describe organizations along three key dimensions: the density of membership, the diversity of membership, and the extent of participation in the decisionmaking process.

DENSITY OF MEMBERSHIP. At the level of the community, density of membership is measured simply by the number of existing organizations (for comparability, best normalized by population size). At the level of the household, it is measured by the average number of memberships of each household in existing organizations (this can be normalized by household size). This basic indicator can be cross-tabulated by location (region, province, urban/rural) or socioeconomic characteristics of the households (income groups, age and gender of the head of household, religion, ethnic groups) to capture the distribution of memberships. An example for Indonesia is given in table 3.2, which classifies memberships by type of group and province. The types of groups distinguished are of course country-specific, but the table illustrates that large regional variations can exist in the pattern of organizational membership. For example, in the provinces of Jambi and Nusa Tenggara Timur, about 12 percent of memberships were in finance and credit services groups, but in Jawa Tengah these groups accounted for almost one-third of memberships.

An alternative way to display the same information is to ask this question: what percentage of households participates in what types of local organizations? This shifts the focus of analysis from memberships to the household. Table 3.3, which is based on the same data as table 3.2, indicates that in Jambi 32.3 percent of households belong to finance and credit services groups, compared with 56.5 percent of households in Nusa Tenggara Timur (even though, as table 3.2 shows, the share of all memberships accounted for by finance groups is the same in both provinces). This reveals that financial group membership is more concentrated in Jambi and that financial services delivered through local organizations reach a much smaller share of households in Jambi than in Nusa Tenggara Timur.

The classification of associations in tables 3.2 and 3.3 is functional—focusing on the prime objective of the association. Other classifications

Table 3.2 Active Memberships in Local Organizations in Indonesia, by Province

Type of organization	Jambi Number	Jambi Percent	Jawa Tengah Number	Jawa Tengah Percent	Nusa Tenggara Timur Number	Nusa Tenggara Timur Percent	All Number	All Percent
Social service	346	27.2	616	26.1	733	28.4	1,695	27.3
Production	45	3.5	61	2.6	129	5.0	235	3.8
Occupational	113	8.9	41	1.7	206	8.0	360	5.8
Finance/credit	148	11.6	740	31.4	307	11.9	1,195	19.2
Religious	348	27.3	272	11.5	527	20.4	1,147	18.5
Natural resources	19	1.5	89	3.8	65	2.5	173	2.8
Environmental	1	0.1	9	0.4	0	0.0	10	0.2
Government affairs	189	14.9	418	17.7	572	22.2	1,179	19.0
Recreation	63	5.0	97	4.1	37	1.4	197	3.2
Others	1	0.1	16	0.7	2	0.1	19	0.3
Total	1,273	100	2,359	100	2,578	100	6,210	100

Source: Grootaert 1999a.

Table 3.3 Percentage of Households Participating in Local Organizations in Indonesia, by Province

Type of organization	Jambi	Jawa Tengah	Nusa Tenggara Timur	All
Social service	57.5	72.8	79.0	69.8
Production	10.5	14.3	29.0	17.9
Occupational	25.0	9.8	39.0	24.6
Finance/credit	32.3	84.8	52.5	56.5
Religious	57.8	58.0	89.3	68.3
Natural resources	4.5	18.5	15.8	12.9
Environmental	0.3	2.3	0.0	0.8
Government affairs	43.8	67.5	87.5	66.3
Recreation	14.8	21.3	7.5	14.5
Others	0.3	3.0	0.5	1.3

Source: Grootaert 1999a.

can also be useful, such as whether the groups operate only in the village, are affiliated with other groups (inside or outside the village), or are part of a federated structure. Groups with linkages often have better access to resources, especially from outside the village, such as from government or nongovernmental organizations (NGOs). Such linkages have been described as "bridging" or "linking" social capital, in contrast to the "bonding" social capital that exists within the group (Woolcock and Narayan 2000). Federated structures of associations have often been especially effective at opening up a wide range of resources for their members (Bebbington and Carroll 2000).

The SOCAT asks households to identify the three most important groups to which they belong (question 4A.3). Tabulating the "votes" received by each organization is often useful. The example from Bolivia in table 3.4 highlights the dominant position of the Agrarian Syndicates—considered the most important local organization by 41 percent of respondents. Created by the Bolivian state in 1952 during the land redistribution reform, Agrarian Syndicates have become the central community organizations of farmers to manage land, forests, and water resources, and to resolve conflicts.

The identification of the three most important organizations for each household is followed in the SOCAT questionnaire by a series of supplementary questions about these organizations, relating to the internal diversity of membership (questions 4A.4 to 4A.11) and the decisionmaking process and leadership (questions 4A.12 and 4A.13).

Table 3.4 The 10 Most Important Local Organizations in Bolivia

Organization	Times cited (Percentage of total citations)	
Agrarian syndicate	584	(41.3)
Nondenominational NGO	194	(13.7)
Mothers club	65	(4.6)
Agricultural producers association	60	(4.2)
Denominational NGO	48	(3.4)
Women's center	46	(3.3)
Captaincy	43	(3.0)
Association/federation of rural people	39	(2.8)
Heads of family association	39	(2.8)
Informal education group	23	(1.6)

Source: Grootaert and Narayan 2000.

DIVERSITY OF MEMBERSHIP. It is not immediately obvious whether a high degree of internal diversity is a positive or negative factor from the point of view of social capital. One could argue, on the one hand, that an internally homogeneous association would make it easier for members to trust each other, to share information, and to reach decisions.[3] On the other hand, they may also have similar information so that less would be gained from exchanging information. Furthermore, the coexistence of a series of associations that are each internally homogeneous but along different criteria could render the decisionmaking process at the village level more difficult. The multivariate analysis discussed later is the best vehicle to assess empirically the role of diversity of membership. Tabulations, however, are useful to show any regional or socioeconomic patterns in diversity.

The SOCAT questionnaire makes it possible to rate the internal diversity of an organization according to seven criteria: kinship, religion, gender, age, political affiliation, occupation, and education. If appropriate in a given country context, other dimensions such as race or ethnicity could be added. Diversity information can be used separately or combined in an index. Specific dimensions such as age or gender can be used to refine the profile of organizations, for example, by indicating how many have male-only or female-only membership. In Burkina Faso, for instance, the incidence of gender-segregated associations is related to the province and its ethnic composition (table 3.5). In Yatenga and Sanmatenga, home of the Mossi tribe, more than 90 percent of memberships are in gender-mixed organizations, but in Houet and Sissili, the cultural preferences of other tribes lead to male-only groups in the majority of cases.

A diversity score can be calculated for each organization, ranging from zero to seven (a value of one on each criterion indicates that members of the organization are "mostly from different" kin groups, religious affiliations, and so on). These scores can be averaged over the three most

Table 3.5 Distribution of Associational Memberships, by Gender, in Burkina Faso (percent)

Gender	Houet	Sissili	Sanmatenga	Yatenga	All
Female only	17.2	18.1	2.2	0.8	10.6
Male only	50.4	62.3	6.6	5.3	34.6
Mixed	32.4	19.6	91.2	93.9	54.8
All	100.0	100.0	100.0	100.0	100.0

Source: Swamy, Grootaert, and Oh 1999.

important organizations per household and, for ease of comparison, rescaled from 0 to 100 (with 100 corresponding to the highest possible value of the index).

Returning to the Indonesian example, the data show that organizations are much less diverse in Jambi (average diversity index of 39 out of a maximum of 100) than in Nusa Tenggara Timur (average diversity index of 62). Another interesting finding is that female-headed households belong to less-diverse organizations than male-headed households (table 3.6).

This index procedure assumes that each criterion has the same weight in measuring the overall diversity of membership. Alternative weighting schemes are possible. For example, larger weights can be given to the economic criteria (occupation and education) on the assumption that an organization of people with different occupations or education levels presents greater opportunities for information sharing than, for instance, a group of people with different ages. Weights can also be derived from a

Table 3.6 Dimensions of Structural Social Capital, by Province and Household Characteristics, Indonesia

Category	Diversity index	Index of participation in decisionmaking
Province		
Jambi	38.9	63.5
Jawa Tengah	57.6	55.6
Nusa Tenggara Timur	61.6	71.4
Head of household		
Male	53.6	64.1
Female	49.2	57.1
Religion		
Muslim	49.2	59.5
Catholic	58.7	71.6
Protestant	63.7	70.7
Education of head of household		
None	52.5	53.5
Primary school—incomplete	51.5	60.0
Primary school—complete	53.0	65.7
Secondary school—incomplete	54.1	68.3
Secondary school—complete	64.0	72.9
Vocational	59.2	83.3
University/other	51.9	77.5

Source: Grootaert 1999b.

principal component analysis of the diversity criteria. Sensitivity analysis is recommended to check if results relating to the relevance of the diversity of membership are affected by changing the weights.

PARTICIPATION IN DECISIONMAKING. Organizations that follow a democratic pattern of decisionmaking are generally believed to be more effective than others. Question 4A.12 asks organization members to evaluate the relative roles of the leader and the members in reaching decisions. A complementary question, 4A.13, asks for an overall evaluation of the effectiveness of the organization leader.

Answers to these questions can be tabulated separately by type of organization (to assess whether certain categories of organizations are more democratic than others) or against spatial or socioeconomic variables (to assess whether organizations in certain parts of the country tend to function more democratically, or whether organizations of the poor function differently from those of the rich). The two questions can also be combined in a "democratic functioning score" using a method similar to that used to determine the diversity score:

1. Scale responses to each question.
   Question 4A.12:   0 =   The leader decides and informs the group.
                        1 =   The leader asks group members for their views and then decides.
                        2 =   The group members hold a discussion and decide together.
   Question 4A.13:   0 =   The leader is not effective.
                        1 =   The leader is somewhat effective.
                        2 =   The leader is very effective.
2. Add up the scores and take the average over the three most important organizations.
3. Rescale the total score from 0 to 100.

Table 3.6 shows a striking correlation between gender and education of the head of household and participation in decisionmaking in Indonesia. The index of participation in decisionmaking is 7 points lower for female-headed households than for male-headed households, and 24 points lower for households where the head has no education than for households where the head has postsecondary education.

OTHER ASPECTS OF STRUCTURAL SOCIAL CAPITAL. The three key dimensions of structural social capital discussed so far—density, diversity, and functioning—describe the associations and networks in which social capital is embodied. They are input indicators. It is also useful to consider a few output or effectiveness indicators. The SOCAT contains questions on two such indicators: the extent to which the village or neighborhood is a source of mutual support in times of crisis (questions 4B.1 to 4B.4) and the degree of inclusiveness in access to services (questions 4C.1 to 4C.8).

Two hypothetical crisis situations (chosen to be locally relevant) are proposed to the respondent, who is then asked to indicate the extent to which the village or neighborhood would act collectively to deal with the crisis and who would take the initiative to set up the response. The five possible answers range from no collective action to full collective action. As with previous topics, these questions can be tabulated separately against spatial and socioeconomic variables, or they can be combined in a single "mutual support score." As before, the required assumption for the latter approach is that the qualitative answers to each question can be given a numeric value on a common scale, so that addition or averaging becomes possible. Each analyst needs to decide whether this assumption is acceptable in the context of the specific analysis undertaken. Factor analysis or principal component analysis can also be used to see if the four questions share a common underlying factor.

Questions 4C.1 to 4C.8 probe for the existence of exclusion at the level of the village or neighborhood and for the characteristics that may be the grounds for the exclusion (religion, social status, and the like). The household is also asked directly whether it has ever been the victim of exclusion. The most policy-relevant information will come from the detailed cross-tabulation of the presence of exclusion by type of service against the characteristics deemed to be the grounds for exclusion. This tabulation will reveal whether exclusion exists across the board, due to specific characteristics such as gender or ethnicity, or if the reasons for exclusion vary by type of service. For example, access to education may differ according to gender, but access to credit may be differentiated depending upon political affiliation. Both types of tables have a high diagnostic value in identifying sources of social stress in the community. To compare the incidence of exclusion across communities, an "exclusion score" can be constructed by adding up the answers from several questions; for instance, the 11 subanswers to question 4C.1 can easily be scored on a common scale, as can the 11 subanswers to questions 4C.5 and 4C.6.

Cognitive Social Capital

Measurement of cognitive social capital in the SOCAT is organized around three themes: solidarity, trust and cooperation, and conflict resolution.

SOLIDARITY. Solidarity, as an aspect of cognitive social capital, parallels the issue of mutual support discussed earlier under structural social capital. The mutual support questions (4B.1 to 4B.4) asked the respondent whether the village or neighborhood would get together to deal with a hypothetical crisis affecting everyone. The solidarity questions (5A.1 and 5A.2) present the hypothetical situation of an unfortunate event happening to a neighbor or an individual in the village or neighborhood and then inquire about the degree of solidarity that would be displayed throughout the community to assist that individual. Again, the crisis situations need to be selected carefully so as to be relevant in the local context. The tabulation of this information can follow a pattern similar to that of mutual support, that is, the answers from each question can be tabulated separately against spatial or socioeconomic criteria (table 3.7), or the answers to the two questions can be scored on a common scale and averaged. The latter approach is most useful if one wishes to create a "solidarity score" for each village or neighborhood.

TRUST AND COOPERATION. Trust is an abstract concept that is difficult to measure in the context of a household questionnaire, in part because it may mean different things to different people.[4] The SOCAT approach therefore focuses both on generalized trust (the extent to which one trusts people overall) and on the extent of trust that exists in the context of specific transactions, such as lending and borrowing, or taking care of children during their parents' absence.[5] The generalized trust questions ask respondents to express their agreement or disagreement with general statements such as "most people in this village or neighborhood are basically honest and can be trusted" or "people are always interested only in their own welfare" (question 5C.4). These general questions are balanced by questions asking the respondent to choose between two concrete alter-

Table 3.7 Solidarity in Times of Crisis, in Burkina Faso
(Percent of households who think they can obtain assistance beyond immediate household and relatives)

Response	Houet	Sissili	Sanmatenga	Yatenga	All
Definitely	49.0	32.1	27.2	19.8	32.0
Probably	23.0	22.5	35.0	35.4	29.0
Probably not	7.9	23.3	5.8	16.5	13.3
Definitely not	10.9	18.8	23.0	24.9	19.4
Difficult to answer	9.2	3.3	9.0	3.4	6.3
Total	100.0	100.0	100.0	100.0	100.0

Source: Swamy, Grootaert, and Oh 1999.

natives, such as owning and farming 10 hectares of land by themselves versus owning and farming 25 hectares of land jointly with one other person (question 5B.5). The joint option is clearly more beneficial to each participant, but it requires mutual trust between them. Thus, the assumption is that in an environment characterized by high levels of trust, more people will choose the joint option.

Because trust is difficult to measure, the questions in this section have a certain degree of redundancy to them. In part, this repetitiveness serves the purpose of cross-validating the responses to different questions. It is possible to tabulate the answers to each question against the usual spatial or socioeconomic characteristics, but because of the complexity of the concept of trust, it is recommended that the analyst uses factor analysis or principal component analysis to identify any underlying common factors across the different questions. Including the subanswers to certain questions, the trust module contains 19 items altogether, and, in its unprocessed form, this amount of information is unwieldy. Factor analysis or principal component analysis provides a convenient way to aggregate this information.

This approach was used in a study of social capital in Ghana and Uganda by Narayan and Cassidy (2001). Seven questions on trust were included in the questionnaire for Ghana and nine in the questionnaire for Uganda (table 3.8). Factor analysis revealed that all trust variables for Ghana loaded onto a single factor. This discovery would justify constructing one index for trust and treating it as one variable in the analysis. In contrast, in the Uganda study, three factors emerged, identifying different dimensions of trust. The first factor focused on trust in agencies (police, government), the second on trust in members of one's immediate environment (family, village, tribe). The third factor combined trust in the business community and ward officials.

CONFLICT AND CONFLICT RESOLUTION. The presence of conflict in a village or neighborhood or in a larger area is often an indicator of the lack of trust or the lack of appropriate structural social capital to resolve conflicts or both.[6] As such, conflict must be seen as an output indicator (from that perspective, it leans closer to the collective action indicators discussed in the next section). The SOCAT questionnaire contains a brief module (questions 5C.1 to 5C.7) to determine the extent to which a given village or neighborhood is in conflict and if so, the mechanisms available to help resolve disputes. As a measure of conflict avoidance, two questions are devoted to determining the extent to which people are willing to contribute time or money to common development goals.

Three of the questions (5C.2, 5C.4, and 5C.6) ask respondents to compare their village or neighborhood with others in terms of amount of con-

Table 3.8 Factor Analysis of Trust Variables for Ghana and Uganda

| | Ghana | Uganda | | |
	Factor 1	Factor 1	Factor 2	Factor 3
Variable				
Trust in people in your tribe/caste	0.786	—	—	—
Trust in people in other tribes	0.757	—	0.533	—
Trust in people in your village	0.718	—	0.736	—
Trust in people in same clubs	0.697	—	—	—
Trust in business owners	0.645	—	—	0.427
Trust in politicians	0.585	—	—	—
Trust in family members	0.534	—	0.369	—
Trust in government service providers	—	0.719	—	—
Trust in local/municipal government	—	0.593	—	—
Trust in judges/courts/police	—	0.447	—	—
Trust in community/ward officials	—	—	—	0.612

— *Not applicable.*
Source: Narayan and Cassidy 2001.

flict, amount of contribution to common development goals, and extent of harmonious relations. Clearly, it makes sense to combine these three questions into a single indicator per village or neighborhood to reflect how the community views itself relative to its neighbors. Three parallel questions (5C.1, 5C.3, and 5C.5) ask respondents to assess whether their village or neighborhood is peaceful or in conflict, whether people make any contributions to common goals, and whether relations are harmonious or disagreeable. The answers to these three questions could be aggregated into a total score as follows:

Question 5C.1:	Conflictive = 0	Peaceful = 1
Question 5C.3:	No time or money contributions = 0	Time or money contributions = 1
Question 5C.5:	Disagreeable relations = 0	Harmonious relations = 1

Maximum score per village or neighborhood = 3

This type of aggregation obviously involves strong assumptions about underlying common scales. A priori, there is no reason to assume that the "distance" between disagreeable and harmonious relations is the same as between conflictive and peaceful. Yet, in practice, this aggregation method is quite commonly used, and resulting indicators have proven useful, especially in the context of multivariate analysis. However, as suggested several times previously, factor analysis and principal component analysis are alternative methods (although they are less suitable when the number of questions is small).

Collective Action

Collective action is the third and final type of indicator by which we propose to measure social capital. Unlike most of the indicators of structural and cognitive social capital, collective action is an output measure. Its usefulness stems from the fact that in the vast majority of settings, collective action is possible only if a significant amount of social capital is available in the village. The major exception occurs in totalitarian societies where the government can force people to work together on infrastructure projects or other types of common activities. Thus, the validity of the collective action indicator as a measure of social capital needs to be evaluated against the political context of a society. The indicators of structural and cognitive social capital discussed previously can be helpful here.

Collective action is an important aspect of community life in many countries, although the purposes of the action may differ widely. In Indonesia, for example, collective action is part of village tradition and consists primarily of community-organized activities for building and maintaining infrastructure (roads and bridges, community buildings, water supply systems) and for providing related public services (Werner 1998). Table 3.9 shows that in Indonesia the frequency of participation in collective action, both at the level of the neighborhood and the village, is quite high, although it varies significantly across provinces. In other countries, collective action is more politically oriented, used primarily to lobby elected officials to provide more services to the community.

The collective action module of the SOCAT (questions 4D.1 to 4D.8) aims to collect three items of information: the extent of collective action, the type of activities undertaken collectively, and an overall assessment of the extent of willingness to participate in collective action. The extent of collective action is captured by questions 4D.1 to 4D.3. Questions 4D.4 and 4D.5 list 13 types of activities that can be undertaken collectively or are for the collective benefit. The prototype module focuses on political actions such as participating in an election campaign or protest demonstration, but this focus may need to be modified in different social and cultural contexts. The final three questions, 4D.6 to 4D.8, assess the overall spirit of participation in the community. Questions 4D.1 and 4D.3 have a common set of answers and thus can readily be aggregated or averaged to provide a community-level indicator of the extent of collective action.

Table 3.9 Participation in Collective Action (Gotong Royong) in Indonesia, by Province (percent)

Frequency of participation (per year)	Jambi	Jawa Tengah	Nusa Tenggara Timur	All
At neighborhood level				
0	30.5	9.8	17.5	19.3
1–6 times	51.3	19.8	31.3	34.1
7–12 times	9.0	15.8	13.8	12.8
13–24 times	3.5	15.5	12.5	10.5
25–48 times	4.8	22.3	15.8	14.3
49+ times	1.0	17.0	9.3	9.1
Total	100.0	100.0	100.0	100.0
At village level				
0	27.8	55.5	17.3	33.5
1–6 times	51.8	29.5	40.3	40.5
7–12 times	12.3	11.0	19.3	14.2
13–24 times	2.0	1.8	7.8	3.8
25–48 times	5.5	1.3	10.8	5.8
49+ times	0.8	1.0	4.8	2.2
Total	100.0	100.0	100.0	100.0

Source: Grootaert 1999a.

Combining the Different Indicators of Social Capital

The proposed indicators of structural social capital, cognitive social capital, and collective action can be tabulated separately or combined into a single index of social capital. We profess a preference for separate tabulation—as discussed in the previous three sections—because the indicators capture different dimensions of social capital that are each relevant in their own right for understanding social capital. Still, a number of studies have constructed aggregate social capital indicators across various aspects of social capital, usually by means of factor analysis.

A study of watershed management in Rajasthan, India, selected three indicators of structural social capital and three indicators of cognitive social capital to define a single index of social capital (Krishna and Uphoff 1999). The structural indicators tried to capture the extent to which informal networks and established roles helped the community deal with crisis situations and disputes and whether the village had a tradition of looking after common goods. The cognitive indicators captured certain norms and attitudes that represent a sense of solidarity and mutual trust. As table 3.10 shows, factor analysis indicated that the six variables loaded onto a single common factor, which accounted for about 55 percent of the combined variance. Hence, the six separate variables can validly be combined into a single social capital index, which can be used as an explanatory variable as well as a dependent variable in multivariate analysis (see table 3.19).

The study of social capital in Ghana and Uganda by Narayan and Cassidy (2001) combined a much larger number of social capital variables and used factor analysis to identify common factors (table 3.11). In Ghana, ten factors were identified capturing five dimensions of social capital: group characteristics (structural social capital), trust (cognitive social capital), everyday sociability, volunteerism, and togetherness. The ten factors explained 48 percent of the variance. In Uganda, the structure of social capital proved simpler, with four factors capturing 64 percent of the variance. In both countries, structural social capital as measured by group characteristics was found to be the principal factor.

Multivariate Analysis of Social Capital Data

The tabulations discussed in the previous section map the different dimensions of social capital across spatial and socioeconomic characteristics. This section focuses on three questions that can be addressed only by multivariate analysis:

• What is the contribution of social capital to household well-being, that is, are households with a higher level of social capital, as measured by the various indicators proposed in the previous section, better off?
• What is the importance of social capital for poverty reduction?
• What are the determinants of social capital?

Table 3.10 Structural and Cognitive Social Capital in Rajasthan, India: Factor Analysis

Item	Factor 1
Dealing with crop disease	0.73052
Dealing with common pastures	0.64826
Settling disputes	0.73272
Dealing with errant children	0.72029
Value placed on unity	0.78680
Trust placed in others	0.66859

Source: Krishna and Uphoff 1999.

Table 3.11 Factor Analysis of Multiple Social Capital Variables, Ghana and Uganda

Factor	Eigenvalue	Percent of variance	Cumulative percent
Ghana			
GC	3.03	9.19	9.19
Trust	1.95	5.91	15.11
ES	1.84	5.58	20.69
ES	1.65	5.01	25.71
Volunteerism	1.63	4.94	30.66
ES	1.60	4.85	35.51
GC	1.25	3.80	39.32
Togetherness	1.18	2.59	42.90
ES	0.857	2.59	45.49
GC	0.772	2.34	47.83
Uganda			
GC	7.86	41.36	41.36
GN and togetherness	1.59	8.40	49.77
NC	1.49	7.88	57.65
Trust	1.17	6.19	63.85

GC = Group characteristics; ES = Everyday sociability; GN = Generalized norms; NC = Neighborhood connections.
Source: Narayan and Cassidy 2001.

These questions address the role of social capital in the poverty reduction strategy set forth by the *World Development Report 2000/2001* (World Bank 2001), as discussed in chapter 1. The first question focuses on the role of social capital in creating opportunities for enhancing income and improving other dimensions of well-being such as health and education. We also look at the extent to which social capital improves access to credit and thus contributes to reducing vulnerability. The second question looks at the relative importance of social capital in the asset portfolio of poor households. The third question addresses the critical issue of building social capital, a core element of the empowerment pillar of the *World Development Report's* poverty reduction strategy.

The Contribution of Social Capital to Household Welfare

To analyze the contribution of social capital to household welfare, we propose a simple conceptual framework whereby social capital is seen as one class of assets available to households for generating income and making consumption possible.[7] The household disposes of an asset endowment consisting of physical assets (land, equipment, cattle), human capital (years of schooling and work experience), and social capital. The household combines these assets to engage in productive activities, either in enterprises within the household or in the external labor market. This process involves making decisions about the labor supply of each household member and acquiring a number of productive inputs (agricultural inputs, credit) and services (education, health), which may need to be combined with labor supply in order to generate income. In this conceptual framework, each decision in the income-generating process is determined by the household's asset endowment, including social capital, in conjunction with the social and demographic characteristics of the household.

This model can be formalized in a set of structural equations making up a conventional model of household economic behavior under constrained utility maximization. By recognizing that the households' consumption behavior is a function of the level and composition of its income, the set of structural equations can be summarized by a reduced-form equation that expresses household consumption directly as a function of the asset endowments and other exogenous characteristics of the household, and of the economic environment in which it makes decisions. This leads to the following estimation equation:[8]

$$(3.1) \quad \ell n E_i = \alpha + \beta SC_i + \gamma HC_i + \delta OC_i + \varepsilon X_i + \eta Z_i + u_i$$

where E_i = household expenditure per capita of household i,
SC_i = household endowment of social capital,
HC_i = household endowment of human capital,
OC_i = household endowment of other assets,
X_i = a vector of household characteristics,
Z_i = a vector of village/region characteristics, and
u_i = error term.

The key feature of this model is the assumption that social capital is truly *capital* and hence has a measurable return to the household. Social capital has many features of capital: it requires resources (especially time) to be produced, and it is subject to accumulation and decumulation.[9] Social capital can be acquired in formal or informal settings, just like human capital (for example, schools versus learning-by-doing). Much social capital is built during interactions that occur for social, religious, or cultural reasons. This is reflected clearly, for example, in the pattern of organizational memberships in Indonesia, where almost one-half of all memberships are in organizations that pursue social, religious, or recreational purposes (Grootaert 1999a). Other interactions occur in settings specifically aimed to yield economic benefits. In Bolivia, for example, this is the case with the Agrarian Syndicates and other production-oriented groups (Grootaert and Narayan 2000).

The key assumption is that the networks built through these interactions have measurable benefits to the participating individuals, and lead, directly or indirectly, to a higher level of well-being (Putnam 1993). This is the proposition that can be tested empirically by means of equation 3.1.[10]

The dependent variable of equation 3.1 is the natural logarithm of household expenditure per capita.[11] The explanatory variables consist of the asset endowment of the household, demographic control variables, and locational dummy variables. Household assets consist of physical assets, human capital, and social capital. Relevant physical capital variables include the amount of land owned or operated by the household, ownership of a house (and its characteristics), farm equipment and tools, equipment and inventory that is part of a nonfarm household enterprise, and cattle.[12]

As the earlier discussion has made clear, numerous social capital variables are available for use in the regression. Following are a few examples of multivariate analyses that have used different combinations of variables capturing structural and cognitive social capital. One basic question that each analysis needs to address is whether different social capital dimensions should be introduced separately or as an index. The literature contains examples of both approaches. A study of Tanzanian villages by Narayan and Pritchett (1997) used a multiplicative index of social capital, capturing the density of associations, their internal diversity, and a measure of effective functioning. The justification for using a multiplicative index is that the effect of the number of organizations to which one belongs may not be independent of the internal degree of diversity or the type of functioning of the organization. The effects are assumed to interact.

The analysis in Tanzania found strong empirical support for the use of this type of index. A similar study for Indonesia also found a multiplicative social capital index to be significantly and positively related to household expenditure per capita, but in a study for Bolivia only an additive index was found to be significant (Grootaert 1999b, Grootaert and Narayan 2000). Unfortunately, the conceptual and theoretical literature on social capital has not yet provided a sufficiently refined model to justify one approach or the other. In part it remains therefore an empirical question to be tested in each case. Existing empirical analyses of social capital data have found support both for the use of an aggregate index (either multiplicative or additive) and for the inclusion of separate social capital dimensions.

Table 3.12 shows a basic application of equation 3.1 to data from Indonesia. It is useful to compare the model estimated with and without the social capital variable in order to highlight the relative contribution of social capital to household welfare. Including social capital increases the R-squared from 0.21 to 0.24. More important, it reduces the coefficient of human capital by about one-third. This suggests that at least some of the human capital effects operate through the networks and associations captured in the social capital index.

One interesting observation following from table 3.12 is that the estimated returns to human and social capital are quite similar. A 10 percent increase in the household's human capital endowment would lead to an increase in expenditure per capita of 1.65 percent, compared with a 1.18 percent increase stemming from a 10 percent increase in social capital endowment. This result is not unusual and was also obtained in similar empirical analyses for Bolivia and Burkina Faso (see Grootaert 2001 for a synthesis of these results). We emphasize here that this interpretation of the regression results critically depends upon the assumed exogeneity of social capital. This is a key assumption that is discussed more fully later in this chapter.

The main drawback of using a single index for social capital is that it provides little guidance as to which of the included aspects of social cap-

Table 3.12 Household Welfare and Social Capital: The Index Model

Variable	Coefficient	t-statistic	Coefficient	t-statistic
Intercept	12.7948	69.65	12.6782	67.59
Social capital index	0.0069	6.52	—	—
Household size	−0.0972	10.23	−0.0923	9.59
Years of education per adult	0.0343	4.49	0.0454	6.11
Female head of household	−0.0463	0.67	−0.0551	0.81
Age of head of household	0.0309	3.75	0.0354	4.20
Age of head of household squared	−0.0003	3.30	−0.0003	3.71
Farmer household	−0.2311	5.73	−0.2417	5.89
Jawa Tengah	−0.1630	3.90	−0.0987	2.40
Nusa Tenggara Timur	−0.3271	7.24	−0.2201	5.21
Number of observations	1,137		1,137	
R-squared	0.24		0.21	
F-statistic	33.6		31.3	

Notes:
1. Dependent variable = ln(household expenditure per capita).
2. t-statistics are based on robust standard errors (Hubert-White estimator for nonidentically distributed residuals).
Source: Grootaert 1999b.

ital produce the beneficial effect on household welfare. For example, is it more important to belong to many organizations, or is it more important to belong to democratic or internally diverse organizations? To address this question one needs to assume that each social capital dimension acts independently and that the effects are additive. This proposition can be empirically tested by including a series of variables that capture the different dimensions separately in the regression model. Table 3.13 shows the results of this exercise using seven different dimensions of social capital and the same data for Indonesia that underlie table 3.12. [13]

Note that the variables in this example include only structural social capital dimensions. The results suggest that the most important aspects

Table 3.13 Household Welfare and Social Capital: Disaggregating the Social Capital Index

Variable	Coefficient	t-statistic
Intercept	12.5318	64.66
Social capital dimensions		
Number of memberships	0.0146	2.43
Diversity index	0.0031	3.16
Meeting attendance	−0.0020	0.81
Index of participation in decisionmaking	0.0025	4.29
Cash contribution score	0.0113	1.46
Work contribution score	−0.0008	0.27
Community orientation	0.0000	0.01
Household characteristics		
Household size	−0.0947	9.87
Years of education	0.0322	4.22
Female head of household	−0.0303	0.44
Age of head of household	0.0298	3.62
Age of head of household squared	−0.0003	3.15
Farmer household	−0.2182	5.23
Province		
Jawa Tengah	−0.1686	3.56
Nusa Tenggara Timur	−0.3446	6.17
Number of observations	1,137	
R-squared	0.25	
F-statistic	21.7	

Notes:
1. Dependent variable = ln(household expenditure per capita).
2. t-statistics are based on robust standard errors (Hubert-White estimator for nonidentically distributed residuals).
Source: Grootaert 1999b.

of structural social capital are the number of memberships, internal diversity, and extensive participation in decisionmaking. The coefficient of the membership variable indicates that in Indonesia an additional membership in local organizations is associated with a 1.5 percent higher household expenditure level.[14]

The results also indicate that the benefits from participating in internally diverse organizations are higher than from participating in organizations whose members are more alike than different. The reasons for this may have to do with the exchanges of knowledge and information that occur among members. Members from different backgrounds may learn more from each other because they have different knowledge to start with. Similarly, people with different backgrounds may be able to pool risk more effectively because they are more likely to have different sources of income. The role of the different dimensions of diversity can be examined further by including each dimension as a separate regressor in the model. The Indonesian data suggest that the economic dimensions of diversity (occupation, education, and economic status) matter the most: organizations whose members differ in economic attributes yielded more benefits to their members than organizations whose members differed primarily in demographic attributes. Of course, whether this result for Indonesia applies elsewhere remains to be investigated.[15]

Finally, the results in table 3.13 suggest that active participation in the decisionmaking process of an organization increases benefits to households. In Indonesia, the coefficient of this variable is quite large: a 10 point increase in the active participation score (which is a 15 percent increase) corresponds with a 2.5 percent higher expenditure level—a larger effect than from adding a membership.

One of the important ways in which social capital can contribute to household welfare is by making household enterprises more profitable. For farmers, greater profitability can occur through better access to agricultural technology, inputs, and credit (discussed further below—see table 3.16). In the case of trading activities, good networks of clients and suppliers constitute social capital that complements a trader's financial, physical, and human capital. In situations where contract enforcement is often difficult and costly, these networks lower transaction costs and increase profitability. A study of agricultural traders in Madagascar by Fafchamps and Minten (1999) measured the extent of traders' networks and estimated the contribution of these networks, over and above that of working capital, equipment, labor, and management, to value added and sales. The two most important dimensions of social capital were the number of traders known and the number of people the trader could count on in times of trouble. A doubling of each of these networks would add 19 percent and 29 percent, respectively, to total sales (table 3.14).

Table 3.14 Determinants of Total Sales of Trading Firms in Madagascar

Variable		Coefficient	t-statistic
Capital and equipment			
Working capital	ln	0.3519	4.649
Dummy if subsidiary	1=yes	0.9538	4.290
Value of equipment	ln	0.0313	1.114
Storage capacity	ln	0.0438	0.767
Number of vehicles	ln	−0.4861	−2.191
Utilization of telephone	1=yes	0.5986	2.186
Labor and management			
Manpower (in months/year)	ln	0.7236	3.234
Dummy if full-time trader	1=yes	0.1340	0.854
Dummy if trader all year round	1=yes	0.3834	2.412
Years of schooling of owner/manager	level	0.0218	1.299
Years of experience in agricultural trade	ln	0.0913	1.199
Speak another language	1=yes	−0.2227	−1.876
Social capital			
Number of relatives in agricultural trade	ln	−0.2737	−2.794
Number of traders known	ln	0.1924	2.837
Number of people who can help	ln	0.2875	3.270
Number of suppliers known personally	ln	0.0721	1.149
Number of clients known personally	ln	0.1103	1.704
Shocks			
Aggregate sales shock	ratio	0.1926	2.235
Theft in the last 12 months	1=yes	−0.2560	−1.518
Location			
In capital city	1=yes	−0.5231	−1.482
In another city	1=yes	0.1792	1.386
In Vakinankaratra region	1=yes	−0.4315	−1.292
In Fianar/Haut Plateaux region	1=yes	−1.2057	−3.403
In Fianar/Côte et Falaise region	1=yes	−1.1150	−3.038
In Majunga/Plaines region	1=yes	−0.4667	−1.250
In Majunga/Plateau region	1=yes	−0.9785	−2.610
Intercept		4.5114	7.447
Number of observations		681	
F-value		32.47	
R-squared		0.568	
Joint test of nonfamily social capital	F-stat	p-value	
	4.59	0.0012	

Note: Dependent variable = ln (total sales)
Source: Fafchamps and Minten 1999.

The multivariate analysis discussed so far aimed to determine the impact of social capital on household welfare in general, as captured by income or expenditure. It is also useful to investigate whether social capital improves the nonmonetary dimensions of welfare, especially health and education. We give an example of each. In many poor countries, access to potable water is a critical determinant of health. A study of water supply systems in Central Java, Indonesia, found that social capital had a positive effect on the design, construction, and maintenance of water supply systems in villages, which in turn improved household health (Isham and Kähkönen 1999). Interestingly, these effects were observed only for piped water systems and not for public wells (table 3.15). It appears that piped systems require more collective effort and cooperation to construct and maintain, and thus the role of social capital is more critical for their success.

Table 3.15 The Effect of Social Capital on Household Health in Central Java, Indonesia

	Type of water supply	
Social capital variable	Public wells	Piped connections
Social capital index	−0.008	0.021 ***
	(0.011)	(0.005)
Density of membership	0.033	0.061 ***
	(0.041)	(0.016)
Meeting attendance	0.078	0.106
	(0.157)	(0.117)
Participation index	−0.120	0.159 ***
	(0.119)	(0.056)
Community orientation	−0.077	0.031
	(0.127)	(0.136)
Number of activities	0.062	0.093 ***
	(0.067)	(0.025)
Social interaction	−0.081	0.157 ***
	(0.074)	(0.057)
Neighborhood trust	0.004	−0.094
	(0.049)	(0.071)

Notes:
1. Dependent variable is improved household health. Sample sizes are 289 and 588 households, respectively. Other independent variables in the model (not reported) are agricultural land, years of schooling, household size, and previous use of river or pond.
2. Reported are marginal changes in the probability of the independent variable, calculated from probit estimation (Huber-adjusted standard errors are in parentheses). Significance levels are *** (99%), ** (95%), * (90%).
Source: Isham and Kähkönen 1999.

Better access to education often holds the key to the next generation's ability to escape from poverty. A higher involvement of the community and parents in the schools can improve the quality of schooling and reduce dropout rates. Coleman (1988) first made this observation about the role of social capital in the acquisition of human capital in the context of U.S. high schools, and it has proved valid in many other countries as well. For example, a study of Burkina Faso used the village average of the number of times households attended parent-teacher association (PTA) meetings during the year as an education-specific indicator of social capital (Grootaert, Oh, and Swamy 1999). A probit model of school attendance, which controlled for many household and village characteristics, found that one extra PTA attendance per household was associated with an increase of 3.5 percentage points in the probability that the child attended school. In light of the low school attendance rates in Burkina Faso, this is a substantial effect.

Is Social Capital Exogenous?

All the methods and results discussed so far depend critically on the assumption that social capital is part of the household's exogenous asset endowment, that is, those assets that determine income and consumption. This assumption needs to be carefully examined. The formation of networks and associations of different kinds can be costly in terms of time and other resources. Conceivably, therefore, households with higher income can devote more resources to network formation and thus acquire more social capital more easily. This is not unlike the situation of human capital, the demand for which also increases with income. The possibility exists, then, that social capital, like human capital, can be at least partly a consumption good. The extent to which this is the case depends in part on the type of network or association. For example, demand for participation in social groups pursuing leisure activities is quite likely to rise with income because leisure is usually a luxury good. If social capital is in part a consumption good, then reverse causality, from welfare level to social capital, is possible. In econometric terms, social capital becomes endogenous in equation 3.1, and its estimated coefficient will be upward biased if the equation is estimated by Ordinary Least Squares (OLS).

The standard solution to endogeneity problems is the use of instrumental variable estimation, which provides an empirical test of the extent of two-way causality. The real challenge in applying this method is to find a suitable instrument set for social capital: instruments must determine social capital, but not household welfare (nor be determined by household welfare). It is not an easy task to identify such instruments, and only a limited number of empirical studies have had any measure of success with this approach. Narayan and Pritchett's (1997) study of social capital in Tanzania used a measure of generalized trust as an instrument for their social capital index that captured dimensions of structural social capital. They contend that generalized trust is built over time, is a function of village cohesion and norms, and is independent of the income level of a specific household. While this argument has a certain validity, the difficulty is that essentially one type of social capital (cognitive social capital) is used as an instrument for another type (structural social capital). A similar approach was followed in a study on Burkina Faso by Grootaert, Oh, and Swamy (1999), who constructed an index of trust derived from questions about whether people perceived others to be making fair contributions to collective activities and whether people thought they could get emergency help from villagers. The limitations of the instrument notwithstanding, both studies found that it passed standard statistical tests used to check the validity of instrumental variables and supported the interpretation that social capital is a causal factor of household welfare and not the other way around.

The Burkina Faso study also proposed two other instruments:

- *Length of residency in the village.* Building a social network takes time, and thus the longer the household resides in the village, the greater the potential for building social capital through interaction with other villagers.
- *Trend of membership in associations.* Households were asked whether they were currently members of more, the same, or fewer organizations than five years earlier. The retroactive nature of this information makes it an ideal instrument since it clearly cannot be influenced by current income.

It is possible to search for instruments at the level of the village or neighborhood. Each of the following variables can arguably be seen as affecting the household's endowment of social capital but not its income:

- *Ethnic and religious diversity of the community.* This variable affects directly the potential diversity of associations, but there is no reason to assume that the village's ethnic or religious composition would directly affect a given household's income.
- *Density and effectiveness of institutions in the community.* Clearly, the possibility for a given household to join an association increases as more associations exist in the community. The likelihood of joining and being active can also be expected to increase as organizations are perceived to be effective.

- *The community's involvement in the procurement of social services and infra-structure.* Such involvement is likely to encourage people to join organizations dealing with education, health, roads, or other infrastructure. It does not, however, have a direct effect on household income, which stems from the use of such services or infrastructure.
- *Traditional authority.* The existence of a traditional council of village elders or similar institution mandated to deal with conflict or contract enforcement may be a sign of respect for tradition and adherence to norms.
- *Past community involvement in the creation of associations.* The perception that the community is actively involved in the creation of local organizations may increase the level of trust in these organizations and make it more likely that households would join. Since this is a historical variable, there is no possibility for reverse causation.

Each of these candidates for instrumental variables can be subjected to standard econometric tests that will indicate whether the variable in question is a valid instrument.[16] It is recommended that analysts test each potential instrument separately as well as in different combinations to determine how sensitive the results are to the selection of specific instruments.

Most studies using the instrumental variables method have found that it led to higher coefficients for the social capital variable compared with the OLS model. This finding suggests that equation 3.1 is correctly specified and that social capital is an exogenous determinant of household welfare. If reverse causality were significant, the coefficient of the social capital index in the instrumental variables regression would be lower than the OLS coefficient. The substantive interpretation of this result strengthens the case for viewing social capital as an input in the household production function and as a causal factor of household welfare. However, the same econometric result would be obtained if social capital is measured with a high degree of error.[17] Unfortunately, it is generally not possible to provide independent verification of the latter. One hopes that the use of multiple indicators for social capital as well as multiple instruments reduces the possibility that measurement error drives the result.

Instrumental variable results are, of course, only as good as the instruments are believable, and it is desirable therefore to address the issue of causality in different ways. The theoretical ideal would be to have historical data available, since no reverse causality is possible from current income to past indicators of social capital. Both the community profile and the organizational profile of the SOCAT contain several questions about the historical evolution of organizations and the community's role in creating them. This information captures elements of the creation of social capital in the past and is ideally suited to test whether a tradition of collective activities and social capital building has an impact on current welfare. Many of the questions in the community and organizational profiles lend themselves fairly easily to quantification, and variables could be constructed that can be added into equation 3.1.

The Indonesian study from which several of the earlier examples in this chapter were drawn illustrates the potential value of such data. The Indonesian village data files include information on the major development projects undertaken in the sample villages during the past 10 years and on the degree of community involvement in the design, funding, and implementation of the project. These data made it possible to construct an index of past community involvement for each village as a variable measuring historical social capital. This variable was added to equation 3.1, along with a number of village-level control variables, including one for the number of development projects that the village undertook. The results indicated that past social capital had positive effects on current incomes over and above those stemming from current social capital and over and above the effect of the development projects themselves (Grootaert 1999b). This finding could reflect the fact that projects with high beneficiary participation are more effective (Isham, Narayan, and Pritchett 1995); it is also in line with Putnam's (1993) position that it is the history of civic engagement that explains differences in the economic performance of communities.

After the use of instrumental variables and historical data (where available), a third way to tackle the potential endogeneity of social capital is to move away from the reduced-form model of equation 3.1 and attempt to estimate structural equations; they capture directly one of the pathways through which social capital affects welfare. Structurally, social capital achieves improvements in welfare through various channels: better access to information, better ability to cope with risk, better collective decisionmaking. It is possible to construct variables for each of those channels. Narayan and Pritchett's 1997 study on social capital in Tanzania estimates several equations that explain farmers' access to new agricultural technology. The results indicate that households living in villages with high levels of social capital have a higher probability of using agrochemicals or fertilizer, although social capital was not found to be related to the adoption of improved seeds (table 3.16).

Access to credit is an important way in which households improve their ability to manage income risk (World Bank 2001). The Tanzania study found that high village-level social capital led to better access to credit, although the effect was not very large (table 3.16). A study for Indonesia, however, found strong household-level effects of membership

Table 3.16 Household Probability of Adopting Improved Agricultural Practices in Tanzania (calculated from probit estimates)

Variable	Used agrochemicals	Used fertilizer	Used improved seeds	Used credit for agri-cultural improve-ments
Village social capital	0.057	0.075	0.015	0.027
	(2.35)	(2.45)	(0.737)	(1.66)
Household size	0.012	−0.006	0.004	−0.0019
	(3.25)	(1.43)	(1.03)	(0.742)
Average household adult education	0.019	0.0078	0.010	0.0044
	(5.00)	(1.56)	(2.30)	(1.21)
Female head	−0.102	−0.112	−0.114	0.0035
	(2.89)	(3.46)	(3.51)	(0.143)
Assets	0.049	0.110	0.058	0.0069
	(2.45)	(6.28)	(2.63)	(0.606)
Self-employed in agriculture	0.046	−0.035	−0.037	0.027
	(1.49)	(0.958)	(1.06)	(1.03)
Median distance to market	−0.013	0.005	−0.005	−0.0052
	(2.34)	(0.855)	(1.16)	(1.51)
Observed probability	0.217	0.197	0.169	0.093
Pred. probability at means	0.155	0.129	0.125	0.078
Number of observations	772	734	765	842
Pseudo R-squared	0.204	0.254	0.147	0.71

Notes:
1. In parentheses are the Huber-corrected t-statistics of the probit regression coefficients (not the t-statistics of the reported marginal effects).
2. Included in the regression but not reported were dummy variables for agro-climatic zones, and for missing values of the assets, schooling, and distance to market variables.
Source: Narayan and Pritchett 1997.

in organizations on access to credit (Grootaert 1999b). The study separat-ed memberships in financial associations from those in nonfinancial asso-ciations and found that memberships in both types of organizations con-tributed to access to credit. This is an interesting example of why social capital is truly "social": the building of networks and trust among mem-bers in the context of a nonfinancial social setting spills over into finan-cial benefits, such as easier access to credit.[18]

In summary, this section has proposed a multivariate analysis to assess the contribution of social capital to household welfare. Two approaches are possible. The first one relies on a social capital index combining different dimensions, usually in a multiplicative way. An alternative method is to include different dimensions of social capital as independent regressors in the model. This method brings out more clearly those aspects of social capital that contribute to household welfare. Either method assumes that social capital is part of the exogenous asset endowment of households. This assumption needs to be tested empirically. We discussed three methods for testing: instrumental variables estimation, the use of historical data, and the estimation of structural equations. The empirical evidence from studies that have undertaken these methods generally suggests that the overwhelming direction of causality is from social capital to household welfare. However, the number of case studies for which this type of analysis is currently available is fairly limited, and we hope that the increased availability of the Social Capital Assessment Tool will lead to future analyses that will further validate these findings.

Social Capital and Poverty

The analysis suggested in the previous section can furnish evidence of the extent to which social capital has positive effects on household welfare and which dimensions contribute the most to that effect. One question remaining is whether social capital helps the poor to the same degree as it does the rich and whether investments in social capital can help poor groups escape from poverty. A useful starting point for answering this question is the distribution of the ownership of social capital relative to other types of assets. An example from Bolivia is given in table 3.17.

Table 3.17 Ownership of Assets, by Quintile of Household Expenditure per Capita, in Bolivia

Variable	1 (Poorest)	2	3	4	5 (Richest)	All
Social capital index						
Multiplicative index	19.7	20.1	20.2	18.2	16.2	18.9
Additive index	21.4	22.7	24.1	24.7	25.0	23.6
Years of education	3.3	3.8	3.9	4.1	4.5	3.9
Land ownership (hectares)	2.7	3.9	2.9	2.7	4.8	3.4
Animal ownership (number)	19.1	16.6	19.9	19.4	22.4	19.5
Farm equipment ownership (number)	0.5	0.4	0.5	0.5	0.5	0.5
Household durables	1.7	1.9	2.2	2.4	3.0	2.2

Source: Grootaert and Narayan 2000.

The poorest quintile of households has only 3.3 years of education, compared with 4.5 years for the richest quintile. Land and household durables are distributed more unequally. In contrast, the additive social capital index is only slightly below average for the poorest quintile, and the multiplicative index is even above average—indicating that poor households in Bolivia have *relatively* more social capital than other assets. The question is whether this accumulation of social assets by the poor is rational, in the sense that it indeed helps them escape poverty or at least provides them with relatively higher returns than other assets.[19]

This question can be addressed by three complementary methodological approaches: a probit model of the likelihood of being poor, quantile regressions, and split-sample estimation of equation 3.1.

The probit model collapses the distribution of expenditure into a binary variable that takes a value of one if the household falls below the poverty line. This approach is potentially useful when the underlying expenditure data may contain nonrandom measurement error that is eliminated when the distribution is collapsed (except for some possible misclassification around the poverty line).[20] The explanatory variables of the model are the same as those for equation 3.1. Studies that have used this method have typically found that social capital does significantly reduce the probability of being poor. Memberships in internally diverse associations were especially helpful, particularly if members came from different educational and occupational backgrounds. This suggests that the mechanisms at work are primarily those of exchanging information and knowledge and perhaps also the pooling of risks over households with different sources of income (Grootaert 2001).

Quantile regressions are a further way to explore differences between the poor and the rich in the role of social capital. Quantile regressions estimate the regression line through given points on the distribution of the dependent variable (while an OLS regression line goes through the mean) and can assess whether certain explanatory factors are weaker or stronger in different parts of the distribution.[21] Results for Bolivia, Burkina Faso, and Indonesia all suggest that the returns to social capital, as measured by an aggregate index, are highest at the bottom of the distribution (table 3.18).

The third method available to investigate differential returns to social capital is the split-sample approach. The sample should be split according to an exogenous variable, such as education or landholdings. Splitting the sample into poor and nonpoor subgroups is not advisable, because it is likely to introduce selection bias into the results. Split-sample estimation of equation 3.1 for the same three countries indicated that the returns to social capital were in each case larger for smallholders than for households with higher amounts of land (Grootaert 2001).

Table 3.18 Poverty and Social Capital: Quantile Regression Results

Location	10th percentile	25th percentile	Median	75th percentile	90th percentile
		Coefficient of social capital index at			
Bolivia	0.0059*	0.0052*	0.0055*	0.0055*	0.0044*
Burkina Faso	0.0062*	0.0047*	0.0027*	0.0014	-0.0003
Indonesia	0.0096*	0.0090*	0.0078*	0.0048*	0.0049*

Note: * indicates significance at the 90% level.
Source: Grootaert 1999b; Grootaert, Oh, and Swamy 1999; Grootaert and Narayan 2000.

Taken together, findings from the available studies suggest that returns to social capital are generally higher for households in the lower half of the distribution, whether by expenditure per capita or land ownership. This is perhaps the sense in which social capital is the capital of the poor; they do not necessarily have more of it, but it provides them with greater returns and hence occupies a more prominent place in their portfolio of assets. These results, like all the other examples in this chapter, are country-specific. However, in the settings investigated, they make the case that promoting the participation of poor households in local organizations is a potentially valuable ingredient of poverty alleviation policy.

The Determinants of Social Capital

All the analyses proposed so far have focused on the potential contribution of social capital to household welfare and other outcomes, that is, they have treated social capital as an explanatory variable. This treatment is consistent with the conceptual framework in which social capital is seen as part of the asset endowment of the household. Although social capital shares many attributes with other forms of capital, it is fundamentally different in one respect, namely, its creation can never be the result of one individual's action. It requires interaction between at least two people and usually among a larger group of people.[22]

If social capital is not subject to the same person-to-person market exchanges through which, for example, physical capital can be acquired or sold, then how does it come about? The literature has emphasized that the creation of social capital is a complex process heavily influenced by social, political, and cultural factors as well as by the dominant types of economic activities. The construction of empirical models with social capital as a dependent variable will therefore have to be much more complex than models that merely seek to assess the relative contribution of social capital together with other determinants of well-being. Hence, great caution is needed if data from the SOCAT are used for multivariate analysis with social capital as a dependent variable. The number of determinants of the creation of social capital that could actually be captured in such a model based on the SOCAT data (or, for that matter, based on data collected by almost any practical instrument) is likely to be a small subset of the total set of relevant variables, so any such model would be subject to significant specification bias.

Nevertheless, efforts have been undertaken in the empirical literature to see to what degree certain observable factors can explain various indicators of social capital. One example is a study of the role of collective action for conserving and developing watersheds in Rajasthan, India (Krishna and Uphoff 1999). Although the study focused on examining how much social capital contributes to the development and the maintenance of watersheds, it also looked at the factors (at the level of the household and the community) that were associated with higher levels of social capital. Specifically, the study examined the relevance of eight possible determinants: (1) prior experience with collective action, (2) existence of rules of behavior in the community, (3) extent of participatory decisionmaking, (4) number of sources of information, (5) education, (6) economic status, (7) demographic characteristics, and (8) district history. As table 3.19 shows, the first four of these factors turned out to be highly significant predictors of the amount of social capital, as did district history. The coefficients of these four significant variables added up to more than one standard deviation in the household distribution of social capital. In contrast, attributes such as education, economic status, and demographic characteristics did not prove to be significant predictors.

Another study used a multi-equation system to analyze the determinants of three types of social capital and their role in explaining why some communities in Dhaka, Bangladesh, were able to organize themselves to arrange for the private collection of solid waste (Pargal, Huq, and Gilligan 1999). Solid waste collection is a public good that involves positive externalities and thus the role of the community is vital since incentives for individual action are limited. The study hypothesized that three aspects of social capital would be relevant, namely, trust, reciprocity, and willingness to share goods with people in need. The study explicitly recognized two-way causality whereby each of these three factors determines the probability that a trash collection system would be orga-

Table 3.19 OLS Regression of the Determinants of Household-Level Social Capital in Rajasthan, India

Variable	Coefficient	Standard error
Intercept	27.38***	2.49
Prior experience		
Experience of collective action within the last 12 months	5.27***	0.27
Prior collective management of common lands	0.74*	0.30
Rules		
Clear and fair rules relating to common land development	4.85***	0.66
Participation		
Participative decisionmaking vs. decisions by chiefs alone	1.09*	0.58
Decisions made by all vs. decisions by technical specialists	2.09***	0.57
Information		
Number of sources of information	0.80***	0.15
Education		
Number of years	−0.59	0.45
Status		
Landholding	0.04	0.02
Caste status	−0.16	0.27
Demographic variables		
Gender	0.41	0.56
Family size	0.08	0.12
Length of residence in the village	−0.25	0.20
History (district dummy variables)		
Bhilwara	−1.69*	0.81
Rajsamand	8.60***	0.83
Udaipur	8.03***	0.84
Number of observations	1,451	
R-squared	0.453	
F-ratio	79.24	
F-probability	0.0001	

Note: Significance levels are *** (99%), ** (95%), * (90%).
Source: Krishna and Uphoff 1999.

nized and that once such a system existed, it would contribute to enhancing trust, reciprocity, and willingness to share. The authors therefore estimated a simultaneous equation system consisting of four equations, as summarized below.

$$Trust \ = \ f(\text{existence of trash collection;}$$
$$\text{household characteristics;}$$
$$\text{community characteristics})$$
$$Reciprocity \ = \ f(\text{existence of trash collection;}$$
$$\text{household characteristics;}$$
$$\text{community characteristics})$$
$$Sharing \ = \ f(\text{existence of trash collection;}$$
$$\text{household characteristics;}$$
$$\text{community characteristics})$$
$$\text{Existence of trash collection} \ = \ f(\text{trust, reciprocity, sharing;}$$
$$\text{household characteristics;}$$
$$\text{community characteristics}).$$

The study found that reciprocity and norms of sharing have a significant positive effect on the probability of organizing for trash collection. In terms of the determinants of social capital, the share of households with a business and the share of residents that own their home were positively and significantly associated with all three measures of social capital (table 3.20). This may reflect that the business community in Dhaka is fairly close-knit, but it also implies that the members of the business community foster trust and norms of reciprocity among other community members including those not involved in business. Likewise, homeowners appear to have a stronger effect on community social ties than tenants, who may be more temporary residents.

While such studies illuminate the relative importance of personal attributes, the household's experience with past collective action, and institutional factors such as the presence of rules and participatory mechanisms, still the studies cannot explain why some communities have clearer and fairer rules than others or why they have a stronger past experience with participation and collective action. It is doubtful that a quantitative analytic approach is likely to shed much further light on this question beyond the kind of results provided by the previous examples. Progress will have to be made by an integration of quantitative and qualitative analytic methods. Much of the existing social capital literature can be classified as either quantitative or qualitative, but there are very few examples where the complementaries between the two methods have been successfully exploited.

Caveats

This chapter on the analysis of social capital data closes with a few caveats, specifically about how *not* to use the data from the Social Capital Assessment Tool. The prime objectives of the tool are to measure struc-

Table 3.20 OLS Regression of the Determinants of Social Capital in Dhaka, Bangladesh

Variable	Trust score	Reciprocity score	Sharing score
Intercept	0.8427**	1.8705**	1.4387**
	(0.1966)	(0.1398)	(0.1523)
Presence of voluntary solid	0.1348	0.0916	0.1022
waste management system	(0.0839)	(0.0596)	(0.0650)
Median tenure	0.0041	0.0040*	0.0024
	(0.0029)	(0.0021)	(0.0023)
Origin = Chittagong	0.1388	0.1641**	0.2580**
	(0.0889)	(0.0632)	(0.0688)
Homeowners (%)	0.0104*	0.0074*	0.0167**
	(0.0061)	(0.0043)	(0.0047)
Business jobs (%)	0.0076**	0.0070**	0.0111**
	(0.0037)	(0.0027)	(0.0029)
Number of meeting places	−0.1318**	0.0702**	0.0138
	(0.0378)	(0.0269)	(0.0293)
Number of private organizations	0.0736	0.0274	0.0915
	(0.0841)	(0.0598)	(0.0652)
Number of public organizations	0.0286	−0.0499	−0.0376
	(0.0492)	(0.0350)	(0.0381)
Adjusted R-squared	0.2626	0.2611	0.3819
Number of observations	65	65	65
t-statistic for exogeneity test	0.6050	1.4345	1.8791

Note: Standard errors in parentheses. Significance levels are ** (95%), * (90%).
Source: Pargal, Huq, and Gilligan 1999.

tural and cognitive social capital at the levels of the household and the community. The community and organizational profiles also contribute to understanding the links between different organizations and their relevance for the provision of various services in the community. Both the quantitative and the qualitative data can be used to assess the impact, positive or negative, of social capital on a range of outcomes at the household and community levels. The analysis discussed in this chapter has largely stayed within this framework. As we have pointed out, efforts at explaining how the observed levels and types of social capital come about have been successful only to a very limited degree. We caution therefore against expectations that the data from the SOCAT can be used to explain how social capital is created and why it is weak or strong in certain communities. The dynamics of the creation of social capital are complex and involve many political, social, and cultural factors. Efforts to analyze these dynamics need to rely on a wider range of tools than the SOCAT. We emphasize that the tool was primarily designed to assess the contribution of social capital and not the process of its creation.

One of the important findings of the empirical social capital literature is that the social capital characteristics of a community can make a great difference in project outcomes. Communities that have strong social capital are more successful in managing irrigation projects, water supply and sanitation projects, and many other types of infrastructure projects. Education projects benefit from the presence of cohesive and well-functioning parent-teacher associations. There are many such examples. It is therefore tempting to target interventions to communities that have strong social capital and to use tools like the SOCAT as a screening or targeting device. In principle, the SOCAT can be used for this purpose, but the danger of this application lies in the lack of available benchmarks.

Consider the parallel with poverty targeting. Data from instruments such as the Living Standards Measurement Surveys are routinely used to calculate household expenditure per capita and, on the basis of this, the incidence of poverty in different communities. Interventions are then frequently targeted based on the extent of poverty. This targeting can be done because poverty benchmarks are well understood and well established. The literature as well as the development practice of using poverty thresholds has a tradition of several decades. This is not the case with social capital. Even if an instrument like SOCAT were able to measure social capital perfectly, using the information as a targeting device would still be dangerous because there is insufficient knowledge about which dimensions of social capital are important for project success and what the critical levels are for each of them. As we have documented in this chapter, the different dimensions of social capital have different effects on outcomes, and these effects are not constant across countries. For example, the internal diversity of associations was found to be a critical determinant of outcomes in Indonesia and Burkina Faso but not in Bolivia.

Hence, at the current stage of knowledge, it would be extremely risky to set benchmarks for the density of networks and organizations or their internal diversity and then attempt to target project interventions to communities meeting these targets. Of course, this does not constitute an argument for not using the SOCAT and similar tools; quite the opposite. Only through frequent applications of the tool will a caseload be built up from which generalizations will become possible and that might at some point in the future lead to sufficient knowledge to identify those aspects and levels of social capital that are responsible for success in project outcomes. That knowledge would provide valuable information for future efforts to strengthen social capital.

Notes

1. For further information on these activities, see Grootaert (2001), Grootaert and van Bastelaer (2001), and World Bank (1998). On the World Wide Web, see www.worldbank.org/socialdevelopment and www.iris.umd.edu/adass/proj/soccappubs.asp.

2. See also the reviews of the social capital literature in Grootaert (1997), Portes (1998), Woolcock (1998), and Woolcock and Narayan (2000). Many case studies are also discussed and cited in Krishna, Uphoff, and Esman (1997); Narayan (1995); Uphoff (1993); and Uphoff, Esman, and Krishna (1998).

3. Evidence indicates that homogeneity facilitates the adoption of new technology (Rogers 1995, Isham 1998).

4. For a further discussion on trust, see, for example, Dasgupta (1988), Fukuyama (1995), and Granovetter (1973).

5. The SOCAT questionnaire does not include questions about trust in specific individuals or types of individuals (relatives, friends, teachers) or about trust in institutions (police, courts, the government).

6. The genocides in Cambodia and Rwanda are extreme examples of the link between violence and the lack of inclusive social capital (Colletta and Cullen 2000).

7. As explained in chapter 1, the SOCAT is an instrument for collecting social capital information, and as such, it does not contain modules to capture information on land and physical assets, nor does it contain modules to capture income or expenditure variables. The analysis discussed in this section thus requires that the SOCAT be combined with modules from other surveys to collect the necessary information. Chapter 1 lists several surveys available for this purpose.

8. This reduced-form model has been used by a number of studies on social capital, such as Grootaert (1999b); Grootaert and Narayan (2000); Maluccio, Haddad, and May (2000); and Narayan and Pritchett (1997).

9. Events in transition economies such as Russia and former Yugoslavia are powerful evidence of the effects of the decumulation of social capital (Rose 1995).

10. As said, equation 3.1 is a reduced-form model. In structural terms, the returns to social capital could be measured in earnings functions (for instance, if one's network helps in getting better-paying jobs or promotions) or in the various functions that determine access to credit, agricultural inputs, or other factors that enhance the productivity of a household enterprise.

11. An alternative specification would be to use the natural logarithm of household expenditure per equivalent adult if data are available to support the estimation of an adult equivalency scale. In countries where regional price variation is significant, the expenditure variable should be deflated by a regional price index. If such an index is not available, regional dummy variables can be included in the regression to capture price differences and other differences not observed across regions.

12. The inclusion of physical asset variables in a regression with consumption as dependent variables could be problematic due to possible endogeneity. Some households may indeed sell assets to pay for current consumption. Ideally, this problem can be addressed by including variables that capture the stock of assets at the beginning of the consumption reference period. In practice, this type of information is rarely available, and the analyst will need to make a judgment as to whether possible endogeneity bias would be outweighed by the specification bias resulting from dropping such variables. In practice, it is recommended that equations be estimated with and without problematic asset variables to see if key results remain unchanged.

13. Some of these dimensions can be derived from the information collected by the SOCAT, notably the number of memberships, the diversity index, and the index of participation in decisionmaking. Other variables, such as meeting attendance and community orientation were not included in the SOCAT, in part because previous analyses did not systematically support their relevance.

14. There is a close parallel in the interpretation of the coefficients of human and social capital variables. The former represents the returns to years of investment in education through school attendance. In the case of social capital, the main input is also time, and the coefficient measures the returns to the time spent in developing networks, attending association meetings, and the like. This time can be spread over many years.

15. A similar finding was obtained for Burkina Faso (Grootaert, Oh, and Swamy 1999), but an analysis for Bolivia did not support the importance of internal diversity for outcomes (Grootaert and Narayan 2000).

16. Commonly used is the test for overidentifying restrictions proposed by Davidson and MacKinnon (1993). For applications of this test see, for example, Grootaert (1999b) and Narayan and Pritchett (1997).

17. In that case, the instrumental variable method merely corrects for the attenuation bias in the OLS results.

18. This interpretation of social capital has been proposed by several authors, including Dasgupta (1988), Fukuyama (1995), and Putnam (1993).

19. The ideal data set for answering these questions is a panel data set, which follows the same households over time. However, since panel data sets with social capital data are very rare, we focus on the analysis of cross-sectional data.

20. There is some evidence to suggest that measurement error is strongest at the two extremes of the distribution. The probit model is especially useful in such a circumstance. For further discussion, see Grootaert and Braithwaite (1998).

21. However, the estimation is conditional upon the values of the independent variables and hence coefficients from quantile regressions are not comparable with those of OLS regressions. Specifically, the coefficients show the effect of a marginal change in an explanatory variable on the xth conditional quantile of the dependent variable (Buchinsky 1998).

22. This issue is related to, but nevertheless distinct from, the question of collective versus individual ownership of social capital. Both positions have been advanced in the literature, with Putnam (1993) being perhaps the most noted proponent of the view that social capital is a collective asset. Others, such as Portes (1998), suggest that social capital may well be individually owned even though the creation of social capital requires interaction among multiple individuals. Thus, the process of asset creation should be distinguished from its ultimate ownership. The model underlying the analysis proposed in this chapter clearly takes the position that social capital can be individually owned.

References

The word *processed* describes informally reproduced works that may not be commonly available through libraries.

Bebbington, Anthony J., and Thomas F. Carroll. 2000. "Induced Social Capital and Federations of the Rural Poor." Social Capital Initiative Working Paper 19. World Bank, Social Development Department, Washington, D.C.

Buchinsky, Moshe. 1998. "Recent Advances in Quantile Regression Models." *Journal of Human Resources* 33 (1): 88–126.

Coleman, James. 1988. "Social Capital in the Creation of Human Capital." *American Journal of Sociology* 94 (Supplement): S95–S120.

Colletta, Nat J., and Michelle L. Cullen. 2000. "The Nexus between Violent Conflict, Social Capital, and Social Cohesion: Case Studies from Cambodia and Rwanda." Social Capital Initiative Working Paper 23. World Bank, Social Development Department, Washington, D.C.

Dasgupta, Partha. 1988. "Trust as a Commodity." In Gambetta, D., ed., *Trust: Making and Breaking Cooperative Relations*. Oxford: Blackwell.

Davidson, Russell, and James MacKinnon. 1993. *Estimation and Inference in Econometrics*. New York: Oxford University Press.

Fafchamps, Marcel, and Bart Minten. 1999. "Social Capital and the Firm: Evidence from Agricultural Trade." Social Capital Initiative Working Paper 17. World Bank, Social Development Department, Washington, D.C.

Fukuyama, Francis. 1995. *Trust: The Social Values and the Creation of Prosperity*. New York: Free Press.

Granovetter, Marc. 1973. "The Strength of Weak Ties." *American Journal of Sociology* 78: 1360–80.

Grootaert, Christiaan. 1997. "Social Capital: The Missing Link?" Chapter 6 in *Expanding the Measure of Wealth—Indicators of Environmentally Sustainable Development*. Washington, D.C.: World Bank.

————. 1999a. "Local Institutions and Service Delivery in Indonesia." Local Level Institutions Working Paper 5. World Bank, Social Development Department, Washington, D.C.

————. 1999b. "Social Capital, Household Welfare, and Poverty in Indonesia." Local Level Institutions Working Paper 6. World Bank, Social Development Department, Washington, D.C.

————. 2001. "Does Social Capital Help the Poor? A Synthesis of Findings from the Local Level Institutions Studies in Bolivia, Burkina Faso, and Indonesia." Local Level Institutions Working Paper 10. World Bank, Social Development Department, Washington, D.C.

Grootaert, Christiaan, and Jeanine Braithwaite. 1998. "Poverty Correlates and Indicator-Based Targeting in Eastern Europe and the Former Soviet Union." Policy Research Working Paper 1942. World Bank, Washington, D.C.

Grootaert, Christiaan, and Deepa Narayan. 2000. "Local Institutions, Poverty, and Household Welfare in Bolivia." Local Level Institutions Working Paper 9. World Bank, Social Development Department, Washington, D.C.

Grootaert, Christiaan, Gi-Taik Oh, and Anand Swamy. 1999. "Social Capital and Development Outcomes in Burkina Faso." Local Level Institutions Working Paper 7. World Bank, Social Development Department, Washington, D.C.

Grootaert, Christiaan, and Thierry van Bastelaer. 2001. "Understanding and Measuring Social Capital: A Synthesis of Findings from the Social Capital Initiative." Social Capital Initiative Working Paper 24. World Bank, Social Development Department, Washington, D.C.

Isham, Jonathan. 1998. "The Effect of Social Capital on Technology Adoption: Evidence from Rural Tanzania." University of Maryland, Department of Economics, College Park, Md. Processed.

Isham, Jonathan, and Satu Kähkönen. 1999. "What Determines the Effectiveness of Community-Based Water Projects? Evidence from Central Java, Indonesia, on Demand Responsiveness, Service Rules, and Social Capital." Social Capital Initiative Working Paper 14. World Bank, Social Development Department, Washington, D.C.

Isham, Jonathan, Deepa Narayan, and Lant Pritchett. 1995. "Does Participation Improve Performance? Establishing Causality with Subjective Data." *World Bank Economic Review* 9 (2): 175–200.

Krishna, Anirudh, and Norman Uphoff. 1999. "Mapping and Measuring Social Capital: A Conceptual and Empirical Study of Collective Action for Conserving and Developing Watersheds in Rajasthan, India." Social Capital Initiative Working Paper 13. World Bank, Social Development Department, Washington, D.C.

Krishna, Anirudh, Norman Uphoff, and Milton Esman, eds. 1997. *Reasons for Hope—Instructive Experiences in Rural Development*. West Hartford, Conn.: Kumarian Press.

Maluccio, John, Lawrence Haddad, and Julian May. 2000. "Social Capital and Household Welfare in South Africa, 1993–98." *Journal of Development Studies* 36 (5): 56–81.

Narayan, Deepa. 1995. "Designing Community-Based Development." Environment Department Paper 7. World Bank, Washington, D.C.

Narayan, Deepa, and Michael Cassidy. 2001. "A Dimensional Approach to Measuring Social Capital: Development and Validation of a Social Capital Inventory." *Current Sociology* 49 (2): 49–93.

Narayan, Deepa, and Lant Pritchett. 1997. "Cents and Sociability— Household Income and Social Capital in Rural Tanzania." Policy Research Working Paper 1796. World Bank, Washington, D.C.

Pargal, Sheoli, Mainul Huq, and Daniel Gilligan. 1999. "Social Capital in Solid Waste Management: Evidence from Dhaka, Bangladesh." Social Capital Initiative Working Paper 16. World Bank, Social Development Department, Washington, D.C.

Portes, Alejandro. 1998. "Social Capital: Its Origins and Applications in Modern Sociology." *Annual Review of Sociology* 24: 1–24.

Putnam, Robert D., with Robert Leonardi and Raffaela Nanetti. 1993. *Making Democracy Work: Civic Tradition in Modern Italy*. Princeton, N.J.: Princeton University Press.

Rogers, Everett M. 1995. *Diffusion of Innovations*. New York: Free Press.

Rose, Richard. 1995. "Russia as an Hour Glass Society: A Constitution without Citizens." *East European Constitutional Review* 4 (3): 34–42.

Swamy, Anand, Christiaan Grootaert, and Gi-Taik Oh. 1999. "Local Institutions and Service Delivery in Burkina Faso." Local Level Institutions Working Paper 8. World Bank, Social Development Department, Washington, D.C.

Uphoff, Norman. 1993. "Grassroots Organizations and NGOs in Rural Development: Opportunities with Diminishing States and Expanding Market." *World Development* 21 (4): 607–22.

Uphoff, Norman, Milton Esman, and Anirudh Krishna. 1998. *Reasons for Success—Learning from Instructive Experiences in Rural Development*. West Hartford, Conn.: Kumarian Press.

Werner, Silvia. 1998. "Local Level Institutions and Collective Action." World Bank, Social Development Department, Washington, D.C. Processed.

Woolcock, Michael. 1998. "Social Capital and Economic Development: Toward a Theoretical Synthesis and Policy Framework." *Theory and Society* 27 (2): 151–208.

Woolcock, Michael, and Deepa Narayan. 2000. "Social Capital: Implications for Development Theory, Research, and Policy." *World Bank Research Observer* 15 (2): 225–50.

World Bank. 1998. "The Local Level Institutions Study: Program Description and Prototype Questionnaires." Local Level Institutions Working Paper 2. World Bank, Social Development Department, Washington, D.C.

———. 2001. *World Development Report 2000/2001: Attacking Poverty*. New York: Oxford University Press.

4

Qualitative Analysis of Social Capital: The Case of Agricultural Extension in Mali

Catherine Reid and Lawrence Salmen

This chapter focuses on the cognitive dimensions of social capital, that is, interpersonal trust expressed through the relationships among a society's members, institutions, and organizations. The manner in which people relate to one another in and through institutions affects the quality of their lives and the degree to which they are able to improve them.

Development becomes more effective when it is based on an understanding of the trust placed in institutions and their intermediaries. This is particularly true of poverty reduction activities because of the lack of trust in formal institutions among the poor.

The objective of the research reported in this chapter was to gain an operationally useful understanding of trust. We did so by studying the relationships between agricultural extension agents and contact groups (working groups of 8 to 15 villagers) in the training and visit system of agricultural extension in Mali. We sought to determine if the trust between farmers and agricultural extension agents contributes to increasing agricultural production and if the trust between contact groups and other members of the community determines the effectiveness of the groups as catalysts of community development.

The very nature of the object of inquiry—trust—is one about which little useful information will be revealed unless a high degree of trust is established between the interviewer and interviewee. To identify the people and institutions one does and does not trust and why—topics heavily laden with social, economic, and political implications—one must first trust that the person to whom one is divulging such information will not use it in harmful ways.

To achieve this goal, we used beneficiary assessment methodology, which builds on the establishment of trust to derive insights. Beneficiary assessment contributes to the creation of trust between interviewer and interviewee by using qualitative research techniques meant to instill confidence and create rapport. These include using an interview guide for conversational interviewing, which allows the interviewee to become the subject of a discourse he or she leads; keeping paper and pencil out of sight as much as possible during the interview in order not to create the impression of an interrogation; and beginning interviews with questions that establish the interviewer's concern for the interviewee. These and similar techniques show respect and put the interviewee at ease.

We focused on three aspects of trust. The first is the trust between the agricultural extension agent and the farmer. Such trust may be necessary before farmers are willing to follow extension agents' advice. The second is the trust that binds the members of the contact group into a cohesive whole. The third is the trust that transcends the group and allows it to act for and serve the interests of the larger community to which it belongs.

The Extension System in Mali

Information about agricultural techniques in Mali is disseminated by traveling extension agents, who meet with small groups of villagers, who then share what they learn with the rest of the village. Extension agents first meet with villagers during a general assembly to explain the training and visit approach. During the general assembly, the extension agent explains that contact groups act as conduits for passing technical information on to the rest of the village and asks interested villagers to organize themselves into small working groups of 8 to 15 members.

The extension agent visits each of the three or four contact groups in a village every two weeks to discuss technical themes and demonstrate new techniques. Specific agricultural techniques are taught during hands-on demonstrations in the fields of a contact group member. In theory, demonstrations are open to anyone interested, whether or not the person belongs to a contact group. In practice, the process for inviting nonmembers is left to the discretion of contact group members and the extension agent.

Technical themes address specific agricultural problems that are common in the area or that the village has identified during an annual diagnostic exercise that brings together the community, the extension agent, the agent's direct and regional supervisors, and various technical specialists (for agriculture, environment, and animal husbandry). Information from the diagnostic exercise is then centralized and the upcoming year's themes are chosen at the regional level. Extension agents attend monthly training sessions that give them information about the technical subjects and themes chosen for the year.

Research Design

This study of the relation between social capital and the effectiveness of extension service is based on information collected through fieldwork in six villages in Mali. In each village, we collected data on four variables that may influence the effectiveness of agricultural extension: regional variation; the performance of the village (the ease with which villages created contact groups, attendance at biweekly meetings, and receptivity to and acceptance of new agricultural themes); social cohesion; and the quality of agricultural extension agents' work.

SELECTION OF REGIONS. Two regions in Mali, Kayes and Ségou, were chosen for study. Results from the two regions differed widely. Villagers in Kayes appeared to adopt technical themes less often than villagers in Ségou, and contact group members in Kayes were less willing to diffuse information to others. Only a quarter of the farmers in Kayes who were not contact group members reported receiving most of their agricultural information from contact group members living in their communities. In contrast, farmers in Ségou adopted new techniques more often, and contact group farmers served very effectively as intermediaries, with 76 percent of farmers reporting contact group farmers as the source of most of their agricultural information. Different levels of social capital may explain the differences in information transfer, thus making Kayes and Ségou interesting choices for this study.

Kayes and Ségou also differ in other respects. Kayes is nearly inaccessible, with a rocky, mountainous terrain that makes agriculture and travel difficult. In contrast, Ségou is the rice basket of Mali, and agriculture there can be economically rewarding. Many development projects are taking place in the region. Unlike Kayes, where a significant proportion of the male working population emigrates permanently, emigration from Ségou is seasonal.

SELECTION OF VILLAGES. Villages were selected on the basis of performance variables related to agricultural extension. Documentation of village benchmarks by the regional directorates of the extension service provided information only on technical aspects of extension, such as hectares planted and number of demonstration plots. The regional director and supervisory staff were therefore asked to list 10 villages they considered to be high performers and 10 they considered low performers using three criteria: the ease with which villages created contact groups, attendance at biweekly meetings, and receptivity to and acceptance of new agricultural themes. Villages were then randomly selected from these lists (table 4.1). The research team decided to include one high-performance and two

Table 4.1 Villages Included in the Study

Type	Kayes	Ségou
High performer	Tantoudji	Kolodougou Coro, Soké
Low performer	Kassama, Sambaga	Tingoni Bamanan

low-performance villages in Kayes and one low-performance and two high-performance villages in Ségou, in keeping with the results of an earlier beneficiary assessment.

SAMPLE SELECTION. Within each village, in-depth interviews were conducted with male and female contact and noncontact group members (table 4.2). In all, 90 individual interviews were conducted (see annex 4A for interview guide). Contact group members were selected randomly from the extension agent's list of contact group members. Other villagers were selected from census information, from the extension agent's recorded data, and from information provided by the local government.

The team also completed a simple mapping exercise with key informants to gain insight into each village's dynamics. Informants were asked to draw the different sectors of the village and then describe the population living there (by ethnicity, clan relationships, economic activity and level) and how that population differs from that of the other sectors. The homes of contact group members were then indicated on the map. It quickly became apparent whether all contact group members were clustered within one sector or population—an issue that could then be explored by the interview team. Mapping proved essential to understanding the inclusion and exclusion of different populations in the contact groups and ensured that each subset was interviewed.

Two focus groups—one for men and one for women—were conducted in each village. Fifteen people attended each focus group—5 contact group members and 10 other villagers. Bringing together members and

Table 4.2 Distribution of Interviews

Village	Contact group men	Contact group women	Nonmember men	Nonmember women
Tantoudji	3	2	5	5
Kolodougou Coro	3	2	5	5
Soké	5	0	5	5
Kassama	3	2	7	3
Sambaga	3	2	5	5
Tingoni Bamanan	5	0	5	5
Total	22	8	32	28

nonmembers created a dynamic tension that fueled a productive dialogue about the principles and reality of diffusion as seen from each side. Two of the three villages visited in the Ségou region had no women contact groups. In these villages, women's focus groups were held with each village's traditional women's organization (about 50 women participated in each group). Extension agents were also interviewed in each village about their experiences working in the area. In all, roughly 220 people were interviewed through focus groups.

The Role of Social Cohesion

The importance of another variable, not originally included in the study, became apparent while conducting interviews. Village cohesion, or unity, was not specifically addressed in the definition of performance, but there appeared to be a very strong correlation between the two factors. All three high-performance villages showed numerous indications of social cohesion; the three villages rated low performers showed evidence of lack of cohesion.

Interviewers recognized the relationship between performance and a preexisting fabric of relationships through an inductive process of observation and open-ended interviews. Cohesive and fractured villages differed strikingly, for example, in their ability to meet community needs (table 4.3). In every village with low cohesion there were stories of failed attempts to construct or maintain public goods. Further discussion revealed that each failure was rooted in the lack of unity within the community. Open conflict or subtle dissension among ethnic groups, clans, or family groupings often centered on the placement of public goods. In Tingoni Bamanan, for example, a local nongovernmental organization offered to provide the village with a water pump. The village elders could not agree on whether the pump should be placed in the older part of the village or in the new, more populated sector, which had recently been settled near a national road. Lack of agreement resulted in the cancellation of the project by the NGO (two neighboring villages received pumps).

Similar incidents took place in each of the socially fractured villages. Each failure seemed to create more distrust and dissatisfaction, which in turn reduced the possibility of future success. In Tingoni Bamanan, the undercurrent of recrimination and hopelessness that followed the failure of the water pump project was exacerbated by seeing neighboring villages with pumps. This village's experience stood in contrast with the cohesive villages, in which infrastructure (water pumps, health clinics, community grain storage facilities) were visible proof of villagers' ability to work together.

Table 4.3 Differences between Villages with High and Low Levels of Social Cohesion

Attribute	Tantoudji (high level of social cohesion)	Kassama (low level of social cohesion)
Village cleanliness	Village association weeds monthly.	Main paths covered with weeds and trash.
Distribution of infrastructure according to need	Most infrastructure is in village center, equidistant from the different village sectors, other infrastructure spread throughout village.	Only two water pumps, both located at an administrative building 3 kilometers from village. Each half of village did not want to allow the other half to have access to the water pump.
Ability to organize for maintenance or construction of public goods	Village built two literacy centers and a communal grain storage facility. Youth group purchased antenna and television for village. Village credit association functions.	Loss of outside funding for road construction due to lack of organization. Bridge in village washed away because work was never completed. Three school classrooms left unfinished.
Number of organizations	Village association, youth group, and very dynamic women's group. Traditional groups have been transformed to meet development purposes.	One informal women's group, one informal family farming group. Village meetings rarely called.
Leadership	Village chief delegated responsibilities to members of different clans and ethnic groups.	Two uncles fighting over chiefdom.
Physical condition of mosque	Several mosques in good condition.	Mosque roof caving in.
Friday afternoon prayer attendance	Filled to capacity.	Very few people present.

The presence of social cohesion cannot predict individual interest and ability to adopt technical themes, but it does indicate the ability to mobilize for group activities (such as contact groups) and to diffuse information within communities. It therefore becomes an extremely important element in the planning and supervision of development projects. As one woman put it, "Community cohesion is like a rope. If it breaks, water can no longer be drawn from the well."

Quality of the Agricultural Extension Agent's Work

The final variable to be considered is the competence of the extension agent and the quality of the agent's work. This variable consists of two components. The technical component considers whether the agent understands agricultural principles and the technical themes taught. The second component, which concerns rural development in a broader sense, considers whether the agent is able to understand a village's sociocultural context and group dynamics and to motivate others.

Assessment of the capacity of each of the six extension agents studied was made in the field by the interview team, which included two agroeconomists and two rural development experts. The opinions of the team were then supplemented by each agent's supervisor. Villagers also evaluated the technical and pedagogical abilities of their extension agents.

The training and backgrounds of extension agents differed widely. Of the six agents studied by the team, two were not formally trained in agriculture (one had been a forester, the other was trained in animal husbandry). While agent background did appear to affect the technical themes on which the agent spent the most time, all agents appeared to have a firm grasp of the content and criteria of each theme.

The interview team did notice considerable differences between effective agents and ineffective agents in maintaining and updating their documents (village history, contact group member list, activities per agricultural season) and their regularity in keeping biweekly appointments with contact group members. In two villages with ineffective agents, neither contact group members nor the agent could firmly recall the appointment schedule.

The more glaring differences between effective and ineffective agents were at the pedagogical level. The National Extension Service provides agents with only a few general guidelines about development principles; even some supervisors appear inadequately trained in this subject. Supervisory visits appear to focus exclusively on technical matters. Agents record observations and comments made by supervisors and other official visitors in their notebooks. The interview team did not find a single remark in any of these notebooks regarding either diffusion of information or community concerns and dynamics. Comments were limited to technical matters, such as growth rates of different rice and millet varieties. Moreover, in two of the villages visited, the extension agent undermined trust with key segments of the village by forming contact groups exclusively with certain castes and ethnic groups, neglecting others.

The ineffective agents also had a poor understanding of the yearly diagnostic meeting and were unable to identify opportunities for appropriate activities. In short, they appeared to care little about the success of the people with whom they worked. Effective agents felt a responsibility toward their contact group members and to the village as a whole. Even villages with little internal cohesion responded with trust to this conscientiousness. As one villager from a socially fractured village said, "Our agent's door is always open, even at midnight we could wake him to ask a question." Similarly, another contact group member said, "He never leaves until he's sure that everyone understands the technical message."

Results and Analysis

Two variables—the cohesiveness of the village (relative internal trust) and the quality of the extension agent—seem to have the greatest impact on the success or failure of agricultural extension and other development efforts (table 4.4). While the caliber of the extension agent is clearly important to bringing about grassroots development, our evidence suggests that community cohesion is the foundation on which sound, lasting development must be built.

Development agencies have traditionally placed primary attention on technical matters and the agents who transmit them. They have devoted little or no time and resources to gaining an operationally relevant understanding of the social and institutional fabric of the places where they work or to training agents to enhance this local context so that villagers are more receptive to technical themes. The need for this sensitization and capacity building on the part of development institutions and their agents became very apparent during this study. This finding suggests that an understanding of the level of social cohesion in each locale should orient the steps to be taken by the agent.

The results shown in table 4.4 constitute an interesting and potentially important addition to our understanding of social capital. Cohesion is largely embedded in a village's history and culture (box 4.1). It evolves over time, as it is affected by forces and changes from inside the village and from the world beyond. These changes facilitate movement from one category to another: a cohesive village could become less cohesive, just as a socially fractured village could become more unified. Through its policies and the actions of its agents, agricultural extension is one of the factors that can encourage, reinforce, or damage the level of cohesiveness. The synergistic effects of a cohesive village and a dynamic agent (or any

Table 4.4 Extension Agent-Village Interaction Outcomes

	Extension agent	
Village	*Competent, dynamic*	*Marginal, unmotivated*
Socially cohesive/ high performer	Significant successes in agricultural production; synergy with other projects; informal diffusion. Villagers talk about developing new planning and management capacities, more confident in themselves and their abilities to find solutions. *Examples:* Tantoudji, Kolodougou Coro	Significant impact on contact group members' agricultural production. Some damage to social cohesion through unintentional discrimination and lack of inclusion. Neglect of social principles hinders deeper and more integral development progress. *Example:* Soké
Socially divided/ low performer	Contact group becomes internal unifier; nascent cohesiveness, but very little diffusion except through informal women's group. Extension agent successfully balanced membership in contact groups between quarreling factions of village. *Example:* Kassama	Nonfunctional contact groups, no adoption or diffusion. Technical themes proposed are not adapted to village needs and therefore damage trust. *Example:* Sambaga and Tingoni Bamanan

of the other outcome possibilities) illustrate some of the intricacies of the development process.

The experiences of the six villages in our study strongly suggest that social cohesion is significantly influenced by the design and implementation of development policies. Kassama, for example, a highly fractured village, had not held an assembly in two years because each of the factions wanted the meeting to be on its side of the village. The extension agent for Kassama, a competent, low-key individual, held a general assembly in front of the administrative offices that was attended by more

Box 4.1 Social Cohesion in the Village of Tantoudji

While Tantoudji's history has much in common with other villages in Mali, the continuing observance of its founding principles and traditions stands out. Although dramatic changes have taken place, Tantoudji's people have adapted technologies and outside interventions to meet their own priorities and values, reinforced by appropriate training and some very talented development workers. Understanding how Tantoudji's social capital successfully channeled outside forces should help identify best practices for use in other villages.

The village of Tantoudji was founded in 1898 by two family groups, the Nomoko and the Sissoko. The two patriarchs discovered the site of the future village while hunting together. The two friends decided that one family would settle to the east and the other to the west and that the village chiefdom would be passed through the Sissoko family, where it remains to this day. Over time, the two families invited four other family groups to settle with them.

Villagers trace their cohesion to actions taken by their ancestors: "even before unpacking, our forefathers made sacrifices to ensure that Tantoudji would be a village of understanding and agreement," one villager explained. Basic principles were also agreed on at this time, such as hospitality and respect for elders. The vision of grand hospitality extended to everyone is expressed through village sayings such as "the person who comes to visit you is better than you are" and "you should act as a slave to your guest."

External organizations, including the National Extension Service and various NGOs, use traditional organizations to help them conduct their activities—often overwhelming these small local institutions with new rules and priorities—or create new groups, undermining traditional institutions. The strength of Tantoudji's traditional organizations is that they participate in new activities without allowing outside forces to change their priorities. For example, the National Extension Service requires that a contact group have no more than 15 members, which effectively precludes most traditional groups. Benkadi, Tantoudji's traditional women's group, allowed the extension agent to write down the names of 15 women for reporting purposes but required all 60 women to be present at meetings and demonstrations under threat of fine.

There are two traditional organizations in Tantoudji. The first, Benkadi, is an association for all married women in the village. This dynamic group collaborates with the National Extension Service and several NGOs, from which its members learn skills. Currently, Benkadi's activities include a collective field and weekly street cleaning. Training sessions in children's nutrition and cooking demonstrations, soap making, cloth dyeing, and literacy are provided at regular intervals with the help of NGOs.

The pride of the group is the two members who were sent to another town to be trained as midwives.

Sansene Ton is the other association in Tantoudji. Its membership includes the entire village, but the active members are in their teens. Girls enter at puberty and leave when they marry (often because they move to their husbands' village). The association hires out its services during the agricultural season, with young men doing fieldwork and young women bringing them a noon meal, paid for by the women's families. Money earned is used to build infrastructure in the village and to match funds for NGO interventions. In addition, Sansene Ton pays all taxes owed by the village, something never seen before by any of the researchers. It also finances village festivities, organizing an enormous event on each girl's wedding day.

Honorary titles are held by the village elders. The executive president is recommended by the age group or generation currently running activities and is approved by the elders before being solemnly announced to the village during an assembly. The executive president has authority over all active members and is chosen by his peers for moral qualities, such as courage, seriousness, industriousness, and strength of character. Active members are organized into work groups, with each group headed by a member who functions as a supervisor. Members who are absent during work activities or who do not follow codes of conduct are sanctioned. Sanctions range from a fine of 10 kola nuts to a goat or corporal punishment of up to 20 strokes of a whip. Violations for which the lowest sanction is appropriate are judged and administered by the immediate age group, the next highest by the next oldest generation, going all the way up to the elders for the most serious decision (to use the whip).

With the help of one of the National Extension Service's rare rural organization subject matter specialists, in 1986 the Sansene Ton was formally recognized by the government as a village association, allowing it to become a legal cooperative. Recognition as a legal cooperative has many benefits, some logistical, some financial. For example, a cooperative is eligible for certain government programs and funding and can also secure a loan from a formal bank. Recognition as a village association led to the creation of a village bank, with both savings and lending components, and a store, with grain storage facilities. The creation of each of these new institutions was preceded by a villagewide workshop to explain procedures and responsibilities. The village-level managers of each institution received extensive training in accounting, stock control, and other relevant areas. The entire village is extremely proud that members of their community have gained these new skills. A synergy has been created in which the viability of the village initiatives reinforces the traditional structures and moral code without which these actions could not have taken place to begin with.

than 300 people. While this might appear to be a simple decision, the villagers talked for days about the "miraculous" meeting and vowed to hold all meetings there in the future. Through his careful actions, the agent appeared to be nurturing the early stages of a new beginning for the village. This is an essential task—and one that is far from standard development practice.

Cohesiveness can be damaged by technical messages that do not respond to the communities' perceived needs or that exclude women or other groups within the village. The extension agent in Soké, a cohesive village, had worked with one contact group for more than 10 years (6 of the 10 current members had been present at the founding of the group). There had been significant increases in agricultural production, but members had become so familiar with the themes that they conducted biweekly demonstrations without even waiting for the extension agent to arrive. The rest of the village had become increasingly hostile to the lack of turnover, especially since two of the three sectors of the village were not represented in any of the three contact groups. Clustering three contact groups in one sector effectively excluded two ethnic groups, since each sector of the village is populated with a different ethnic group. As one nonmember commented, "It's time that the extension agent starts looking around at all the villagers that haven't benefited one bit and replaces members that have been in the group for 10 years." By disregarding a foundation of development—community cohesion—the agent and his supervisors focused on existing, successful contact groups, failing to address the impact of exclusion on the village.

Development projects create programs that deal with all communities uniformly. Yet villages are clearly not all the same. Nor do they have the same innate promise for advancement. Some villages are like dry, seasoned wood that lights easily at the touch of a match. Others are like green wood, requiring kindling, attention, and patience to become a blaze. Both types of wood have the inherent potential to fuel a campfire, but each must be treated differently. In this analogy, the age and quality of the wood represent the cohesion of the village, while the lighting techniques represent the extension agent (as a proxy for the larger development program). Lighting a match to green wood and walking away would result in a smoldering mess that would soon be extinguished. Similarly, creating contact groups to distribute technical information without taking into consideration the cohesiveness of the village results, in many cases, in frustration and failure.

Development projects need to adapt to the different levels of cohesion and what they mean for planned activities. This requires a level of understanding and analysis about the communities in which they work. Rather than coming in with assumptions, extension agents need to have a questioning attitude. The village is not neutral territory, but an organic and changing set of relationships.

It may be argued that an agent beginning work in a new village may find it difficult, if not impossible, to understand these relationships. But it should be noted how much this research team discovered in less than a week in each village by focusing on levels of cohesion. Extension agents could spend the first few months gathering such information and working on easy, successful group activities, such as poultry vaccination, which does not require a learning group. This time could also be spent visiting groups, *ton* (peer-group organizations), and associations to see what possibilities for collaboration exist. Villages identified as cohesive (dry wood) could move on to more technically challenging activities, using traditional groups wherever possible. Villages identified as lacking internal cohesion (green wood) could begin literacy projects and spend more time on high-impact, large-group activities. By acknowledging the importance of cohesion, the development worker would not be pressured to perform the same functions in all villages.

Village Organizations That Manifest and Affect Social Capital

Various organizations and groups, formal and informal, exist in each of the villages studied. This section describes these organizations and examines how they could become more efficient at diffusing agricultural information.

VILLAGE ORGANIZATIONS AND TRADITIONAL GROUPS. Among traditional groups in Mali, the *ton* is one of the most important across villages and regions. A *ton* is organized by age groups and allows all boys (and girls in the case of Tantoudji) of about the same age to join together for work and recreation. Relationships based on age groups tend to be very strong and last a lifetime.

In the three villages considered high performers, two were using *ton* for agricultural extension, transforming traditional groups into engines for development. These groups were perceived by members and non-members alike to be the most dynamic actors within the village setting.

Traditional groups, including *ton*, are often larger than the contact groups recommended by the extension service. This could explain some of the noticeably greater diffusion of technical themes when such groups are used, but the implicit trust in such organizations seems to play a large role in their success. *Ton* were functioning even in two of the low-performance, socially fractured villages, although they had never been contacted by an extension agent.

CONTACT GROUPS AND THE DIFFUSION OF INFORMATION. While the importance of diffusion is discussed and emphasized within government and
the National Extension Service, the reality in the field is very different.
Field agents often do very little to encourage information transfer, implicitly or explicitly, from contact group members to others in the village.
During an initial village assembly the role of the contact group as an
intermediary is discussed. But in some of the study villages, the assembly had taken place as much as 10 years earlier, and no one remembered
what had been said. Extension agents are not evaluated on diffusion, and
supervisors seem to emphasize purely technical aspects of their work.

There was little apparent difference in the method of creating contact
groups between high- and low-performance villages: 60 percent of contact group members and 23 percent of noncontact group members in all
villages report that the contact group was created after a large assembly
where the system was explained to the village. The relatively small percentage of people (especially nonmembers) who remember the formation
of the contact groups appears significant because this assembly is often
the only time when the contact group's role as an intermediary is
explained to the whole community. Significantly, it appears that in most
villages contact group members were designated by the village elders
rather than self-selected.

During interviews some contact group members said that they were
hesitant to diffuse new information without permission from the extension agent. Most members reported that they did not know that one role
of the contact group was to diffuse information. Diffusion among men
was taking place at a noticeable level only in the two cohesive villages
that had both *ton* and competent dynamic extension agents. In the third
cohesive village, there was built-up frustration among many noncontact
group members because they could see the impact of the new technical
themes but did not feel welcome to participate in the sessions at which
their use was explained. Their sense of exclusion discouraged diffusion
and may have hurt village cohesion.

The training and visit system of extension is based on the theory that
contact group members change as different topics are introduced. This
concept does not appear to have translated well in Mali, where very little
turnover was observed within the contact groups studied. Because there
are so few opportunities to gain new knowledge in most villages, the contact group becomes a permanent, often stagnant, structure.

Contact group members' perceived need for the extension agent's permission to diffuse information, villagers' need to feel directly solicited for
participation, and the lack of turnover among contact group members are
aspects of communication and information transfer that have not been
considered by extension projects. These problems reflect issues concern-

ing information exchange that are endemic to Malian society. Such issues can only be discovered by paying attention to the cultural dimension of information transfer, as expressed in each local context.

LITERACY AND TRUST. Literacy programs often seem to promote trust and development. Many more villagers in cohesive, high-performance villages (76 percent) reported the presence of a literacy program than did residents of fractured, low-performance villages (22 percent). The presence of newly literate people within the village is testimony to the impact of these programs. Among those interviewed in high-performance villages, 22 percent spoke of being aware of the presence of newly literate people in the village. In low-performance villages, the figure was only 7 percent.

Literacy relates to trust in three ways. First, participants in the programs spoke of increased self-confidence, or "self-trust," and the role it played in encouraging them to try new ideas and techniques. Second, the role of the National Extension Service in promoting literary increased trust in agricultural extension activities. Third, and perhaps most important, literacy has synergistic effects on other development activities, including agricultural extension. A male contact group member in Tantoudji commented on the way literacy reinforced other programs: "I am a true product of the literacy program. I have never attended even one day of formal schooling, but today I manage the paperwork for our village bank."[1]

WOMEN'S RELATIONSHIPS AND COMMUNICATION AS AN UNRECOGNIZED INSTITUTION. Women participated in activities of the agricultural extension system in four of the six villages visited, but in only two of these villages did agents make any real attempt to collaborate with women and respond to their needs. Yet women appear to be the only consistent diffusers of information and technology. They also play a key role in tapping into and generating social capital.

Women's groups emphasized the importance of increased solidarity when asked to name the strong points of contact group functioning. In the most contentious village visited, Kassama, women appeared to be outside the traditional power struggle. They were able to maintain their working and social relationships with one another in a village physically and socially divided by a road.

Even in the midst of quarreling factions, women still spent time together in common work areas, such as the water source and the marsh, which provided gardening sites for the community. Kassama's proactive extension agent built trust with women through his respectful behavior and willingness to address their concerns. Although the women are not formally organized, diffusion of new information nevertheless takes place, facilitated by the fact that their gardening plots are located side by side. In several other villages, the men gave credit for the success of several development projects to the unity of the women's traditional *ton*. If harnessed, this untapped resource could enhance the effectiveness of the extension service and strengthen the villages in which it works.

Some National Extension Service policies seem to discourage extension agents from working with women. In Soké, for example, a women's group with 200 members worked on a four-hectare gardening site with no technical assistance from the extension agent. When asked to explain this neglect, the agent responded that he was told by his supervisor to work with only 1 of the 24 women's groups in his sector, which he was already doing.

Perhaps even more alarming, some of the agricultural extension techniques are increasing the hardships of women's work. A very popular technical theme is composting. Millet stalks are gathered after the harvest and layered into large compost pits, thus removing an important source of fire material for women and greatly increasing the time and distance required to gather adequate firewood. No compensating technologies, such as improved cookstoves that require less firewood, have been introduced.

Another problem is the extension service's lack of awareness of women's activities and how they differ in each village—a problem that makes it difficult to see or look for alternatives. Gardening is the only technical theme encouraged for women, even when they are involved in other activities or where gardening is not environmentally feasible. In two of the villages visited, the extension agent had created gardening contact groups even though there was no water source. The women interviewed voiced frustration and disappointment that they had organized themselves only to have the extension agent suggest inappropriate themes. Even more striking to the research team was the fact that women in these villages were heavily involved in intensive animal husbandry. Significant opportunities for improvement in this area existed, but the extension program provided no encouragement.

RELATIONSHIP BETWEEN EXTENSION AGENTS AND CONTACT GROUP MEMBERS. Extension agents were judged to be serious, available, and patient by 80 percent of villagers in high-performance villages and by only 47 percent of villagers in low-performance villages. As might be expected, the perception of the agent's capability correlated with technical performance within the village.

Another striking difference between high and low performers was how the villages perceived the relevance of technical themes. In the three high-performance villages, 67 percent of contact group members cited the pertinence of the technical messages; in low-performance villages, the figure was just 20 percent. It appears that if the technical themes are not pertinent—that is, if they do not respond to farmers' perceived needs—a loss of trust ensues, making it more difficult for agents to succeed with later activities.

Unfortunately, the extension agent does not always control the pertinence of technical themes being taught. Although much time is spent at the yearly diagnostic meeting eliciting the agricultural problems confronting farmers and their priorities for the coming year, decisions for future technical themes are made by regional authorities, without input from farmers, based on how many villages have the same problem and the availability of technical solutions from the research station. The extension agent is then informed of the technical package for the coming year.

The six extension agents interviewed all expressed frustration with this system, acknowledging that some proposed technical themes were of little interest to the communities in which they work. Trust is betrayed at two levels during this process. First, the community feels that the effort to understand its problems is somehow insincere. Second, extension agents feel let down by the organization.

Another important aspect of the relationship between extension agents and their contact groups is the extent to which agents keep appointments. In high-performance villages, 87 percent of contact group members reported that extension agents kept their appointments in the village; in low-performance villages, the figure was just 53 percent. Keeping one's word is extremely important within Malian society. The serious and conscientious behavior of an agent can be an important factor determining village performance. In divisive villages, it can be pivotal.

Conclusions and Recommendations

Our results show that the single most important factor determining the success of an external intervention such as agricultural extension is the degree of social cohesion already existing in a community. The predisposition of a community's residents to attend association meetings, gather together in places of worship, build and maintain public infrastructure— these are the things that create the fertile ground in which external inputs, such as agricultural extension agents and contact groups, take root. The study's four major findings reveal the importance of this social fabric.

Social Cohesion Is the Primary Precondition for Development

External agents, or project managers, should understand the fabric of the village before they intervene. If the village has both social cohesion and a qualified, dynamic external agent, there can be significant success in agriculture and other development endeavors. In such a situation, the presence of several development projects can create a synergistic effect, resulting in new planning and management capacities.

Although social cohesion is difficult to engineer, it can be enhanced by community organization and local institution building, as well as by literacy programs, public health programs, and other basic development assistance that can increase the capacity for mutually reinforcing social interaction. Agents must be observers as well as actors within their communities. Sociocultural training, including tools such as mapping, participant observation, and conversational interviewing, should be included at all levels of intervention.

Women and Women's Associations Are an Important Source of Social Cohesion

Women and their associations are a vital and often overlooked source of social cohesion, representing latent social capital with great potential for mobilization and development in most villages. Where this potential is recognized and capitalized on, development is more likely to become a reality.

Women's participation depends greatly on the external agent's comportment and willingness to work with women. Development institutions need to encourage and train agents in both these areas. The amount of time an agent spends working with women can be affected positively or negatively by the supervisor's attitude and the quality of the diagnostics conducted.

Trust Must Be Established between External Agents and Their Agencies

Trust between an external agent, such as an agricultural extension worker, and the community is important, as is the internal trust that underlies community cohesion. However, it is also important that trust be established and reinforced between agents and the central government agency for which they work. In the absence of such trust, the agent becomes demoralized and less effective in communicating with villagers. Low trust between agents and their agencies can thus reduce trust between agents and the people they serve. Direct supervision of both the technical and sociocultural aspects of agents' work is crucial and should be emphasized.

Beneficiary Assessment Is Useful in Investigating Social Capital

The qualitative research tool known as beneficiary assessment proved to be particularly well suited to the investigation of social capital, as its reliance on qualitative research techniques enables it to probe, and reveal, the nature of people's relationships with one another and with important institutions. This inductive approach allowed the team to identify important factors as they presented themselves and to adapt the design of the study accordingly.

Appendix 4A: Village Interview Guide

Interviewer:

Date:

Village: Region:

Interviewee:

Sex: (M) _____   (F) _____

Working with the extension agent: Yes _____   No _____

If yes, method of extension (*check one that applies*):

   (a)   Contact group _____, membership (in numbers):
         (M) _____ (F) _____

   (b)   Association _____, membership (in numbers):
         (M) _____ (F) _____;

   (c)   Individual family _____, membership (in numbers):
         (M) _____ (F) _____

1.   **Assessment of extension agent**

   (a)   Professionalism (keeping appointments, knowledge of
         technical themes, pertinence of technical themes, availability,
         technical support, etc.).

   (b)   Involvement in village social life (behavior, attitude,
         reputation, integration into village life).

2.   **Assessment of village organization specialist** (*answer for
     associations only*)

   (a)   Professionalism (availability, technical support, management
         training, etc.).

   (b)   Involvement in village social life.

3. **Relationship between women and extension agents** (extension possibilities, availability, acceptance by husbands, etc.)

4. **Relationship among contact group members (or association members)**

    (a) Formation of the contact group (or association). How formed? By whom? Inclusiveness (gender/income/ethnicity).

    (b) Personal ties among members (friendship, neighbors, type of farming, family).

5. **Evaluation of contact group** (strong points and weak points)

6. **Relationship between the contact group (or association) and the rest of the village population**

    (a) Diffusion of technical themes between villagers working with extension agents and villagers who are not.

    (b) Motivation for diffusion of technical themes.

    (c) Reasons for lack of diffusion of technical themes.

    (d) Suggestions for improving diffusion.

7. **Impact of the contact group (or association) on the rest of the population**

    (a) Impact of extension on the village (agricultural production, revenue, health, literacy).

    (b) Impact on village attitudes (receptivity, social cohesion).

8. **Technical themes that inspire or reinforce trust**

    (a) Agricultural themes (insecticide treatment for seeds, composting, transplanting in line, etc.).

    (b) Animal husbandry themes (improved feed, improved pastures, vaccinations, etc.).

(c)   Environmental themes.

(d)   Rural organization (management, marketing).

9.   **Suggestions for improving the level of trust**

(a)   Between group members and the extension agent.

(b)   Between group members and the village organization specialist.

10.   **Observations of the interviewer**

Appendix 4B: Description of Villages

Kassama, Kayes region, population 1,300

Low performer. Extremely troubled village with almost no village-level social cohesion. Very talented, patient extension agent. Three contact groups, one male (nonfunctional), one female (using traditional women's working group), and one mixed.

Tantoudji, Kayes region, population 360

High performer. Very unified village, despite many different ethnic groups. Dynamic extension agent. Only village with a village organization specialist (also very dynamic). Two newly literate men and two newly literate women give weekly classes in reading and writing for the community. Four contact groups (two male, two female). Female contact groups use traditional women's associations.

Sambaga, Kayes region, population 480

Low performer. Some internal cohesion, although it is hampered by severe water shortages and an ineffective, negligent extension agent. Strong traditional groups have not been used for agricultural extension. Huge potential in women's aviculture is not being exploited. Three contact groups, one male, one female, one mixed. Only one is functional.

Soké, Ségou region, population 1,700

High performer; socially cohesive village. Extension agent of average competence but no initiative. Three contact groups, all male. All contact group members live in one sector of village, that of the village chief.

Tingoni Bamanan, Ségou region, population 385

Low performer. Some tension between sectors of village. Below-average extension agent who was previously forest inspector. Two contact groups, both male, both barely functional. Dynamic youth group not being used for extension. Huge potential in women's small animal husbandry not being exploited.

Kolodougou Coro, Ségou region, population 661

High performer. Highly cohesive village with motivated agent who is somewhat constrained by lack of training in agriculture (his background is in animal husbandry). Five contact groups, four male, one female. Women's group frustrated by lack of extension themes.

Notes

Field research for this study was conducted by Mamadou Camara, Cheick Kamaté, Catherine Reid, and Maimouna Sow Sangaré.

1. This finding was echoed in Anirudh Krishna and Norman Uphoff's 1999 study "Mapping and Measuring Social Capital: A Conceptual and Empirical Study of Collective Action for Conserving and Developing Watersheds in Rajasthan, India," Social Capital Initiative Working Paper 13. World Bank, Social Development Department, Washington, D.C.

Qualitative Analysis of Social Capital: The Case of Community Development in Coal Mining Areas in Orissa, India

Enrique Pantoja

The rediscovery of social capital has seemingly provided a missing and powerful explanation of how development processes work and how they may be used to strengthen related policy, programs, and projects.[1] The potential contribution of social capital to development appears to be immense, as corroborated by rapidly growing empirical knowledge (Putnam 1998). This potential contribution acquires even greater significance under current efforts to make development more equitable and democratic (Stiglitz 1998). International organizations, national governments, and nongovernmental organizations (NGOs) have embraced social capital as an important form of capital, indispensable to making development possible and sustainable. Yet the successful utilization of social capital may not be possible without understanding its potential negative as well as positive effects, and without promoting enabling environments that facilitate participatory, community-driven efforts.

The study described in this chapter explores the concept of social capital through the analysis of two coal mining areas in the state of Orissa, India. The qualitative analysis is of community development processes structured within the broader political economy of poverty. One of the main goals in poverty alleviation is the provision of access to sustainable income sources and reliable and safe basic services. To help achieve this goal, it is assumed that poverty alleviation strategies should support existing forms of social capital and promote the formation of new ones. The study described here approaches this assumption critically by looking at the various forms, dimensions, and effects of social capital. It accepts the notion that social capital is a common resource (even if privatizable in certain instances) that can provide access to other resources. But the study also considers that under scarcity conditions, such as those prevalent in developing economies and particularly among the poor, social capital can become an integral part of the structures of constraint created by gender, class, ethnicity, and in the case of India, religion and caste. For these reasons, the study pays close attention to issues of access to social capital resources and to control of resources once such access has been facilitated. Furthermore, the study analyzes the role social capital plays in the structures of facilitation or constraint that characterize a particular society at the local level.

The unique "enclave development" characteristics of the coal mining areas makes them an ideal research setting. Coal production activities in India take place in remote areas, where coal mining has become the center of economic life while changing the local labor market structure, the social fabric, and the natural environment. After India nationalized most coal mines in the 1970s, Coal India Limited was established, and along with its subsidiaries soon became the most influential institutional and developmental actor in these remote areas. The mining areas have become de facto company enclaves as direct government intervention has diminished and the presence of the state has been rendered almost invisible. Coal India, in turn, has increasingly acquired community development responsibilities and become the repository of peoples' expectations regarding employment generation and service provision.

Interest in the coal mining areas increased when the World Bank financed investments to improve the profitability of 25 of Coal India's opencast mining operations (the Coal Sector Rehabilitation Project, or CSRP) and the company's capacity to deal with social and environmental issues (the Coal Sector Environmental and Social Mitigation Project, or ESMP). Investments in these mines, as in any others across the various coalfields, were likely to affect (positively or adversely) traditional sources of income and employment opportunities, social networks and structures, and the form and quality of social capital. The ESMP did not entail specific activities related to social capital, but it did include social mitigation measures that affected the relations between the coal company and the communities (vertical articulations), and within the communities themselves (horizontal linkages).[2] The CSRP and ESMP are explained in more detail later.

Database and Methodology

This exploratory study identifies hypotheses and indicators that will help future researchers investigate more rigorously the concept of social capital within the framework of community-based development and better distinguish, as Portes (1998) advises, the concept itself from its alleged effects. Specifically, the methodology is responsive to field conditions, including (1) *the need to avoid interfering with project implementation activities*, since the two Bank-financed projects were still being implemented, and many of their social mitigation measures were being tried by Coal India for the first time; (2) *the need to obtain and maintain the collaboration of Coal India and the concerned subsidiary* in doing fieldwork and deploying members of the local team; and given these requirements, (3) *the need to find "safe" study areas* with low levels of conflict between the mine and the villagers, where proj-ect implementation was advancing relatively unencumbered.

The study team identified 13 mines that were receiving World Bank financing and 30 that were not as eligible for the study. The following criteria were used to determine eligibility: (1) the mine affecting the study area had to be an opencast operation, since opencast operations are more likely than underground mines to affect the social and natural environment; (2) one of the mining areas had to come from the set included under the ESMP, while another one, of similar age, had to be from the rest of opencast mines; and (3) the mines had to have created the need for resettlement, rehabilitation, and community development.[3]

After considering particular factors such as geography, regulatory environment, and social, political, and economic context, the Talcher and Ib Valley Coalfields located in the state of Orissa and managed by the subsidiary Mahanadi Coalfields Limited were identified as the most suitable areas in which to undertake the study (see map). In consultation with Coal India and Mahanadi Coalfields representatives, one mining area was finally selected in each coalfield: Samaleswari in the Ib Valley was the study area with a mine receiving bank financing, and Kalinga in Talcher was the area with a mine without bank financing. The study areas' boundaries followed the definition given in the ESMP as the mine's zone of influence for community development, which included all settlements within one kilometer of the boundary of the mine holding (World Bank 1996).

A major advantage of undertaking the study in Samaleswari was the existence of socioeconomic baseline data, social and environmental reports, and project progress reports prepared for the Bank-financed projects. Most of the information for Samaleswari was collected through surveys in 1994 and 1995 during project preparation, but an exercise to update the information on project-affected people was conducted in 1998. Not nearly as much information was available for Kalinga.

To supplement the existing data and further the study's objectives, the following activities were undertaken:

- *A household survey in each of the study areas* to update the socioeconomic data and obtain a first insight into the social capital of the communities;
- *Focus group sessions*;
- *Unstructured interviews* with relevant stakeholders, including officials of Coal India and Mahanadi Coalfields, government officials, and NGO and community representatives;
- *A stakeholders workshop* (in Samaleswari only).

Many of these activities were developed in collaboration with a team from the local consulting firm Operations Research Group, who periodically visited the study areas between July 1998 and February 1999 to follow everyday events in the communities and maintain contact with the NGO operating in Samaleswari. As a member of the World Bank's supervision team for the ESMP, the author visited Orissa on multiple occasions in 1997 and 1998, where he met with Coal India and Mahanadi Coalfields officials, government officials, and community members.

Context: Overview of Orissa

Orissa, located along the Bay of Bengal, occupies 156,000 square kilometers of India's territory. Despite having huge mineral resources, Orissa is one of the poorest, most rural, and least developed states (Crook 1997, Repetto 1994). Eighty percent of the state's population depends on the agricultural sector, which has one of the lowest yields in the country. More than one-fourth of the 34.2 million people living in Orissa in 1996 were officially designated as scheduled tribes, and about 15 percent were considered scheduled castes. The majority of the scheduled tribes are poor and illiterate (Fernandes, Menon, and Viegas 1988). Significantly, most of Orissa's coal belt, as well as other sources of raw materials, corresponds to its forest and tribal regions.

Under the constitution of 1950, those groups belonging to the lower levels of the caste system and persons of tribal origin were classified into separate schedules. The scheduled castes and tribes were officially identified as the most underprivileged groups in the country (World Bank 1996). Some poor groups that did not fall into either of these categories were classified as "backward," and the state assumed responsibility for advancing the economic, social, and educational welfare of the "backward" classes, including the scheduled castes and tribes. In contrast, the general castes were considered "socioeconomically advanced" and no special provision was made for them.

Profile of the Study Areas

The coal mines in the Ib Valley and Talcher fall under management of Mahanadi Coalfields Limited, which operates 21 mines and projects across these two areas.

Samaleswari, Ib Valley Coalfield

Coal mining operations in the Ib Valley area began more than 50 years ago and accelerated with the nationalization of the mines in the 1970s and the implementation of opencast projects in the 1980s. In the Ib Valley, Mahanadi Coalfields runs five underground mines and five opencast mines. Three of the opencast mines, including Samaleswari, received World Bank financing (World Bank 1996, 1997). The Samaleswari opencast mine is located in Jharsuguda revenue district, between Sambalpur and Sundargarh revenue districts. Actual coal mining in Samaleswari started in 1993, although preparation work began in 1987. The mine has an estimated project life of about 23 years.

The study area in Samaleswari includes four villages, which in turn comprise seven habitations: Ainapalli, Karapalli, Kudapalli, Lajkura, Mundapara, Orampara, and Sukhpara.[4] Total population within the study area is approximately 2,751 (or 470 households). About 46.7 percent of the total population belongs to scheduled tribes, while 12.7 percent belongs to scheduled castes. The rest belong to other backward castes (35.4 percent), who are the second largest group, and to general, upper castes (5.2 percent). According to the 1994 socioeconomic baseline survey, an estimated 1,655 persons (398 families) would be affected by the mining operations due to land acquisition, of whom 232 were tribals (Vivekananda Palli Agragami Seva Pratishan [VPASP] 1994a, 1994b). The total number of entitled project-affected persons in Samaleswari was estimated at 986.[5] Land acquisition had been finalized along with payment of compensation, except in cases where the ownership of the land was under legal dispute or tenure was not clear. Ironically, many families who had to resettle because of the mine project had been resettled into this area after their native places were submerged during construction of the Hirakud Dam.

Kalinga, Talcher Coalfield

The Talcher-Angul area is industrializing rapidly. Several large industries in the area, such as the National Aluminum Company and the National Thermal Power Corporation, and a good number of medium and small industries, depend on the coal company for their power. Three opencast mines, also under the management of Mahanadi Coalfields, are receiving Bank financing here. The selected study area, Kalinga, is adjacent to one of them, Bharatpur. The first coal mine in the area opened, although on a very small scale, in 1926, but it was not until 1960 that coal mining began to intensify. The Kalinga Opencast Project, located in Angul District, had been started about 8 years before the study. The expected life of the mine was 27 years.[6]

In Kalinga, eight habitations are included in the study: Bramhanbahal, Danra, Kalam Chhuin, Majhika, Nakeipasi, Natada, Nathgaon, and Solada. The study area has a population of 15,095 (or 2,351 households). The majority of the population (65.5 percent) belongs to the other backward castes. Scheduled tribes are second (15.2 percent), followed by general castes (9.7 percent) and scheduled castes (9.6 percent). Bramhanbahal was scheduled to be resettled completely, while Majhika and Solada were scheduled to be partially relocated. The other five habitations were not directly affected by the mine's land acquisitions but were receiving community development assistance.

Social Organization in the Study Areas

In 1995, when the area was surveyed in preparation for developing the ESMP, the economy of Samaleswari, although still predominantly agrarian, was changing rapidly (ORG 1995). Over time, the mining industry had created many new activities in the area, transforming what had been a subsistence economy into a market-driven one. The coal company had also acquired a significant amount of land, and many inhabitants had lost their agricultural plots. More than half of the male population had found employment in the mines in 1995, and some had become daily laborers in mine-related activities, but others had been left without access to income-generation opportunities. ORG's initial survey also indicated that inequality was increasing because those working at the mines had steady incomes and job security, while the livelihood of those left without land and alternative income-generation opportunities was deteriorating. A change in the leadership pattern was also observed, as the Mahanadi Coalfields employees began to take power away from the traditional leadership.

The caste hierarchy has historically been strong in Orissa, and it is through this hierarchy that village-level intercaste relations and sociability must be viewed (Lerche 1991). With mining development and agricultural transformation, the study areas' prevailing social orders and rules for social exchange have certainly changed. But a villager's position in the social hierarchy continues to be determined largely by the same factors that have long defined it: power, wealth, and ritual prestige. The socioreligious network structuring the villages' caste-based division of labor has proved to be highly impervious to change, and many of the changes in intercaste relations have occurred within this system's framework.

Historically, the degree of ritual purity or pollution of each caste has been related to specific occupations, and specific exchanges and services have been derived from this relationship.[7] The purity-pollution hierarchy is also expressed in a number of norms regarding what a given person is allowed to do and not to do (such as eating rules and whom one may associate with). Changes in occupations in the study areas, especially the decline in and even extinction of many traditional caste occupations, have undermined caste differentiation and accelerated social change. With the loss of land, traditional farm-labor arrangements have declined, albeit more in Samaleswari than in Kalinga, where agriculture is still more relevant to the local economy. Long-term relationships between employers and laborers have decreased in both study areas, while more casual, impersonalized contracting and subcontracting in various sectors has increased.

Despite these changes, two main divisions established by the ritual hierarchy are still remarkably strong: the dividing line between Brahmin and everyone else, and the dividing line between clean castes and polluted castes ("untouchables," or *Harijans*) (Neale 1990). The hierarchy establishes the Brahmins at the top, followed by the clean general castes, then the unclean general castes, and at the bottom, the peripheral castes, including the *Harijans*. Although the unclean general castes are considered a part of the village, the peripheral castes are marginalized spatially and socially, living in hamlets of their own located at some distance from the other villagers.

Coal India Limited

Coal India Limited, established in 1975, is, in terms of outputs and employment, the world's largest coal company and India's largest public sector enterprise.[8] It has about 490 mines under its command, of which approximately 140 are opencast operations. Structured as a holding company, Coal India has eight subsidiaries, which operate with relative autonomy. Like other large, complex, and hierarchical organizations, Coal India is characterized by imperviousness to change and obvious challenges regarding information flows and delegation of authority. A subsidiary, for instance, has three layers of management: corporate level, area level, and mine level. Mahanadi Coalfields, which became a subsidiary company in 1992, manages mines in five areas.

Coal India is a *coal company*, so, not surprisingly, its management and officers see the production of coal as their primary mission. The company cannot ignore, however, the social and environmental issues intrinsic to coal mining. In the long run, the company becomes closely identified with the particular regions where its operations take place, to the extent that the mining areas themselves, including the surrounding villages, become implicitly company grounds, at least in the eyes of state and local government officials and those living within their confines.[9] The futures of most of the individuals living in the mining areas are closely tied to the mining operations, through direct and indirect employment or through the ways their lives are changed by the new social, economic, and environmental conditions created by such operations.

Paradoxically, the coal company's capacity to address the demands of the surrounding communities, let alone to fulfill its promises regarding community development, resettlement, and rehabilitation, is limited. In turn, a relationship of dependency and a sense of distrust tend to develop, often simultaneously, between the affected communities and the coal company. This relationship is complicated by the fact that everyone knows the coal company will eventually leave the area, returning the land to the state government once mining operations have been completed and the area has been restored.[10]

The establishment of de facto company domain over a region starts with the decision to acquire land in areas with commercially exploitable coal resources. Coal India and its subsidiaries acquire the land for mining under the Land Acquisitions Act of 1904 and the Coal Bearing Areas Act of 1957.[11] Holders of the land must give it up to the coal company, and the Land Acquisition Act requires that the company compensate all landowners.

The company's interaction with the local population thus starts years before the actual mining operations begin. Local labor is usually recruited early on by the company, mainly for semiskilled and unskilled jobs. Further along in the process, the state and local governments tend to scale down their level of intervention in the social and economic development in the mining areas. With time, the centrality of the mine economy increases. A more defined market economy emerges as agriculture and other traditional forms of livelihood decline while more and more local people start working at the mine. The company also builds new facilities and improves the existing infrastructure to facilitate the movements of goods in and out of the mining areas, while carrying out community development activities in villages near the mines. Expectations and a sense of entitlement simultaneously increase among local communities. Since most of these areas, at least initially, are isolated, a clear case of "enclave development" takes place.

The World Bank–Financed Projects

The Coal Sector Rehabilitation Project, or CSRP, aimed at assisting Coal India to make coal production financially sound and more efficient. The project, with an estimated cost of US$1.6 billion (of which the World Bank was financing US$500 million), was approved in September 1997 and was expected to close in June 2003. Specifically, through the investment component, the Bank loan was financing the cost of a large fleet of heavy earth-moving equipment to modernize or expand 25 opencast mines. In addition, the CSRP also supported coal sector reform and the restructuring of Coal India through technical assistance and training.

The Coal Sector Environmental and Social Mitigation Project, or ESMP, was approved in May 1996, and its activities were to finish by June 2001.[12] A complement to the CSRP, this project supported Coal India's efforts to make its production more environmentally and socially sustainable, while ensuring that any possible negative effects of coal mining expansion would be alleviated.[13] Total project cost was estimated at US$84 million, of which the World Bank was financing US$63.3 million.

An important change induced by the project, and key for the study, was Coal India's adoption of a new corporate resettlement and rehabilitation policy and the revision of its community development guidelines, which all subsidiaries would eventually have to follow. Social mitigation measures included individual assistance through specific rehabilitation and compensation packages. In general, depending on the category a project-ed-affected person was in (landowner, landless, or member of a tribe using common resources), Coal India would offer assistance for establishing nonfarm employment through the provision of infrastructure, small contracts, and establishment of cooperatives; would pay the replacements costs of homesteads, where applicable, and provide an alternative housing site; and would offer employment in the mines when feasible. Moreover, Coal India would offer village-level assistance through community development plans (known as indigenous peoples development plans) that included provision of physical and social infra-structure, training for self-employment, and support for community activities such as watershed management and reforestation.

Coal India's new resettlement and rehabilitation policy and community development guidelines were likely to have several effects on the social capital resources of the mining areas with World Bank–financed mines, including Samaleswari. These effects included the establishment of new cadres of environmental officers and community development, resettlement, and rehabilitation officers; the hiring of an NGO to facilitate community participation in and implementation of social mitigation measures; enhanced consultation with people affected by the project; and creation of a community development council and village working groups to identify and carry out development activities. Previously, community development was ad hoc and the assets provided by the company to the beneficiaries were absolutely free. Under the new guidelines, the coal company was requiring payment from the communities in the form of mandatory contributions in kind or labor. The most important changes related to the resettlement and rehabilitation policy, however, counted loss of economic assets as well as loss of land in the compensation process; expanded the definition of a project-affected person to cover not only landowners, but any adult whose livelihood was affected, including the landless, and entitled all eligible adults to compensation; and replaced jobs in the mines as the major form of rehabilitation with multiple rehabilitation options.

The mines receiving World Bank financing were considered to be a testing ground for the new social and environmental measures that the coal company was planning to apply eventually to all mines. Problems with implementation of the new measures arose immediately. This was not the first time that Coal India had changed its practices for dealing with the effects its mines had on the surrounding populations, and people were understandably confused over what to expect. Moreover, confusion and potential for conflict was destined to arise because adjacent communities were being treated differently even though they were experiencing similar conditions.

Analysis

The study of social movements and collective action has long required social scientists to pay attention to issues of cooperation, social cohesion, and conflict. In general, however, sociologists have tended to oversocialize individuals' actions. Conversely, economics has tended to undersocialize these actions (Granovetter 1985). The works on social capital by Bourdieu (1986), Coleman (1988, 1990) and Putnam (1993, 1995), among others, have provided new conceptual and analytical elements to balance the two. Their work provides valuable new and relevant insights to supplement narrowly constructed economic models whose limitations in explaining social and political behavior of individuals and groups have long been evident. The work on social capital contributes significantly to the effort to overcome these limitations by integrating nonmarket factors into the analysis of political and economic life.[14]

The coal mining areas in Orissa provide an excellent opportunity to explore the concept of social capital. The study areas, Samaleswari and Kalinga, as part of de facto "company enclaves," represent a scaled-down model of the working of social capital in Indian society as a whole. Although it would be misleading to extrapolate from the particular findings in the study areas to the country level, the relative isolation of the study areas allows researchers to explore certain dynamics more clearly and to identify issues critical to a better understanding of the nature and effects of social capital in general and of social capital at the community level in particular.

Specifically, the study focuses on the vertical articulations and nonarticulations between the coal company and the concerned communities, understood as a replication of state-civil society relations. The study also examines horizontal interactions among community members, that is, the local civil society. As mentioned above, the focus is on community-based development, but within the broader framework of the political economy of poverty. The analysis is developed as a *virtual matrix* that takes a particular form of social capital and looks at its width and depth, at the way the issues of power and politics weigh in to give it a relative use value depending on who is assessing this value, and at its relevance for community-based development. The virtual matrix is thus multilevel and multidimensional, targeting the structures of facilitation and constraint that affect access to resources (including social capital resources), control of access to resources, and control of the resources once access is obtained or granted. Through the development of this matrix, the main assumptions of the study are iteratively tested against the findings.

Forms of Social Capital

All forms of social capital can affect collective action, governance, and economic performance in many ways, and all of them have a role to play in the creation and maintenance of generalized trust as well. These forms vary from one socio-organizational setting to the next (Eastis 1998). They do not exist in isolation, many do not have clear or real boundaries, and many are embedded in other forms of social capital or are necessary inputs to or outputs of other forms of social capital. Following Harriss and De Renzio (1997), Portes (1998), Putnam (1993, 1998), and Rose, Mishler, and Haerpfer (1997), the forms of social capital considered in this study are:

- *Family and kinship connections*, including the single household, the extended family, and the clan, based on "strong" ties of blood and affinity. An important factor is that family and kin relationships are created mainly by birth, not by choice.
- *Wider social networks, or "associational life,"* including networks of individuals, groups, and organizations that link individuals from different families or groups in common activities for various purposes. This is the form of social capital closest to Putnam's 1993 definition of social capital in terms of "networks of civic engagement" or "local associations." This form of social capital covers a full range of formal and informal horizontal arrangements.
- *Cross-sectional linkages, or "networks of networks,"* including the networks that link organizations from various sectors of society (for example, NGOs, grassroots organizations, government agencies, private firms) and allow them to combine resources and different types of knowledge to find solutions to complex problems. Through these networks, public-private cross-sectoral linkages and mutually supportive and complementary relations are established. This form of capital provides the articulations between horizontal and vertical associations and organizations.
- *Political capital*, including the norms and networks shaping relations between civil society and the state, thereby allowing a society to mediate conflict by effectively responding to multiple citizen demands. Political capital is related to informal institutional arrangements that

may result in clientelism, rent-seeking, and exclusion, or in effective representation, accountability, and participation.

- *Institutional and policy framework*, including formal rules and norms (constitutions, laws, regulation, policies) that regulate public life. Generally identified as macro-level social capital, this form has a double nature, since it may induce the creation of other forms of social capital, while it constitutes in itself a resource that facilitates coordinated actions. Moreover, existence of a consistent institutional framework is necessary to generate and strengthen generalized social trust.
- *Social norms and values*, including widely shared cultural beliefs and the effects such beliefs have on the functioning of society at large. Norms and values support other forms of social capital as well as representing the most general form of social capital.

Institutional and Policy Framework: The Extent of Generalized Social Trust

Hatti and Heimann (1992, p. 62) explain that "one of the most important concepts in the Indian value system is the one of trust." Accordingly, trust or the lack of trust is a critical component in evaluations of relationships among Indian people. Descriptions of family members, friends, or strangers always include an assessment of the specific individual's trustworthiness, which according to Hatti and Heimann is usually assumed to be lacking. Historical and contemporary forces both have exacerbated ethnic, class, gender, and familial tensions in India, which, combined with the scarcity of resources, have made access, distribution, and use of existing social capital highly contested and social capital resources themselves fragmented (Morris 1998).

In India, communalism has translated into conflict and violence across religion-based communities, such as Muslims, Hindus, and Sikhs. Generalized social trust has been weakened by the deeply ambivalent relationship between secularism and religion (Basu and Subrahmanyam 1996). A high level of "abstract trust" has resulted in strengthened identities based on mechanisms of inclusion and exclusion. Diversity of voices and interests has resulted, in India, in a pluralist democracy that with all its limitations may be its greatest strength. At the same time, the modus operandi of this pluralism may be India's greatest weakness.

Institutional and Policy Framework: Civil Society in the Study Areas

Samaleswari and Kalinga are characterized by a weak civil society, a weak state, and a weak state–civil society synergy, all of which are strongly mediated by the highly bureaucratic, justifiably profit-oriented, and complex organization that is Coal India. In the study areas, the institutional and policy framework that could potentially foster generalized trust and promote cooperation among individuals and social groups lacks cohesiveness and consistency. The coal company's influence is so strong here that its policies and programs are perceived by local residents as integral to, if not a replacement for, the larger institutional and regulatory context enabling social exchange in Indian society.

For instance, the only NGO that operates regularly in either of the study areas is CART, the NGO brought in by Mahanadi Coalfields to Samaleswari as part of the World Bank–financed projects. The new village working groups created in the Bank-financed mines to implement community development activities officially came into being when they signed an agreement with the company. As a result, these groups tend to be perceived as a contracting agency for the company, while CART is often seen as an agent of the company. Moreover, most of the new leaders in the villages are employed by the coal company and tend to identify themselves strongly with its interests. In general, then, the interests of the company have permeated civil society in the mining areas. These circumstances provide the specific context for studying how social capital works in the study areas.

The social environment that prevails in Samaleswari and Kalinga is not conducive to generalized social trust. Granted, given the larger conditions affecting generalized trust in India, promoting an enabling environment where generalized trust can grow and solidify is not an easy task or an effort that can render immediate results. At a minimum level, however, and within its capabilities, "any institution with a developmental agenda must be at once engaged with the communities it seeks to serve *and* capable of maintaining its own credibility and effectiveness." (Woolcock 1998, p. 178). Yet Coal India has been unable to cement trusting relationships or maintain credibility with the communities affected by its operations. One of the main constraints is that the coal company is simultaneously the main agent affecting the social, economic, and natural environments of these communities and the agency in charge of helping those affected by these impacts. The relation of dependency and sense of mistrust that develops between the affected communities and the coal company shape the ways the company's policies and programs are applied. The communities' demands and attempts to bargain with the company test the limits of the company's commitments and cooperation, causing the "rules of the game" guiding intervention strategies to change constantly.

Multiple sets of game rules were in fact found to coexist in Samaleswari and Kalinga, which undermined coherent social interaction and increasingly disconcerted local civil society. Financing requirements, state policies, and the relative autonomy of the coal company subsidiary all prevented the development of a single, consistent, and clear policy for handling the community development responsibilities assumed by the company. Before 1980 there were no clear guidelines for community development. With the Bank-financed projects, Coal India prepared coherent guidelines for community development, for guiding the actions of company officers, and for informing communities about what to expect from the company. But these guidelines were applied only to 24 mines and to those villages located within 1 kilometer of the mines' lease-holds, and not to other mines or villages in the region, and that differentiation represented, at least during the study, an additional source of contradiction and inconsistency. As Hyden (1997) explains, individuals cannot be persuaded to cooperate genuinely or respect each other where *the institutional framework* is neglected.[15] These inconsistencies created different expectations that have not been completely met by the coal company or the government.

Family-Kinship: The Weaknesses of Strong Ties

According to Buckland (1998), in South Asia, cooperation beyond the extended family unit is relatively uncommon. In the study areas, as for other regions in India (see Hatti and Heimann 1992), the household is central to an individual's life, and a generalized sense of distrust toward nonhousehold members prevails. In this context, the social capital created within this family or kinship circle may not be as valuable as is often assumed (Putzel 1997). A key issue that hinders the evolution of informal institutions—of norms and values—is precisely that they are constantly reproduced within the family realm and enforced through strongly held ties based on dependency relationships that demand submission from certain members. Often, then, collective action for community development is not based completely on voluntary participation or is not as collective as it seems. Any assessment of the nature of social capital in a given community must thus probe into the strong ties created by family and kinship relations, and the extent to which these ties influence the access to and control of resources, including social capital itself.

Family structure in both Samaleswari and Kalinga has changed significantly with the development of coal mining. The number of nuclear families has increased, in part because of the presence of the mines. Often, when one brother gets a job, for example, and another does not, tension and a diversion of interests develop, and the extended family disintegrates. This is perhaps more pronounced in Orissa, where the resettlement and rehabilitation guidelines stipulate a "one family–one job" approach. The 1994 survey of project-affected persons in Samaleswari indicated that the number of nuclear families increased from 39.7 percent before mining operations to 47.7 percent at the time of the survey. Simultaneously, the percentage of joint families had decreased from 60.3 percent to 52.5 percent (VPASP 1994b). Incidence of female-headed households remained very low.

Power of decision—that is, "the room for agency" of particular social actors—is highly concentrated within the nuclear families in the study areas, especially since high levels of dependency are common. As this study corroborates, one of the main variables affecting these dependency levels is gender (Kapadia 1997, World Bank 1991). Like Singh (1995), this study found that mining operations have limited women's economic opportunities and correspondingly increased their levels of dependency and vulnerability within the household and the community. Before the mines opened, women found jobs as agricultural workers and earned income from collecting forest produce. More recently, access to the forests has been restricted, and agricultural work has decreased significantly, while the mining economy has not managed to offer sufficient "suitable" occupations for women, primarily for cultural reasons. The rate of female employment is thus dramatically lower than male employment, while self-employment is practically nonexistent among women.

The structures of constraint affecting women at the family-kinship level tend to be stronger among caste Hindus than among scheduled tribes and castes. They also tend to be stronger among landowning culti-vators than among landless laborers or marginal farm families.[16] In part, this may be because women have a higher status among the scheduled tribes and castes, where they are appreciated as an economic asset, than among the middle and higher castes (see also Fernandes and Raj 1992). Although tribal and lower-caste women are not considered equal to their husbands, they do seem to have greater freedom than the middle and upper-caste women, who might go through life subordinated first to their fathers, then to their husbands, and then, in widowhood, to their sons. These differences notwithstanding, as social capital resources undergo cycles of contraction due to economic stress, households in general tend to withdraw from the larger community, furthering the isolation of women (Moser 1996).

In summary, at the intrafamily level, the use value of social capital varies for each member depending on his or her gender. Furthermore, a family and the community to which it belongs may have plenty of social capital resources but this may not provide access to resources that will help women and other vulnerable family members overcome poverty or benefit them directly. Access to forms of social capital outside the house-hold and to other resources depends, in this context, on the degree to which one's links with the outside world are mediated by other family members. Availability of social capital resources may therefore be independent of opportunities for access and control of resources. This is particularly important for women, since the power of mediation of males is likely to increase with contractions in social capital resources, particularly under conditions of stress, scarcity, and poverty like those found in Samaleswari and Kalinga.

Horizontal Networks: Social Capital at the Community Level

It is generally agreed that social capital, particularly among poor communities, is scarce in South Asia (Woolcock 1998). Upon a cursory look, India does not seem to be an exception. The study found, however, that mutual trust within the community is plentiful in the study areas, and that there might even be an oversupply of certain forms of social capital.[17] Yet, while social capital resources in both Samaleswari and Kalinga may be abundant, they correspond to bonding social capital, which is not always conducive to the cohesiveness of the community at large.[18] Moreover, extreme poverty has probably discouraged collective action and curtailed its effectiveness by limiting people's time horizons and social interaction while augmenting self-interest and distrust toward outsiders. The considerable lack of horizontal linkages in the two villages most likely stems from a highly fragmented social structure, characterized by closed groups with high entry costs. The pattern of segregation that emerges from this is both social and spatial.

COMMUNITY LIFE. The village system, although certainly in flux due to the changes triggered by the mining industry, has maintained a set of structural rules (that is, guidelines or external norms and values) that influence what people do for and receive from other community members (Neale 1990). The distinct social stratification pattern characterizing the villages located in the study areas is a direct reflection of these rules.

In Samaleswari, social and spatial segregation are high. In two habitations, Sukhpara and Orampara, the entire population belongs to a single scheduled tribe, while in Mundapara most of the population belongs to a single scheduled tribe. (table 5.1). Although they are a minority of the population, the *Dixits* (Brahmins) dominate local politics and village management. They are the main landholders and have traditionally been the major decisionmakers of the area.

Lajkura has the highest concentration of scheduled castes, who are still restricted to an isolated hamlet and treated as untouchables by the upper caste group. Because of the rigid social norms and values imposed on them by the community at large, scheduled castes are not allowed to

Table 5.1 Total Population of Samaleswari, by Category

Village	Scheduled castes	Scheduled tribes	Other backward classes	General castes	Total
Kudapalli	41	345	260	77	723
Lajkura	219	190	254	61	724
Sukhpara	0	130	0	0	130
Mundapara	7	229	27	0	263
Ainapalli	48	183	200	0	431
Orampara	0	112	0	0	112
Karapalli	34	96	232	6	368
Total	349	1,285	973	144	2,751

enter the temple of the main village or to use the bathing platform (*ghat*). Nor are they allowed to participate in the main village functions or in any collective decisionmaking process. As a group, the scheduled caste population displays high degrees of internal social connectedness and relative cooperation. Despite these characteristics, they are still highly dependent on the higher-caste group because they lack economic resources and access to market opportunities, especially employment and credit. The level of dependency has diminished with the consolidation of the coal mining economy.

A higher level of social cohesiveness exists in Kalinga, largely because the traditional power groups have managed to maintain more traditional cooperative arrangements at the village level, and agriculture is still a relevant economic sector. This higher level of cohesion seems to stem from the existence of groups with strong internal ties and the economic and institutional resources necessary to impose their will on the rest of the community (table 5.2). In Kalinga, the *Chasa* (farmers) category—the largest among the "other backward classes" population—is perceived as the main power group. This is not surprising, since the farmers have traditionally been the main landholders in this area and have high social and economic status. Due to their power-wielding status, the *Chasa* appear to dominate the decisionmaking process and to be able to center the community consensus around their own priorities.

According to Grootaert (1997, p. 80), "...the creation of trust and reciprocity is more likely in horizontal groups, especially those based on kinship or other dense networks (for example, based on gender, ethnicity, or caste)." The study found that in this respect, Samaleswari and Kalinga have plenty of social capital resources, but they were fragmented among castes and gender and not always conducive to the cohesiveness of the community at large. Portes (1998) identifies four potential negative consequences of social capital: exclusion of outsiders, excess claims on group

Table 5.2 Total Population of Kalinga, by Category

Village	Scheduled castes	Scheduled tribes	Other backward classes	General castes	Total
Bramhanbahal	140	240	190	160	730
Danra	610	280	3,000	110	4,000
Kalam Chhuin	420	60	2,825	55	3,360
Majhika	70	25	655	0	750
Natada	280	430	1,150	15	1,875
Nathgaon	0	0	63	7	70
Nakeipasi	125	65	80	980	1,250
Solada	650	350	1,925	135	3,060
Total	2,295	1,450	9,888	1,462	15,095

members, restrictions on individual freedom, and downward leveling norms. All of these consequences, except the last one, seem to exist in the study areas.[19] Under the conditions prevailing in Samaleswari and Kalinga, community feeling tends to be fostered by inclusion-exclusion mechanisms, and social capital can become an antidemocratic and potentially disruptive force. When alienation from the community is deep, as is the case with the scheduled castes in Lajkura village, for example, the sense of suspicion can turn into hostile relationships toward "foreign" neighboring communities or individuals. As a group, both men and women belonging to the scheduled caste in Lajkura do not express much sympathy for the upper castes. Exclusionary mechanisms in the study areas discourage the formation of bridging social capital and simultaneously promote the emergence of closed groups. Significantly, the closed nature of these groups tends to exercise excessive claims on some of their members, notably women and disenfranchised social groups. Ethnic and caste divisions constitute an important factor affecting social interaction in the study areas, which has hindered the emergence of generalized trust and increased the transaction costs of social and economic exchanges (see also Collier 1998).

Gender, again, is an important variable. In both Samaleswari and Kalinga, many women have developed very informal, yet relatively strong, "support networks" with other women outside their households, although within the confines of their own social and economic, and often, spatial location. Much as males are isolated in their social interaction by caste, class, and related issues such as occupation and identification with work, women also tend to separate themselves by caste and class. Not only do women continue to occupy a completely separate social dimension from men, even when facing the outside world, but they do not attempt to build bridges either across networks or to groups of women different from "their own kind." Since most local women lack autonomy and economic resources, their social capital represents instrumental potential, but this potential is of little real value. The resources made available to those women when they use their social capital are minimal and insufficient to make a noticeable impact on their lives.[20] Within existing socioeconomic arrangements, their room for action and the chances of improving their well-being through collective action still remain highly constrained.

A sense of "fictive kinship," to apply Kapadia's (1997) term, could be detected among company employees, as evidenced by the tendency to address each other as if they were part of a large family, the coal company "kin." With the entrenchment of the mining economy in the area, many males have acquired a strong sense of identity with the company, while the prevalent aspiration of males—and of many females—not yet working for the company is to become a Mahanadi Coalfields employee. This close identification with the coal company has provided some intervillage linkages of similarly socially and economically positioned men. This is not surprising, since occupation, workplace, and the organization of production are likely to play a key role in the development of social ties and horizontal linkages between individuals and groups of individuals.

In the study areas, the centrality of mining activities may make these factors even more relevant.[21] The networks of fictive kinship found in the study areas, however, are loose and without a strong sense of collective interests. These characteristics are the result of two interrelated factors: first, the ties of fictive kinship do not cross gender or caste divisions, because so few women are regular company employees and certain castes tend to concentrate in certain activities; and second, the interests of mine employees often differ from others in their communities and even from members of their own ethnic or caste groups or family members who are not part of the company. The latter factor directly affects the feasibility and nature of collective action, more so as company employees have increasingly taken power from the traditional leadership (ORG 1995).

The coal company's scheme for compensating people depending on their designation as a formal employee, a daily wage worker, or an entitled project-affected person has created new power relations and furthered inequality. In Samaleswari, the situation is especially precarious. All the villages in Samaleswari are entitled to community development benefits, but many villages coterminous with them fall under the old Coal India policies and residents feel that they are treated differently under the same circumstances. Moreover, because the resettlement and rehabilitation packages benefit individuals rather than the community as a whole, the incentives for cooperation and collective action within the villages are low (Eyben and Ladbury 1995). Instead of working together to try to obtain benefits for everyone in the community, individuals compete for designation as one of the categories of people who receive compensation.

The development of a market economy in the study areas has also been an incentive for individuals to act on their own rather than within a community structure—perhaps even a more important incentive than the divisive compensation scheme. In a traditional village economy, the sense of community is tied not only to the place where people live, but also to a system of traditional economic production and transactions. As the market increasingly provides individuals access to the same goods they once had to obtain through collective action, individuals feel less compelled to cooperate with those outside their close-knit groups. Increasing commercialization of agriculture (in Kalinga) or the virtual disappearance of agricultural activities (in Samaleswari), coupled with the monetization of the economy and the provision of infrastructure and certain services—at least for some people—by the coal company, has dramatically eroded the need for collective action to provide collective goods. In turn, the traditional system of resource sharing and service obligations has given way, and the reciprocal caste-based relationships between landowners and laborers have been replaced by market relations. Lower-caste groups are not compelled to interact as much with the landowner castes. Social cleavages are simultaneously strengthened as the more powerful groups feel threatened and lower groups become more independent of them, albeit more dependent on the coal company.

COMMUNITY-BASED ASSOCIATIONAL LIFE. Social capital in the study areas is high but simultaneously fractured by gender, caste, and class. Significantly, but not surprisingly, the study found that community-based associational life is very low (table 5.3 and table 5.4). Most social interaction takes place outside community-based groups, within the divisions established by the existing social hierarchy. Although most survey respondents in both study areas indicated that they are aware of the existence of the community-based groups discussed below, they were unsure about the groups' functions and showed a low level of interest in getting involved in these types of associations.

The only visible groups in the villages are the *mahila mandals* (women's clubs), most of which have died out due to lack of interest and resources.[22] In Samaleswari, women in four villages organized *mahila mandals*, but only three are relatively active.[23] In Lajkura, a club organized by scheduled caste women in 1987 to raise the social standing of the scheduled castes is no longer in operation, due to lack of guidance, inadequate funding, and internal power conflicts. The situation is similar, if

Table 5.3 Community-Based Groups in Samaleswari

Village	Mahila mandal	Youth club	Village working group
Lajkura	Inactive	Active	Active
Sukhpara	Nonexistent	Nonexistent	Active
Kudapalli	Active	Inactive	Active
Orampara	Nonexistent	Nonexistent	Active
Ainapalli	Active	Inactive	Active
Karapalli	Active[a]	Inactive	Active
Mundapara	Active	Nonexistent	Active

[a] The *mahila mandal* of Mundapara also covers Karapalli.

Table 5.4 Community-Based Groups in Kalinga

Village/town	Mahila mandal	Youth club	Village management committee
Solada	0	4	0
Bramhanbahal	0	0	0
Nakeispasi	0	2	0
Majhika	1	1	1
Kalam Chhuin	3	5	3
Natada	1	1	1
Danra	1	3	1
Nathgaon[a]	0	0	0

a. Nathgaon is a new settlement where all households are still dependent on their respective "mother" villages.

not worse, in Kalinga, where most of the women's clubs found in four of the villages (Danra, Kalam Chhuin, Majhika, and Natada) are inactive.[24]

Youth clubs, common throughout India, also have been established in the study areas to promote youth participation in a broad range of activities including sports, cultural activities, literacy programs, health awareness, and community development activities. In Samaleswari, four villages have youth clubs, but only one, in Lajkura, is registered and active. The others suffer from lack of interest and of any binding force. In Kalinga, youth clubs are found in each village or town except Bramhanbahal and Nathgaon and are much more active than in Samaleswari. In general, clubs in the study areas have between 40 to 50 members, especially in Kalinga, where population density is higher. Most of the members are educated. Membership in the club is restricted to youth of a particular village or hamlet.

An important qualitative difference between the two study sites is that the traditional *grama parichala samiti* (village management committee) has survived in Kalinga but not in Samaleswari. Villages across India were traditionally managed by this type of committee, but their relevance diminished, and many disappeared after the consolidation of the *panchayat* system for managing community development.[25] Contrary to this trend, every village but one in Kalinga has an active village management committee.[26] The traditional village management system has survived in Kalinga because most of the villages are much older and more populated than the ones in Samaleswari, and they are composed of various caste groups. Agricultural work and land-based employment is still significant in Kalinga, where villages are much less dependent on the coal company than they are in Samaleswari.

Village management committees in Kalinga are primarily responsible for resolving disputes and conflicts within the community, managing common property resources and temples, and organizing cultural events.[27] The committees also make sure that the village's pond water is equally shared among villagers for irrigation during the drought season. The committees are informally organized and composed of village elders, following traditional arrangements. The leader is a senior male, who in Kalinga is called *Sabhapati* (President). Most of the presidents and other members of the committees are from the upper-caste "farmers group." Participation of scheduled tribes and castes representatives is, as it has historically been, very low. Members of the *panchayati raj* pay respect to and consult the members of these committees about important decisions such as the selection of beneficiaries for government-funded programs. No horizontal linkages exist between the management committees of the various villages, except for limited agreements among certain villages to guard the nearby forests on a rotating basis. Disputes between two villages are often resolved at a joint meeting of the two committees, while major cases are taken to a court of law. In both study areas, the *panchayats* were the only grassroots institutions with an intervillage character, but they tended to reflect the villages' social structure and its related cleavages, and many people said that they had lost trust in them.

Under Coal India's new community development guidelines, village working groups were promoted in Samaleswari to ensure beneficiaries' participation and enhance their sense of ownership. These working groups are supposed to have 10 to 15 members representative of all castes and tribal populations in the village; at least two of the members are expected to be women. Instead, the groups tend to reflect the existing social structure and power relations of the villages (table 5.5). In Lajkura, for instance, only 1 of the 17 members of the working group belongs to the scheduled castes, even though the scheduled castes represent about

Table 5.5 Composition Profile of Village Working Groups in Samaleswari

| Village | Total members | By gender | | By group | | | | Percentage of scheduled castes and tribes | |
		Male	Female	Scheduled castes	Scheduled tribes	Other backward classes	Others	Percent of scheduled castes in village	Percent of scheduled tribes in village
Ainapalli (431)	14	12	2	1	2	11	0	11	42
Karapalli (368)	10	10	0	0	0	10	0	9	26
Orampara (112)	11	11	0	0	11	0	0	0	100
Mundapara (263)	12	9	3	1	7	4	0	3	87
Lajkura (724)	17	17	0	1	6	9	1	30	26
Sukhpara (130)	10	10	0	0	10	0	0	0	100
Kudapalli (723)	18	13	5	0	5	6	7	6	48

Note: Total population of village is given in parentheses.

one-third of the total village population. In the entire study area, only three working groups had female members at the time of the study; the other villages said there were no "suitable" female candidates. Despite concerted efforts by the facilitating NGO hired by Coal India to "equalize" the village working groups, they tend to be dominated by the already powerful.[28]

Neighboring villages in Samaleswari do not seem to find any common interests. Despite high levels of in-group caste or ethnic solidarity within the habitations, no strong networks of horizontal associations linking the same groups from one village to the next could be identified. Similarly, no horizontal linkages among the various village working groups have developed in Samaleswari, despite the proximity of the villages and of the coal mines themselves. Considering this situation, it is likely that community-based development could achieve only very modest results here. Bargaining power is fundamental to establish respect for freedom of association, which in consequence demands a degree of "scaling up" of organization that must transcend the local level. Regional horizontal networks and organizations are an option for scaling up, since they provide opportunities for linking dispersed solidarities, increasing bargaining power, and facilitating access to information. None of this is present in Samaleswari, or the nearby mining areas that comprise Ib Valley. Nor does the coal company seemed very interested in addressing this issue.

INTERPERSONAL TRUST AND THE NEED FOR COOPERATION. Table 5.6 provides a comparative measurement of degrees of generalized trust in the two study areas. As it indicates, individuals say they count on the entire village to help out in times of personal crises such as a death in the family or a conflict between two individuals or families. Yet cooperative efforts in other situations have not been particularly successful. Indeed, cycles of conflict and cooperation have been a central feature of the interactions among the various social and institutional actors involved in the community development and resettlement and rehabilitation activities in the study areas. Periodic cooperative efforts have failed to resolve issues of power, equity, and access to resources in any lasting way, reinforcing attitudes of suspicion and distrust and creating a vicious circle.

The survey showed that more residents of Samaleswari (84.9 percent) than of Kalinga (74.0 percent) were aware that collective action could improve their communities' quality of life. The higher level of awareness in Samaleswari was to some degree related to the efforts of the facilitating NGO working there. Close to 84 percent of survey respondents in Samaleswari also expressed their willingness to contribute either time or money toward activities that would improve the quality of life in their communities. Considering the level of social fragmentation, this stated

Table 5.6 Degrees of Generalized Interpersonal Trust (percent)

Type of event	Social unit/ institution	Samaleswari (n = 141)	Kalinga (n = 235)
Festivals	Within family	15.0	5.5
	Neighbor	6.8	6.8
	Caste group	7.5	3.8
	Entire village	68.7	82.6
	Neighboring village	2.0	1.3
Economic loss	No one	9.3	13.2
	Relatives	30.5	28.5
	Neighbors	43.7	48.5
	Village money lender	15.2	8.5
	Rural bank	1.4	1.3
Dispute between	Among themselves	18.8	1.7
two individuals/	Neighbors	9.4	3.8
families	Caste group	2.7	0.4
	Entire village	66.5	92.3
	No response	2.7	1.8
In case of	No one	5.2	0
any death	Relatives	12.3	26.4
	Neighbor	26.6	30.6
	Caste group	7.8	7.2
	Entire village	48.1	35.7

Note: Indicator: Whom would people count on in case of various events?

willingness may appear to be some form of cognitive dissonance. A closer probe, though, showed that "community" meant something different to each respondent. In addition, although people expressed willingness to contribute time or money, they expected that the coal company would provide many of the needed public goods and that their contributions would not in fact be required. Finally, despite the realization that cooperation was important, most interviewees rarely interacted with people from other social groups and village clusters, and even felt that other people from their own villages were self-centered and did not care about the welfare of others. Not surprisingly, confidence in the sustainability of group effort was low.

An important area for cooperation is the management of common property resources (table 5.7). In Samaleswari, where these resources have dwindled along with any kind of villagewide management system, a majority of survey respondents still recognized the need for cooperation. Yet roughly only 3 out of 10 respondents were willing to help organize and run this management system. In Kalinga, 6 out of 10 respondents were willing to share this responsibility. Interestingly, despite the low percentage of people in Samaleswari willing to cooperate in managing common property resources, most respondents were willing to contribute money for it. Apparently, many people would not mind paying for provision of collective services, if they could afford it, because in the past collective action was not very democratic. Traditionally, higher-caste groups assumed the role of supervisors, while the actual physical work was done by individuals at the bottom of the social hierarchy. This forced labor has tended to disappear with the increased influence of the mine economy and the related demise of the agricultural sector, and many of the lower-caste groups do not want it back.

In Samaleswari, willingness to contribute money for future infrastructure maintenance was even lower than the willingness to participate in the management of common property resources (table 5.7). Most people felt that operations and maintenance were the responsibility of Mahanadi Coalfields or the government. The coal company had been providing infrastructure for years, and many people in Samaleswari did not agree with the new rules that required them to take on the responsibility, particularly since the coal company was still maintaining the infrastructure

Table 5.7 Attitudes toward Management of Common Property Resources and Village Infrastructure

Attitude	Samaleswari (n = 141) Percent	Kalinga (n = 235) Percent
Felt that community-based management is necessary	58.2	88.1
Willing to participate in the management of common property resources	27.7	60.0
Willing to contribute money for management of common property resources	75.9	62.6
Community-based operation and maintenance (O&M) of village infrastructure perceived to be necessary	31.2	74.0
Willing to participate in O&M	25.5	28.5
Willing to contribute money for O&M	25.5	43.0

in some nearby villages. In Kalinga, people felt stronger about participating in operation and maintenance activities of village infrastructure. Here, the Periphery Development Program—the ad hoc form of community development implemented by Mahanadi Coalfields—continued to operate, and the villages were enjoying its benefits without having to organize for or contribute to it.

Cross-Sectional Linkages:
Vertical Articulations—The Company and "Its" Communities

Largely because Coal India has assumed more and more local community development responsibilities, civil society in Samaleswari and Kalinga has forged few vertical articulations with the local and central government agencies that would have conducted these activities in the coal company's absence. Its mounting responsibilities have gradually overwhelmed the coal company, in part because of its inability to form a partnership with the communities it is meant to assist. The company's own lack of capacity and interest in dealing with community development issues has kept it from promoting the creation of the very community networks that could have facilitated community development activities. But although the company could be doing more to address this situation, it is highly unlikely that it could have been fully successful on its own. Even if stronger horizontal linkages were established across the study areas, not all the development issues could have been solved at the community level, let alone solely by building social capital through the promotion of associations.

On the one hand, local and community development and poverty alleviation are tasks that cannot be assumed entirely by a single agency, even one with an increased capacity to build social capital. That is especially true when the agency in question is a coal company under great pressure to improve the bottom line of its mining operations. On the other hand, by becoming the de facto central agency in the area, the coal company has displaced an important form of social capital: the mutually supportive and complementary relations that could be provided by other sectors of society such as national and international NGOs, government agencies, and private firms. Without these vertical articulations, which are necessary to break down the isolation of local community groups and provide them with better access to other (informational, economic) resources, the potential of the social capital prevalent at the community level to improve people's lives cannot materialize.

To assess social capital in the context of community development, it is essential to look at the actual and potential winners and losers in transactions mediated by social capital. Social capital does not have an absolute value, but a relative one. Whether social capital has a beneficial or detrimental nature depends on the social or institutional actors' stake in the process of community development—a characteristic that makes the valuation of social capital difficult. On the occasions when collective efforts, such as the formation of village working groups, appeared to be compatible with the goals of the company policy, they were well received by mine officials. But on the few occasions when some people in the study areas decided to come together to pool their bargaining power and oppose certain decisions of the company, mine officials perceived this form of social capital development as undesirable. Many mine representatives saw the notion of building bridges across villages as a threat to the smooth operation of the mines and therefore counterproductive.

Implications for Future Research

The study's findings suggest that social capital has a multidimensional nature and a relative and contingent value that depends heavily on the social, economic, cultural, and political context. From these characteristics it follows that individual and group access to a community's social capital reserves are not equally distributed, while, at the same time, each form of social capital can have different, sometimes contradictory, effects. It would be rather limiting, given these conclusions, to assess social capital resources by focusing only on associational membership or norms of reciprocity and trust, and by assuming that social capital always produces beneficial forms of civic engagement (Edwards and Foley 1998) or that more of it is always better (Woolcock 1998). To assess the value of social capital, one should therefore consider its multidimensional nature and its overall distribution and accessibility vis-à-vis particular community and household members. And one should take into account the effects of the nature of distribution and accessibility of these resources on equity—in terms of control of resources and control of access to resources—and democratic outcomes in a community. In this respect, two key sets of variables affecting social capital that need to be investigated more intensively are political engagement and power relations.

Relative and Contingent Value of Social Capital

Social capital may have a different meaning and use value for each of the concerned individuals and groups, depending on their specific social, economic, cultural, and political context (Burt 1997). In the particular case of community development, whether social capital is experienced as beneficial or detrimental varies according to the stakeholder. It would thus be relevant to identify both the range of possible effects of social capital and the particular costs and benefits of social capital for the concerned stakeholders. Social capital at the community level should therefore not be assumed to be the sum of "individual" social capital (Edwards and Foley 1998, Portes and Landolt 1996). And social capital in general should not be assumed always to have a positive value. Under certain circumstances, a form of social capital that might otherwise play a critical role in facilitating certain actions or resources may become useless or even harmful (Coleman 1988, 1990; Harriss and De Renzio 1997).

The use value of social capital is also affected by its own social location, independent of who appropriates it (Edwards and Foley 1997). To put it differently, the value of a given form of social capital for enabling some action depends to a large extent on the social and economic location of the social capital in a community. In fact, the availability of social capital cannot be assumed to be equivalent to the resources obtained through it, given that these resources can be simultaneously limited and constraining (Portes 1998). While some social capital may be nested within dynamic sectors, for instance, other forms of social capital may be connected to declining or contracting sectors. A group that appropriates this latter form may obtain some benefits, but these may be short-lived.

Distribution and Access to Social Capital Resources

Access to and control of social capital resources are not equally distributed within the family or throughout a community (Bourdieu 1986, Granovetter 1985), while social capital is often considered valuable precisely because of its scarcity and exclusivity (Whittington 1998). In particular, access to social capital depends on one's social location and is constrained by various factors such as the level of geographical, cultural, and social isolation; lack of financial resources; and the specific institutional arrangements that structure everyday life (Edwards and Foley 1997). Thus, at the group level, it does not always hold that the resources a person obtains through his or her relationships within a group are available to all members of the group or that all members of a group have equal access to the group's resources (Astone and others 1998).

Effects of Social Capital

The study's findings further suggest that each form of social capital can have different, sometimes contradictory, effects. In the notion of social capital that has developed on the basis of Putnam's work, there has been a tendency to romanticize the image of community and to neglect some of the adverse effects of sociability (Portes and Landolt 1996). This study indicates, as does other recent research (for example, Portes 1998, Woolcock 1998), that sociability can have desirable and not-so-desirable consequences. When evaluating the social capital resources of a given community, the analyst should identify and account for both the positive and the negative effects of social capital (Putzel 1997; Rose, Mishler, and Haerpfer 1997). Social capital can facilitate all kinds of individual and collective efforts, ranging from community development organizations to death squads (Edwards and Foley 1998). Often, though, it has been assumed, misleadingly, that social capital is not just a public good, but intrinsically for the public good (Putzel 1997). The normative underpinnings of what is desirable or undesirable notwithstanding, it is safe to assume that social capital can be a *public good* and a *public bad*, alternatively or even simultaneously. In other words, as a common property (social) resource, social capital may have positive and negative externalities.

Social capital can certainly enhance the efficiency of physical and human capital and can facilitate economic exchange and coordination. But, as observed in the study areas, some forms of social capital are illiberal and socially exclusive. Certain civic society groups can use their social capital resources to exercise control over other community members and secure a considerable share of the community resources (Woolcock 1998). Importantly, as Granovetter (1985) puts it, although social relations are often a necessary condition for trust and trustworthy behavior, they are not sufficient to ensure that behavior. On the contrary, social relations may actually provide opportunities and means for malfeasance and conflict, perhaps to a greater extent than if they did not exist at all. As the case of Kalinga suggests, a group may actually have access to too much social capital. Certain networks of civic engagement may be a source of trust within, but they can also incite distrust from without.

Political Engagement

The networks and relationships created by associations do not guarantee by themselves political outcomes (Putzel 1997). There are significant differences across various kinds of social clubs and organizations regarding levels of political mobilization and community action. In the long run, an individual's rich social life may not necessarily translate into political competence (Almond and Verba 1963). It is relevant for future research, therefore, to distinguish between the "mechanics of trust" (the operation of networks, norms, and the like) and the "political content and ideas" disseminated through these networks and reflected in the shared norms (Putzel 1997).

This distinction implies not only that the capacity of well-mobilized groups to make effective demands on government can remain limited. It also implies, as Whittington (1998) correctly argues, that civic associations can cultivate resentment that leads to political turbulence and distrust. There is no guarantee that demands will always be democratic in nature or that they will not conflict with the social order or, as in this specific case, with the stated objectives of development projects. Mobilization of the population can lead also to the emergence of very particularistic demands that may undermine democracy more than enhance it.

Power Relations

As observed during fieldwork, social capital resources exist within the same social space as power relations. According to Foucault (1980), power is coextensive with the social body, and power relations are intricately woven into other kinds of social relations, such as economic production, kinship, family, or sexuality. Therefore, a full understanding of social capital requires not only an understanding of these relations, but also an understanding of the exercise of power and strategies of resistance that take place at the moment of social exchange. This element of the social exchange involves—or to be more precise, produces and reproduces systematically—relations of inequality intrinsic in power relations (Agger 1992). Simultaneously, people are positioned differently with respect to the resulting power structures, which are constituted by various axes of identity, such as gender, class, and ethnicity (Kapadia 1997). In other words, social relations play a conditioning role for power relations while being simultaneously conditioned by them. This assumption, which implies, in Foucault's words, that "power is always already there" in social exchange, does not mean that it is useless to promote social capital. Foucault understood the extent to which government institutions mattered, but he also realized that the dispersed mechanisms of power that existed outside the state, in civil society, were just as important. Altogether, these power relations constitute, as stated above, structures of facilitation and constraint to access resources and to control the access to and resources available in a society.

Conclusions: Specific Implications for Community Development

Lack of social cohesion represents a major challenge for successful implementation of community-driven development in India. Community development strategies have increasingly become dependent on the social capital of the target beneficiaries. They require community consultation during project preparation and participation during implementation to identify problems and priorities that arise under the constraints imposed by low-cost investments, minimal subsidies, and cost recovery. This approach is also demand-based, requiring a high degree of commitment by the communities to ensure sustainability. All these assumptions lead to one logical conclusion: the standard approach can work best through community-based groups that promote existing social capital or can build the needed social capital.

In India, however, the standard approach has been based on unrealistic notions of the nature of community in the villages and of the possibilities and democratic content of collective action. Communities are assumed to be inherently democratic, and "inclusion" and "participation" guaranteed by promoting new groups that include representatives of all groups in a community. The fundamental constraint identified during fieldwork is that communities—village civic society in this case—are not always structured in a way that facilitates the equal distribution of external resources or any kind of aid across the intended beneficiaries. In India, village civic society remains extremely hierarchical, and despite many positive changes brought about by development, persistent inequalities remain embedded in social capital resources. Under such conditions, villagewide groups, as indicated by the study and corroborated by other research (for example, Jayaraman and Lanjouw 1999; Mosse 1995, 1996), may not be effective mechanisms for democratic planning and collective decision-making. Most villagewide groups tend to ignore certain sections of the population and are dominated by the most powerful groups; women are given a very limited role, if any. If they are not closely monitored, new villagewide groups are also likely to resemble this pattern.

The study also highlights the difficulty of identifying appropriate social and spatial boundaries of the target community, given that these boundaries seldom correlate. Most community development programs in rural India assume that the village *is* the community and should therefore remain or be made self-sufficient. Under this premise, *community* is usually associated with the official boundaries of the Revenue Village, as is the case under the new community development guidelines of Coal India. In reality, the village, composed of several hamlets, does not have a clear physical identity or a homogeneous social identity. The emergence of a sense of community at the level of the village would therefore be better approached as a dynamic process shaped by the various forms of dependence, competition, and factional conflict that characterize the hamlets' relations (Mosse 1996).

Current approaches to community development see the association of beneficiaries as a necessary ingredient to achieving development goals, under the rationale that the social capital produced by these associations makes the provision of collective goods more cost-effective (Stolle and Rochon 1998). Accordingly, the strategy for preparing a community development project has been to search for "developmentally valuable forms of social capital," and in the absence of these, to recommend the promotion of "desirable forms of social capital" (Beall 1997). Social capital in this context acquires developmental value mainly as a compensatory resource to address the deficiencies prevalent in society, including the unmet social needs of the intended beneficiaries. By extension, civic cooperation becomes narrowly defined as a tool to implement development programs and plans, while the use value of social capital is restricted to cooperative and voluntary social relations demanding leisure time. The problem is that in poor communities like those included in this study, distinctions between voluntary and involuntary association and cooperation and between leisure time and working hours are generally moot. As much as sociability and collective action have benefits, they also have costs. Investing in social capital, particularly in voluntary associations to implement community development activities or to manage certain community affairs (such as operating and maintaining community infrastructure assets) puts additional demands on certain individuals and groups in the community—generally the poorer and more disenfranchised households and social groups, who are paradoxically already overworked and underemployed. It is in this context that the promotion of social capital for community development must be understood in order to avoid overburdening the intended beneficiaries with "voluntary" membership in community groups. Finally, the instrumental value of social capital in project implementation has generally been overemphasized to the detriment of the potential use value of translating these relations into political resources.[29]

It is reasonable to assume that NGOs could act as mediators between vertical and horizontal networks. NGOs, however, are often external agents operating in the middle of the delicate balance of interests and power existing in the communities. Like Buckland (1998), this study indicates that the necessary emphasis on short-term objectives, such as income generation and provision of social services, causes NGOs and other agencies working in community development to neglect longer-term issues such as social organizing to maintain and build social capital. Promotion of community networks and extended normative behavior (generalized trust) are generally insufficient, while cultural patterns and social and economic trends hinder the emergence of new forms of civic engagement. Simultaneously, social capital promotion tends to introduce new norms and incentives for interaction that are heavily mediated by the NGO, which makes the sustainability of the enhanced social interaction heavily dependent on such mediations.

In summary, the main implications of the study for social capital and community development are:

1. Social capital cannot be built, promoted, or transformed exclusively from within the community.
2. New types of community organizations should be promoted, but these cannot be designed in isolation from the social and economic context of the community and from the wider institutional framework facilitating or constraining the generalization of trust.
3. Instead of one particular model of local organization (for example, village working groups), a wide variety of community organizations should be promoted, according to the various objectives and activities of the community development strategy. Reliance on group-based activities should be supplemented with other associational forms such as networks of individuals, and ideally these networks should reach outside a particular community.
4. Building social capital through community development requires triggering a process of social reorganization that takes advantage of informal, often invisible, forms of association. New organizations are unlikely to change existing social relations immediately or in a short period of time.
5. When feasible, it may be better to start promoting the creation of small groups within existing social solidarities. In other words, it is critical to start working the existing social structure from the inside out. However, creation of small groups in isolation might exacerbate social cleavages in the long run. Horizontal linkages across these groups should be facilitated, and vertical articulations with state and private organizations deliberately sought.
6. Promotion of social capital must be complemented with concerted efforts to generalize social trust. Inconsistencies regarding the application of procedures, regulations, and requirements that affect the institutional framework supporting the existence of generalized social trust should be avoided. The coexistence of many old and new rules of the game contributes to generalized mistrust. Simultaneously, credibility of the development agency is adversely affected when beneficiaries in similar circumstances are treated differently.
7. Excessive reliance on community-based groups to achieve the objectives of community development might create unidentified dependency relations among individual members, in particular the most vulnerable ones, within the community. The greater the benefits expected from the community group, the more people are willing to tolerate excessive obligations. If the interpersonal bonds of dependency that may already prevail in a given community are transferred into the newly created groups by making them the main or only providers of certain services or public goods, chances are that these relationships of dependency will be strengthened rather than weakened.

8. Sociability has costs as well as benefits, and the costs may be higher for the poor who do not have as much leisure or idle time to invest in building social capital purposely.
9. The external social actors, be they NGOs or other types of organizations, should have as an objective to make themselves redundant in a reasonable time period.

Implications for Policy

Social capital does matter for community-based development, although it might be better understood as one of a variety of assets available in different degrees to individuals and groups in a community (Moser 1998). Social capital by itself cannot provide the solutions to major social and economic problems and may actually be of limited value if not combined with other forms of capital, namely, natural, physical, and human capital (Serageldin 1996).

The structures of facilitation and constraint that characterize a society demand that social capital be promoted simultaneously at the local level through networks of individuals and groups, and at the institutional and policy level. The state still must play a role in diminishing the close and often risky "personalized dependencies" of people on each other. Traditional associations that may have been necessary under certain circumstances but that perpetuated subordinate roles for women and other vulnerable groups may be bound to disappear, and may be replaced by government institutions. The enthusiasm surrounding the concept of social capital stems from the acceptance that it is a resource or asset that provides an alternative to the heavy hand of the central government and an effective tool to improving governance. It is a concept that fits perfectly into the current promotion of decentralization.

However important the features of social organization are to community development policy and projects, they are significantly affected by political institutions and their capacities, including the state. Attempting to create social capital without recognizing this fact is to attack "the symptoms, not the causes of the problem" (Tarrow 1996, p. 396). Societies and communities, such as those in the study areas, may possess abundant—if fragmented—social capital but lack other key resources and assets that would allow certain groups to escape poverty or make significant progress in terms of democratic political participation (Warren 1998, Harriss and De Renzio 1997).

Civic society and its social capital matter for community development, but in the context of government institutions and the general institutional framework of society at large. Associations, albeit not all, may be built up with the support of the state. As Putzel (1997, p. 947) concludes, "a strong state and strong civil society must go together." In general, it appears that all communities are endowed with at least a minimal stock of social capital, from family and kinship ties to cooperative arrangements among friends and neighbors. The difference lies in how social capital is scaled up and whether it is scaled up through the interaction between the state and private and voluntary organizations in order to create solidarity ties and social action that reaches levels of political and economic efficacy. Finally, if the main objective of community-driven development is to empower individuals, to foster autonomy, to promote personal growth and self-realization through market processes, the notion of social capital is relevant in the sense that it underscores the importance of other necessary means of empowerment to support market processes and to facilitate the emergence of democratic, civic communities.

Notes

This chapter draws from a larger Social Capital Initiative study of the Coal Sector Environmental and Social Mitigation Project in India, of which Jelena Pantelic was the task manager. Field research was done in collaboration with Operations Research Group (ORG India) and Jonathan Glass, an international consultant. Christiaan Grootaert and Thierry van Bastelaer provided useful comments and suggestions during the research and preparation of this chapter. Beltrania Scarano contributed maps and graphics. Susan Assaf facilitated the management of the study's funds. David Fissel provided invaluable support during the preparation of this chapter.

1. According to Hyden (1997), the notion of social capital may be traced as far back as the 19th century. The notion of social capital entered development thinking with full force in 1993, after Robert Putnam published *Making Democracy Work*. The notion had been around in contemporary thinking, implicitly or explicitly, many years before, as made evident by the works of Jacobs (1961), Homans (1961), Granovetter (1973), Bourdieu (1986), and Coleman (1988), among others.

2. As in other World Bank–financed projects, these social mitigation measures were consonant with the bank's safeguard policies designed to avoid unnecessary social harm and to mitigate and compensate when needed to ensure that people's livelihoods and overall quality of life are not drastically affected by the new investments.

3. There were 24 opencast mines included under the ESMP scattered across 11 coalfields in 5 states of east and central India, managed by an equal number of subsidiaries.

4. Every village has a given "revenue boundary" that comprises several habitations. In other words, a village in this paper refers to a "revenue village." Information on the study areas, unless otherwise specified, is derived from the household surveys and the database of project-affected people.

5. Entitled project-affected persons in Samaleswari include those individuals affected by the investments financed by the World Bank who were above 18 years of age by January 1, 1994 (assumed as the cut-off date when baseline surveys were undertaken in the area).

6. This information was provided directly by the Chief Mining Officer of the Kalinga area.

7. The most important castes in Orissa have been the Brahmins, the Karans, the Khandayats, and the Chasas. Their traditional occupations have been, respectively, priests and scholars, writers, landholders and warriors, and cultivators (Lerche 1991).

8. Unless stated otherwise, this information comes mainly from the two staff appraisal reports prepared for the projects (World Bank 1996, 1997).

9. The task facing Coal India was enormous; according to Singh (1995), the mines are "spread over 30 districts of different states in India, approximately covering 2000 villages. . . ."

10. The usual active life of an opencast mine is between 25 to 30 years.

11. The Land Acquisition Act has been amended several times since its adoption, the last time in 1984.

12. Implementation of social and environmental measures did not reach full speed until the middle of 1997. The closing date of the project would later be extended until July 2002.

13. Early estimates indicated that about 16,000 persons would be affected by the project, about 10,000 of whom would have to be resettled. The total number of people entitled to rehabilitation assistance was estimated at about 9,200.

14. See Lenci (1997) for a valuable discussion on the "reconvergence" of economics and sociology.

15. Institutional framework in this context means, first, the vertical articulations between the concerned social and institutional actors (for example, Coal India, Mahanadi Coalfields, various levels of government, private sector agencies such as banks, and the horizontal associations, networks, and individuals themselves), and second, the policies, strategies, and instruments that provide a sense of generalized social trust independent of (and that may actually enable the expansion of) interpersonal trust.

16. Similar findings can be found in Fernandes and Raj (1992) and World Bank (1991).

17. In this respect, see also Madsen (1993).

18. This is based on an important distinction established by Putnam (1993) between bridging and bonding social capital. Bonding capital is limited to groups with similar characteristics and may enhance social divisions.

19. Downward leveling norms, according to Portes (1998), take place in cases when group solidarity is based on shared adversity and opposition to mainstream society. In this case, individual success stories are seen as negative because they threaten group cohesion, especially since this cohesion is based

precisely on the alleged impossibility of the individual success of any group member.

20. Incidentally, this finding is congruent with Portes's (1998) assertion that social capital is not equal to the resources made available by accessing it.

21. The study's survey found that in Samaleswari about 50 percent of males between 18 and 55 years of age were employed in the mine. Kalinga has a more diversified economy, and the survey indicated that about 20 percent of 488 males over 18 years of age in the sample were regular mine employees.

22. These organizations have been promoted by the central government to increase women's participation in community development across villages in India. The official objective is to ensure social equity, economic empowerment, and self-reliance of women. In the study areas, few of these clubs were found to be formally registered under the Society Registration Act.

23. The active women's clubs met regularly once a month. The clubs were undertaking similar activities, such as meetings to raise awareness among women regarding health, family planning, and nutrition.

24. In Kalinga, none of the women's clubs has its own building, which made it difficult to conduct meetings and keep records.

25. The *panchayati raj* consists of a three-tiered system of local self-government to administer community development in India: a *panchayat* in each village, a council for each community development block, and a council at the district level (or *zila parishad*).

26. The village is Nathgaon, and the committee's lack of activity is due to its recent creation.

27. Sources of funds for the committees have traditionally included leasing out the village ponds for fish cultivation, charging fines during dispute settlement, and collections during village festivities. These funds are deposited in a common village fund managed exclusively by the members of the management committee.

28. Mosse (1995) similarly concludes that new organizations tend to reproduce existing power structures. For a contrasting view, see Fisher (1994).

29. Buckland (1998) offers a useful distinction in this respect. At the simplest level of analysis, social capital may be seen as central to facilitating cooperation and community participation as a means to reduce project implementation costs and achieve immediate results. However, when the "use value" of social capital is seen as "empowerment," the implication is that social capital in the community will facilitate social and political organization that, in the long term, will provide wider access to other resources.

References

Agger, Ben. 1992. *The Discourse of Domination*. Evanston, Ill.: Northwestern University Press.

Almond, Gabriel A., and Sidney Verba. 1963. *The Civic Culture*. Princeton, N.J.: Princeton University Press.

Astone, Nan Marie, Constance A. Nathanson, Robert Schoen, Young J. Kim. 1998. "Family Demography, Social Theory, and Investment in Social Capital." Working Paper 98-01. Johns Hopkins Population Center, Baltimore. Processed.

Basu, Kaushik, and Sanjay Subrahmanyam. 1996. "Introduction." In Kaushik Basu and Sanjay Subrahmanyam, eds., *Unraveling the Nation: Sectarian Conflict and India's Secular Identity*. New Delhi: Penguin Books.

Beall, Jo. 1997. "Social Capital in Waste—a Solid Investment?" *Journal of International Development* 9 (7): 951–61.

Bourdieu, Pierre. 1986. "The Forms of Capital." In J. G. Richardson, ed., *Handbook of Theory and Research for the Sociology of Education*. New York: Greenwood.

Buckland, Jerry. 1998. "Social Capital and Sustainability of NGO-Intermediated Development Projects in Bangladesh." *Community Development Journal* 33 (3): 236–48.

Burt, Ronald S. 1997. "The Contingent Value of Social Capital." *Administrative Science Quarterly* 42 (2): 339–65.

Coleman, James S. 1988. "Social Capital in the Creation of Human Capital." *American Journal of Sociology* 94 (Supplement): S95–S120.

———. 1990. *Foundations of Social Theory*. Cambridge, Mass.: Harvard University Press.

Collier, Paul. 1998. "The Political Economy of Ethnicity." Paper presented at the Annual World Bank Conference on Development Economics, World Bank, Washington, D.C., April 20–21. Processed.

Crook, Clive. 1997. "Survey of India's Economy." *Economist* 342 (8005): S1–S26.

Eastis, Carla M. 1998. "Organizational Diversity and the Production of Social Capital." *American Behavioral Scientist* 42 (1): 66–77.

Edwards, Bob, and Michael W. Foley. 1997. "Social Capital and the Political Economy of Our Discontent." *American Behavioral Scientist* 40 (5): 669–78.

———. 1998. "Civil Society and Social Capital beyond Putnam." *American Behavioral Scientist* 42 (1): 124–39.

Eyben, Rosalind, and Sarah Ladbury. 1995. "Popular Participation in Aid-Assisted Projects: Why More in Theory than in Practice." In Nici Nelson and Susan Wright, eds., *Power and Participatory Development: Theory and Practice*. London: Intermediate Technology Publications.

Fernandes, Walter, Geeta Menon, and Philip Viegas. 1988. *Forests, Environment, and Tribal Economy: Deforestation, Impoverishment, and Marginalization in Orissa*. New Delhi: Indian Social Institute.

Fernandes, Walter, and S. Anthony Raj. 1992. *Development, Displacement, and Rehabilitation in the Tribal Areas of Orissa*. New Delhi: Indian Social Institute.

Fisher, Julie. 1994. "Is the Iron Law of Oligarchy Rusting Away in the Third World?" *World Development* 22 (2): 129–43.

Foucault, Michel. 1980. *Power/Knowledge*. New York: Pantheon Books.

Granovetter, Mark. 1973. "The Strength of Weak Ties." *American Journal of Sociology* 78 (6): 1360–80.

———. 1985. "Economic Action and Social Structure: The Problem of Embeddedness." *American Journal of Sociology* 91 (3): 481–510.

Grootaert, Christiaan. 1997. "Social Capital: The Missing Link." In *Expanding the Measure of Wealth: Indicators of Environmentally Sustainable Development*. Washington, D.C.: World Bank.

Harriss, John, and Paolo de Renzio. 1997. "Policy Arena: 'Missing Link' or Analytically Missing? The Concept of Social Capital." *Journal of International Development* 9 (7): 919–37.

Hatti, Neelambar, and James Heimann. 1992. "Limits to Cooperation." *Asian Journal of Economics and Social Studies* 11 (1): 55–71.

Homans, George. 1961. *Social Behavior: Its Elementary Forms*. New York: Harcourt, Brace and World.

Hyden, Goran. 1997. "Civil Society, Social Capital, and Development: Dissection of a Complex Discourse." *Studies in Comparative International Development* 32 (1): 3–30.

Jacobs, Jane. 1961. *The Life and Death of Great American Cities.* New York: Random House.

Jayaraman, Rajshri, and Peter Lanjouw. 1999. "The Evolution of Poverty and Inequality in Indian Villages." *World Bank Research Observer* 14 (1): 1–30.

Kapadia, Karin. 1997. "Mediating the Meaning of Market Opportunities: Gender, Caste, and Class in Rural South India." *Economic and Political Weekly* (November 27): 3329–35.

Lenci, Sergio. 1997. "Social Capital? From Pizza Connection to Collective Action. An Inquiry into Power, Culture, and Civil Society." Working Paper 244. Institute of Social Studies, The Hague.

Lerche, Jens. 1991. "Economic Development and Transformation of Traditional Social Relations: A Case Study of the Viswakarma Blacksmith and Carpenter Class of Orissa, India." CDR Project Paper 92.1. Center for Development Research, Copenhagen.

Madsen, Aase Mygind. 1993. "Divisive Cohesiveness and Changing Caste Relations in Karnataka." CDR Working Paper 93.1. Center for Development Research, Copenhagen.

Morris, Matthew. 1998. "Social Capital and Poverty in India." Working Paper 61. University of Sussex, Institute of Development Studies, Brighton, U.K.

Moser, Caroline O. 1996. "Confronting Crisis: A Comparative Study of Household Responses to Poverty and Vulnerability in Four Urban Communities." Environmentally Sustainable Development Studies and Monographs Series 8. World Bank, Washington, D.C.

———. 1998. "The Asset Vulnerability Framework: Reassessing Urban Poverty Reduction Strategies." *World Development* 26 (1): 1–19.

Mosse, David. 1995. "Local Institutions and Power: The History and Practice of Community Management of Tank Irrigation Systems in South India." In Nici Nelson and Susan Wright, eds., *Power and*

Participatory Development: Theory and Practice. London: Intermediate Technology Publications.

————. 1996. "Local Institutions and Farming Systems Development: Thoughts from a Project in Tribal Western India." Network Paper 64. Agricultural Research and Extension Network (AGREN), London.

Neale, Walter C. 1990. *Developing Rural India—Policies, Politics, and Progress*. Glen Dale, Md.: Riverdale Co.

ORG (Operations Research Group). 1995. "Indigenous Peoples Development Plan for Samaleswari Open Cast Project (Mahanadi Coalfields Ltd.)." Coal India Ltd., Calcutta. Processed.

Portes, Alejandro. 1998. "Social Capital: Its Origins and Applications in Modern Sociology." *Annual Review of Sociology* 24: 1–24.

Portes, Alejandro, and Patricia Landolt. 1996. "The Downside of Social Capital." *The American Prospect* 7 (26): 18–22.

Putnam, Robert D., with Robert Leonardi and Raffaella Nanetti. 1993. *Making Democracy Work*. Princeton, N.J.: Princeton University Press.

Putnam, Robert D. 1995. "Tuning in, Tuning out: The Strange Disappearance of Social Capital in America." *Political Science and Politics* 28 (4): 664–83.

————. 1998. Foreword to "Social Capital: Its Importance to Housing and Community Development." *Housing Policy Debate* 9 (1): v–viii.

Putzel, James. 1997. "Policy Arena: Accounting for the 'Dark Side' of Social Capital: Reading Robert Putnam on Democracy." *Journal of International Development* 9 (7): 939–49.

Repetto, Robert. 1994. *The "Second India" Revisited*. Washington, D.C.: World Resources Institute.

Rose, Richard, William Mishler, and Christian Haerpfer. 1997. "Social Capital in Civic and Stressful Societies." *Studies in Comparative International Development* 32 (3): 85–111.

Serageldin, Ismail. 1996. "Sustainability and the Wealth of Nations: First Steps in an Ongoing Journey." Environmentally Sustainable Development Studies and Monographs Series 5. World Bank, Washington, D.C.

Singh, Mahip. 1995. "Study on Impact of Coal Mining on Tribal and Other Backward Communities." Coal India Ltd., Calcutta. Processed.

Stiglitz, Joseph E. 1998. "More Instruments and Broader Goals: Moving toward the Post-Washington Consensus." The United Nations University, World Institute for Development Economics Research, Helsinki.

Stolle, Dietlind, and Thomas R. Rochon. 1998. "Are All Associations Alike?" *American Behavioral Scientist* 42 (1): 47–65.

Tarrow, Sydney. 1996. "Making Social Science Work across Space and Time: A Critical Reflection on Robert Putnam's *Making Democracy Work*." *American Political Science Review* 90 (2): 389–97.

VPASP (Vivekananda Palli Agragami Seva Pratishan). 1994a. "Resettlement and Rehabilitation Action Plan—Samaleswari OCP, Mahanadi Coalfields Ltd." Coal India Ltd., Calcutta. Processed.

————. 1994b. "Baseline Socio-Economic Study on Project Affected Families of Samaleswari OCP—Mahanadi Coalfields Ltd." Coal India Ltd., Calcutta. Processed.

Warren, Mark R. 1998. "Community Building and Political Power." *American Behavioral Scientist* 42 (1): 78–92.

Whittington, Keith E. 1998. "Revisiting Tocqueville's America." *American Behavioral Scientist* 42 (1): 21–32.

Woolcock, Michael. 1998. "Social Capital and Economic Development: Towards a Theoretical Synthesis and Policy Framework." *Theory and Society* 27 (2): 151–208.

World Bank. 1991. "Gender and Poverty in India: Issues and Opportunities Concerning Women in the Indian Economy." Report 8072-IN. Washington, D.C. Processed.

————. 1996. "India: Coal Sector Environmental and Social Mitigation Project—Staff Appraisal Report." Report 15405-IN. Washington, D.C. Processed.

————. 1997. "India: Coal Sector Rehabilitation Project—Staff Appraisal Report." Report 16473-IN. Washington, D.C. Processed.

Annex 1
Instruments of the Social Capital Assessment Tool

This annex presents the full text of the interview guides and the questionnaires of the Social Capital Assessment Tool. In addition, information is provided that can be useful for adapting and implementing the SOCAT, such as a guide for selecting and training interviewers.

The annex consists of the following sections:

The CD-ROM enclosed with this book contains an electronic file of annex 1. Separate files of the five instruments of the Social Capital Assessment Tool (annexes 1A to 1E) are also included. Each instrument is available as a PDF file and as a Microsoft Word 2000 file. The latter makes it possible for the user to adapt and modify the instruments as needed and to print questionnaires ready for use. To start the CD-ROM, insert it in your computer's CD drive. If an index file does not open automatically, click twice on the "My Computer" icon on your desktop, select your CD drive, and click twice on the file "Index.htm." An instructional toolkit for the application of the SOCAT is also available from the World Bank (contact information can be found at www.worldbank.org/socialdevelopment).

Annex 1A
Community Profile And Asset Mapping—
Interview Guide

The community profile is elicited through a series of group interviews conducted in the community during the initial days of field work. The community profile allows the research team to become familiar with community characteristics and issues relating to social capital for reference in later phases of the data collection. The group interviews establish a consensus definition of the "community" in which the research takes place. This definition will be used throughout the community profile exercise and will serve as reference for the interviews of the household survey. It will also define the catchment area of institutions for the organizational profile.

Several participatory methods are used to develop the community profile. In addition to a focus group format, the data collection includes a community mapping exercise followed by an institutional diagramming exercise. The primary data source material generated by these interviewing, mapping, and diagramming exercises are:

- Community maps, indicating location of community assets and services
- Observational notes of group process and summary of issues discussed
- List of positive characteristics of community assets and services
- List of negative characteristics of community assets and services
- List of all formal and informal community institutions
- Case study of community collective action
- Institutional diagrams (Venn) of relative impact and accessibility
- Institutional diagrams (web) of institutional network relationships

Between two and eight group interviews should be conducted in each community. Each group should have 5–12 participants. At least two group interviews should be carried out with women and men separately. Groups may be stratified on other sociodemographic characteristics that may be important within the community context, such as age or ethnicity. Mixed group interviews can also be conducted to assess levels of consensus, but these should be in addition to separate groups.

Each group should have a moderator and two observers. The moderator's role is to facilitate the discussion, probe on key issues, elicit comments from all participants, and focus the discussion on the issues of interest without seeming to interrupt or ignore extraneous comments from participants. The observers' role is to take notes on the content of the discussion and process of group dynamics.

The team should have the following materials available: interview guide, pads of notepaper, writing pens, flip-chart paper, markers (several colors), colored paper circles of different sizes, tape, scissors.

1. Definition of Community and Identification of Community Assets

Bring large sheets of paper and several color markers. Ask the group to draw a map of their village or neighborhood that shows the settlement pattern, sites for productive activities, and locations of various assets and services in the community. A second group may be asked to make modifications to the map developed by the first group or, if they prefer, draw their own. The map is a key reference point for the discussion and should be used throughout the interview process to stimulate discussion, identify critical issues, clarify discussion points, and so on.

1.1   How do you define this village/neighborhood?
        (*Probe on geographical boundaries, place names, and other reference points. Establish consensus on the geopolitical definition of "community" for later use in the household survey.*)

1.2   Where is/are the...
        ...primary school? Secondary school? Childcare centers? Other schools?
        ...health services (both formal and informal)?
        ...sources of water?
        ...waste and garbage disposal sites?
        ...sources of electric lighting?
        ...public telephones?
        ...main streets/roads?
        ...principal means of transportation?
        ...markets, shops, and other commercial establishments?
        ...churches (places of worship)?
        ...cultural and recreational areas? (Where do you spend your free time?)
        ...areas that are less safe?
        RURAL:...irrigation systems?

1.3   How many years has this village/neighborhood been in existence? Has the village/neighborhood grown, gotten smaller, or stayed the same in the last five years? Who are the people most likely to come into or leave the community?

        (*In the case of significant in- or out-migration, have the group draw a second map showing patterns of migration, new settlement, and expansion of community boundaries and land use.*)

2. COLLECTIVE ACTION AND SOLIDARITY

2.1   People from the same village/neighborhood often get together to address a particular issue that faces the community, fix a problem, improve the quality of life, or something similar. Which of the following issues has your village/neighborhood tried to address in the last three years?
(Probe: education, health, public services, roads and transportation, markets, credit, recreational and cultural resources, security, child care, irrigation, agricultural services.)

2.2   Do you think that everyone in this village/neighborhood has equal access to _____?
(Probe: same services as mentioned under 2.1)

Is this also true for the poorest members of the community?

2.3   Have there been any efforts by the community to improve the quality of the ___*(service or benefit)*___ or overcome a problem? Can you describe one instance in detail? (Refer to this case study for specifics of the following questions.) Were there community groups that played an important role? What kinds of responses did you get from the local government? From other organizations? From the rest of the community? What kinds of obstacles did you have to deal with? What was the outcome of the effort?
(Probe for locus of leadership, resources tapped, sources of resistance, who benefited or suffered from the outcome, the kind of follow-up that occurred as a result of the effort, and the mechanisms employed to ensure sustainability of the effort.)

2.4   Has this village/neighborhood ever attempted to make improvements but failed? Why do you think the attempt failed? What would you have done differently to make the effort more successful?
(Probe for constraints on collective action; identify the roles of government, community organizations, and secondary institutions in influencing outcomes; and discuss the relationship between the community, representative organizations, local government, and other civil society actors.)

3. COMMUNITY GOVERNANCE AND DECISIONMAKING

3.1   Who are the main leaders in this community?
(Probe formal and informal leadership.)

3.2   How do they become leaders? How are new leaders selected?

3.3   How are decisions made within this community? What is the role of the community leaders? How are community members involved?
(Probe on role of traditional leaders, informal leaders, elites.)

4. LIST OF COMMUNITY INSTITUTIONS

4.1   What are the groups, organizations, or associations that function in this village/neighborhood?

Have the group list all the organizations, formal and informal, that exist in the community. Make sure all different types of organizations are included (agriculture, credit, religious, recreational, health, education, etc.) and that the list is as complete as possible. Have the group go through the list and identify which institutions are most important in meeting the community's needs. Make sure the list is written with plenty of space between each item.

4.2   Which groups play the most active role in helping improve the well-being of community members?

4.3   How did this group or organization get started (government initiated, through government donations, NGO donations, grassroots initiative, etc.)?

4.4   How are the leaders selected (election, appointment, inheritance)? How stable is the leadership (frequent or sudden changes, normal progressive change, or never changes)? Is leadership generally harmonious or conflictive?

4.5   How are decisions made within these groups or organizations?

5. RELATIONSHIPS BETWEEN ORGANIZATIONS AND THE COMMUNITY

Venn diagram: Cut out (ahead of time) paper circles of three different sizes and lay them out. Ask the group to place the largest circles next to the most important organizations, the middle-sized circles next to the less important organizations, and the smallest circles next to the least important organizations. Write the name of the organization in each circle. Observers should record the group's reasoning as to why organizations are categorized as more or less important.

Draw a relatively large square in the center of the flip-chart paper. Tell the group that this square represents themselves. Have the group place the organization-labeled circles in or around the square at the center. The closer they are to the center square, the more accessible the particular organization is to the community. Let the group discuss among themselves and facilitate as necessary. Record the resulting diagram and reasoning behind the group's discussion on each organization.

5.1   Of the organizations on this list, which are most important? Which are least important? Which are of medium importance?

5.2   Of the organizations on this list, which ones are most accessible to the community? Which are least accessible? Which are somewhat accessible?

6. Institutional Networks and Organizational Density

Flowchart diagram: Have ready a sheet of flip-chart-sized paper and markers. Facilitate a discussion among the group regarding the relationships among the identified organizations, community leaders, and the community. Probe on local government institutions, nongovernmental organizations, base organizations, and other civil society actors. Ask the group to draw each actor and, using arrows or other appropriate symbols, indicate the relationship among them. Probe links among all organizations.

6.1   Which organizations work together? How do they work together (hierarchically, collaboratively)?

6.2   Are there any organizations that work against each other (compete or have some sort of conflict)? Which ones and why?

6.3   Some groups may share the same members and some groups have different members. Which organizations have the same or similar membership?

6.4   Are there organizations that share resources?

Annex 1B
Community Questionnaire

1. COMMUNITY CHARACTERISTICS

1.1   How many years has the community been in existence?

More than 20 years	[ ]	1
Between 10 and 20 years	[ ]	2
Fewer than 10 years	[ ]	3

1.2   How many households are in this community?

Fewer than 25	[ ]	1
Between 25 and 49	[ ]	2
Between 50 and 99	[ ]	3
Between 100 and 249	[ ]	4
More than 250	[ ]	5

1.3   In the last three years, the number of people living in this community has:

Increased	[ ]	1
Decreased	[ ]	2
Remained the same	[ ]	3

1.4   What are the two main reasons for the increase, decrease, or lack of change?

(a) _____

(b) _____

1.5   What are the two principal economic activities for men in this community?

(a) _____

(b) _____

1.6   What are the two principal economic activities for women in this community?

(a) _____

(b) _____

1.7 In the last three years, availability of employment has:

Improved	[ ]	1
Worsened	[ ]	2
Remained the same	[ ]	3

1.8 What is the main route that inhabitants use to reach this community, both during rainy season and dry season?

	(a) Rainy		(b) Dry	
Paved road	[ ]	1	[ ]	1
Dirt road	[ ]	2	[ ]	2
Mixed paved and dirt	[ ]	3	[ ]	3
Footpath	[ ]	4	[ ]	4
Horse trail	[ ]	5	[ ]	5
Sea	[ ]	6	[ ]	6
Other (specify)	[ ]	7	[ ]	7

1.9 In the last three years, the roads leading to this community have:

Improved	[ ]	1
Worsened	[ ]	2
Remained the same	[ ]	3

1.10 The availability of housing in this community is:

Adequate	[ ]	1
Deficient	[ ]	2

1.11 In the last three years, the quality of housing in this community has:

Improved	[ ]	1
Worsened	[ ]	2
Remained the same	[ ]	3

1.12 What are the two main reasons that housing in the community has improved, worsened, or remained the same during the last three years?

(a) _____

(b) _____

1.13   In the last three years, the overall quality of life of the people liv-
        ing in this community has: (*consider job availability, safety and secu-*
        rity, environment, housing, etc.)

        Improved   [   ]   1
        Worsened   [   ]   2
        Remained the same   [   ]   3

1.14   What are the two main reasons that the quality of life in the com-
        munity has improved, worsened, or remained the same during
        the last three years?

        (a) _____

        (b) _____

1.15   Overall, the level of living of this community may be character-
        ized as:

        Wealthy   [   ]   1
        Well-to-do   [   ]   2
        Average   [   ]   3
        Poor   [   ]   4
        Very poor   [   ]   5

1.16   Do people in this community generally trust one another in mat-
        ters of lending and borrowing?

        Yes   [   ]   1
        No   [   ]   2

1.17   In the last three years, has the level of trust improved, worsened,
        or stayed the same?

        Improved   [   ]   1
        Worsened   [   ]   2
        Remained the same   [   ]   3

1.18   Compared with other communities, how much do people in this community trust each other in matters of lending and borrowing?

More trust than in other communities	[ ]	1
Same as in other communities	[ ]	2
Less trust than in other communities	[ ]	3

1.19   Do you agree or disagree with the following statement: People here look out mainly for the welfare of their own families and they are not much concerned with community welfare.

Strongly agree	[ ]	1
Agree	[ ]	2
Disagree	[ ]	3
Strongly disagree	[ ]	4

2. PRINCIPAL SERVICES

2A.   Electricity

2A.1   What fraction of the community has household electrical service?

The entire community	[ ]	1
Most of the community	[ ]	2
About half the community	[ ]	3
Less than half/very few	[ ]	4
No one in the community	[ ]	5 (go to section 2B)

2A.2   In the last three years, the electrical service to this community has:

Improved	[ ]	1
Worsened	[ ]	2
Remained the same	[ ]	3

2A.3   Currently, the quality of electrical service within the homes of this community is:

Very good	[ ]	1
Good	[ ]	2
Average	[ ]	3
Poor	[ ]	4
Very poor	[ ]	5

2A.4   What are the two main problems with the electrical service?

(a) _____

(b) _____

2B.   *Public Lighting*

2B.1   Does this community have street lights?

Yes   [   ]   1
No   [   ]   2 (go to section 2C)

2B.2   In the last three years, the public lighting service has:

Improved   [   ]   1
Worsened   [   ]   2
Remained the same   [   ]   3

2B.3   Currently, the quality of public lighting service is:

Very good   [   ]   1
Good   [   ]   2
Average   [   ]   3
Poor   [   ]   4
Very poor   [   ]   5

2B.4   What are the two main problems with the public lighting in this community?

(a) _____

(b) _____

2C.   *Drinking Water*

2C.1   What part of the community has pipe-borne water?

The entire community   [   ]   1
Most of the community   [   ]   2
About half the community   [   ]   3
Less than half/very few   [   ]   4
No one in the community   [   ]   5

2C.2   What part of the community has access to public standpipes?

The entire community   [   ]   1
Most of the community   [   ]   2
About half the community   [   ]   3
Less than half/very few   [   ]   4
No one in the community   [   ]   5

2C.3   In the last three years, potable water service has:

Improved   [   ]   1
Worsened   [   ]   2
Remained the same   [   ]   3

2C.4   Currently, the potable water service is:

Very good   [   ]   1
Good   [   ]   2
Average   [   ]   3
Poor   [   ]   4
Very poor   [   ]   5

2C.5   What are the two main problems with the potable water service?

(a) _____

(b) _____

2D.   *Home Telephone Service*

2D.1   What fraction of the community has home telephone service?

The entire community   [   ]   1
Most of the community   [   ]   2
About half the community   [   ]   3
Less than half/very few   [   ]   4
No one in the community   [   ]   5 (go to section 2E)

2D.2   Currently, the home telephone service is:

Very good   [   ]   1
Good   [   ]   2
Average   [   ]   3

Poor   [   ]   4
Very poor   [   ]   5

2E.   *Communication Services*

2E.1   Does this community have public telephones?

Yes   [   ]   1
No   [   ]   2 (go to question 2E.3)

2E.2   How many public telephones are in this community?

_____ (go to question 2E.4)

2E.3   What is the distance from this community to the nearest public telephone?

Distance (in walking minutes) _____

2E.4   In the last three years, the public telephone service in this community has:

Improved   [   ]   1
Worsened   [   ]   2
Remained the same   [   ]   3

2E.5   Currently, the public telephone service in this community is:

Very good   [   ]   1
Good   [   ]   2
Average   [   ]   3
Poor   [   ]   4
Very poor   [   ]   5

2E.6   What are the two main problems with the public telephone service in this community?

(a) _____

(b) _____

2E.7   Is there a post office in this community?

Yes   [   ]   1
No   [   ]   2 (go to question 2E.9)

2E.8   What is the distance from this community to the nearest post
        office?

        Distance (in walking minutes) _____

2E.9   In the last three years, the mail service in this community has:

        Improved   [   ]   1
        Worsened   [   ]   2
        Remained the same   [   ]   3

2E.10   Currently, the mail service in this community is:

        Very good   [   ]   1
        Good   [   ]   2
        Average   [   ]   3
        Poor   [   ]   4
        Very poor   [   ]   5

2E.11   What are the two main problems with the mail service in this
        community?

        (a) _____

        (b) _____

2E.12   What fraction of the community has access to public Internet ser-
        vice?

        The entire community   [   ]   1
        Most of the community   [   ]   2
        About half the community   [   ]   3
        Less than half/very few   [   ]   4
        No one in the community   [   ]   5 (go to question 2E.14)

2E.13   Where are public Internet access services available?

        Local school   [   ]   1
        Library   [   ]   2
        Community center   [   ]   3

Training center   [   ]   4
Internet café   [   ]   5
Other (specify)   [   ]   6
                               (go to section 2F)

2E.14   What is the distance from this community to the nearest public
        Internet access service?

        Distance (in walking minutes) ————————————

2F.   *Sewage*

2F.1   What fraction of the community is served by a public sewage
        system?

        The entire community   [   ]   1
        Most of the community   [   ]   2
        About half the community   [   ]   3
        Less than half/very few   [   ]   4
        No one in the community   [   ]   5 (go to question 2F.6)

2F.2   In the last three years, the quality of the public sewage system in
        this community has:

        Improved   [   ]   1
        Worsened   [   ]   2
        Remained the same   [   ]   3

2F.3   Currently, the public sewage system is:

        Very good   [   ]   1
        Good   [   ]   2
        Average   [   ]   3
        Poor   [   ]   4
        Very poor   [   ]   5

2F.4   What are the two main problems with the public sewage system
        in this community?

        (a) ————————————————————————

        (b) ————————————————————————

2F.5   Do the streets of this community have sufficient sewers and drains to handle excess water and prevent flooding when it rains?

Yes   [   ]   1
No   [   ]   2

2F.6   What other sewage and waste water systems are used in this community?

	Yes		No	
a. Latrine	[ ]	1	[ ]	2
b. Septic tanks	[ ]	1	[ ]	2
c. River or sea	[ ]	1	[ ]	2
d. Other (specify)	[ ]	1	[ ]	2

2G.   Garbage Collection

2G.1   What fraction of the community is served by a garbage collection service?

The entire community   [   ]   1
Most of the community   [   ]   2
About half the community   [   ]   3
Less than half/very few   [   ]   4
No one in the community   [   ]   5

2G.2   In the last three years, the quality of the garbage disposal in this community has:

Improved   [   ]   1
Worsened   [   ]   2
Remained the same   [   ]   3

2G.3   In the homes that do not receive garbage collection service, what is the main solid waste disposal method?

Burn it   [   ]   1
Throw on own lot   [   ]   2
Throw on others' lots   [   ]   3
Throw into river/sea   [   ]   4
Bury it   [   ]   5
Pay to haul away   [   ]   6
Other (specify)   [   ]   7

2H.   *Public Market*

2H.1   Does this community have a public market?

Yes   [   ]   1 (go to question 2H.3)
No   [   ]   2

2H.2   The walking distance from the community to the nearest market
is:

Distance (in walking minutes) _____ (go to section 2I)

2H.3   The market is open:

Every day   [   ]   1
Some days of the week   [   ]   2
One day per week   [   ]   3
Other (specify)   [   ]   4

2H.4   In the last three years, the quality and service of this market has:

Improved   [   ]   1
Worsened   [   ]   2
Remained the same   [   ]   3

2H.5   How many people in the community use the market?

The entire community   [   ]   1
Most of the community   [   ]   2
About half the community   [   ]   3
Less than half/very few   [   ]   4

2I.   *Transportation*

2I.1   Is this community served by a public transport system?

Yes   [   ]   1 (go to question 2I.3)
No   [   ]   2

2I.2   The walking distance to the nearest community with public
transportation is:

Distance (in walking minutes) _____ (go to question 2I.7)

2I.3   Public transportation is available:

    Every day   [   ]   1
    Some days of the week   [   ]   2
    One day per week   [   ]   3
    Other (specify)   [   ]   4

2I.4   In the last three years, the quality and service of public trans-
         portation has:

    Improved   [   ]   1
    Worsened   [   ]   2
    Remained the same   [   ]   3

2I.5   Public transportation is used by:

    The entire community   [   ]   1
    Most of the community   [   ]   2
    About half the community   [   ]   3
    Less than half/very few   [   ]   4
    No one in the community   [   ]   5

2I.6   What two main changes can be made to improve public trans-
         portation to this community?

    (a) _____

    (b) _____

2I.7   What other types of transportation do people in this community
         use to go to neighboring communities? (List the two most impor-
         tant ones).

                                        (a)   (b)

    Walking   1
    Bicycle   2
    Horse   3
    Canoe/boat   4
    Car   5

2J.   *Recreation*

2J.1   Does this community have sports fields or recreational areas?

Yes   [   ]   1
No   [   ]   2 (go to question 2J.3)

2J.2   In the last three years, the condition of the sports fields and recreational areas has:

Improved   [   ]   1
Worsened   [   ]   2
Remained the same   [   ]   3

2J.3   Does this community have separate children's play areas?

Yes   [   ]   1
No   [   ]   2 (go to section 2K)

2J.4   In the last three years, the condition of these children's play areas has:

Improved   [   ]   1
Worsened   [   ]   2
Remained the same   [   ]   3

2K.   *Security*

2K.1   Does this community have a security or police force?

Yes   [   ]   1
No   [   ]   2 (go to section 3)

2K.2   This service is provided by:

The police   [   ]   1
The community   [   ]   2
A private company   [   ]   3

2K.3   This security service is provided to:

The entire community   [   ]   1
Most of the community   [   ]   2

About half the community   [   ]   3
Less than half / very few   [   ]   4

2K.4   In the last three years, the quality of the security service has:

Improved   [   ]   1
Worsened   [   ]   2
Remained the same   [   ]   3

3. LABOR MIGRATION

3.1   Are there members of this community who go to other places to work during certain periods of the year?

Yes   [   ]   1
No   [   ]   2 (go to question 3.6)

3.2   Do more women than men leave to work? Do more men than women leave to work? Or equal numbers of women and men?

More women than men   [   ]   1
More men than women   [   ]   2
Equal numbers   [   ]   3

3.3   Where do they go to work primarily?

To a city in this region   [   ]   1
To a city in another region   [   ]   2
To a city in another country   [   ]   3
To a rural area in this region   [   ]   4
To a rural area in another region   [   ]   5
To a rural area in another country   [   ]   6

3.4   What are the two principal jobs women leave for?

(a) _____

(b) _____

3.5   What are the two principal jobs men leave for?

(a) _____

(b) _____

3.6   Are there people from other communities who come to work in
        this community?

        Yes   [   ]   1
        No   [   ]   2 (go to section 4)

3.7   What are the two principal jobs they come for?

        (a) _____

        (b) _____

4. EDUCATION

4A.   *Preschool*

4A.1   Does this community have a public preschool?

        Yes   [   ]   1 (go to question 4A.3)
        No   [   ]   2

4A.2   How far from the community is the nearest public preschool?

        Distance (in walking minutes)_____ (go to section 4B)

4A.3   Is the number of preschools in this community sufficient to serve
        the number of young children in the community?

        Yes   [   ]   1
        No   [   ]   2

4A.4   Is the number of teachers in these preschools sufficient for the
        number of children?

        Yes   [   ]   1
        No   [   ]   2

4A.5   The physical condition of the preschool is:

        Very good   [   ]   1
        Good   [   ]   2
        Average   [   ]   3
        Poor   [   ]   4
        Very poor   [   ]   5

4A.6   What percentage of young children attend public preschools?

    All children   [   ] 1 (go to section 4B)
    Most children   [   ] 2
    About half of the children   [   ] 3
    Less than half   [   ] 4
    Very few / none   [   ] 5

4A.7   What are the two principal reasons that young children from this community do not attend public preschool?

    (a) _____

    (b) _____

4B.   Primary School

4B.1   Does this community have a public primary school?

    Yes   [   ] 1 (go to question 4B.3)
    No   [   ] 2

4B.2   How far from the community is the nearest public primary school?

    Distance (in walking minutes) _____ (go to section 4C)

4B.3   Is the number of primary schools in this community sufficient to serve the number of school-age children in the community?

    Yes   [   ] 1
    No   [   ] 2

4B.4   Is the number of teachers in these schools sufficient for the number of students?

    Yes   [   ] 1
    No   [   ] 2

4B.5   The physical condition of the primary school is:

    Very good   [   ] 1
    Good   [   ] 2
    Average   [   ] 3

Poor   [   ]   4
Very poor   [   ]   5

4B.6   What percentage of eligible school-age children attend public
       primary schools?

       All children   [   ]   1 (go to section 4C)
       Most children   [   ]   2
       About half of the children   [   ]   3
       Less than half   [   ]   4
       Very few / none   [   ]   5

4B.7   What are the two principal reasons that school-age children from
       this community do not attend public primary school?

       (a) _____

       (b) _____

4C.   *Secondary School*

4C.1   Does this community have a public secondary school?

       Yes   [   ]   1 (go to question 4C.3)
       No   [   ]   2

4C.2   How far from the community is the nearest public secondary
       school?

       Distance (in walking minutes)_____ (go to section 4D)

4C.3   Is the number of secondary schools in this community sufficient
       to accommodate the number of secondary-school-age students in
       the community?

       Yes   [   ]   1
       No   [   ]   2

4C.4   Is the number of teachers in the secondary schools sufficient for
       the number of students?

       Yes   [   ]   1
       No   [   ]   2

4C.5   The physical condition of the secondary school is:

Very good	[ ]	1
Good	[ ]	2
Average	[ ]	3
Poor	[ ]	4
Very poor	[ ]	5

4C.6   What percentage of secondary-school-age children attend public secondary schools?

All children	[ ]	1 (go to section 4D)
Most children	[ ]	2
About half of the children	[ ]	3
Less than half	[ ]	4
Very few / none	[ ]	5

4C.7   What are the two principal reasons that secondary-school-age children from this community do not attend public secondary school?

(a) _____

(b) _____

4D.   *Adult Education*

4D.1   Is there an adult literacy campaign or program for the community?

Yes	[ ]	1
No	[ ]	2

4D.2   Are there job training programs for this community?

Yes	[ ]	1
No	[ ]	2

5. HEALTH

5.1   What are the three principal health problems affecting children under six years of age in this community?

(a) _____

(b) _____

(c) _____

5.2   What are the two principal health problems affecting adult men
        in this community?

        (a) _____

        (b) _____

5.3   What are the two principal health problems affecting adult
        women in this community?

        (a) _____

        (b) _____

5.4   Does this community have a health clinic or hospital?

        Yes   [   ]   1 (go to question 5.6)
        No   [   ]   2

5.5   How far is the nearest public health clinic or hospital?

        Distance (in walking minutes) _____ (go to question 5.7)

5.6   Does the health clinic or hospital regularly have sufficient:

	Sufficient	Insufficient	None
a. Basic medicines	[ ] 1	[ ] 2	[ ] 3
b. Equipment/instruments	[ ] 1	[ ] 2	[ ] 3
c. Patient beds	[ ] 1	[ ] 2	[ ] 3
d. Ambulances	[ ] 1	[ ] 2	[ ] 3
e. Physicians	[ ] 1	[ ] 2	[ ] 3
f. Nurses	[ ] 1	[ ] 2	[ ] 3
g. Other health staff	[ ] 1	[ ] 2	[ ] 3

5.7   Does this community have a family planning program?

        Yes   [   ]   1
        No   [   ]   2 (go to section 6)

5.8   Who offers the program?

        Government   [   ]   1
        NGO   [   ]   2
        Private facility   [   ]   3
        Other (specify)   [   ]   4

6. ENVIRONMENTAL ISSUES

6.1   Does this community have:

	Yes		No	
a. Garbage dumping that contaminates rivers or wells	[ ]	1	[ ]	2
b. Garbage dumping that contaminates the ocean	[ ]	1	[ ]	2
c. Junk yards or scrap heaps	[ ]	1	[ ]	2
d. Standing water or stagnant pools	[ ]	1	[ ]	2
e. Slaughterhouses that dump waste in public places	[ ]	1	[ ]	2
f. Mechanics who dump waste oil in soil or water	[ ]	1	[ ]	2
g. Polluting industries	[ ]	1	[ ]	2
h. Clear-cutting or forest burns	[ ]	1	[ ]	2
i. Mining	[ ]	1	[ ]	2
j. Other (specify)	[ ]	1	[ ]	2

6.2   Overall, the current environmental condition of the community
        is:

        Very good   [   ]   1
        Good   [   ]   2
        Average   [   ]   3
        Poor   [   ]   4
        Very poor   [   ]   5

6.3   In the last three years, the environmental conditions in the com-
        munity have:

        Improved   [   ]   1
        Worsened   [   ]   2
        Remained the same   [   ]   3

6.4   What are the two main actions that could be taken to improve the environmental conditions in this community?

       (a) _____

       (b) _____

7. AGRICULTURE (only in rural areas)

7.1   What are the three principal agricultural or livestock activities undertaken in this community?

       (a) _____

       (b) _____

       (c) _____

7.2   Where do the inhabitants of this community generally sell their livestock and produce? (*List up to three venues by order of importance.*)

a	b	c

       Community market   1
       Market in neighboring areas   2
       Domestic middlemen   3
       Exporters   4
       Public institutions   5
       Cooperatives   6
       Local stores and shops   7
       Other (specify)   8
       Only self-consumption/
         no outside sales   9 (go to question 7.4)

7.3   What are the two most important problems facing members of this community for getting their products to the market and earning a profit?

       (a) _____

       (b) _____

7.4   Do the agricultural workers/producers in this community receive technical assistance?

Yes   [   ]   1
No   [   ]   2 (go to question 7.6)

7.5   Who is the main provider of this technical assistance? (*Probe whether the institution is public or private.*)

_____

7.6   Does this community have any type of agricultural cooperative?

Yes   [   ]   1
No   [   ]   2

7.7   Does this community have any institution or person (either in the community or nearby) that provides credit and loans to agricultural producers?

Yes   [   ]   1
No   [   ]   2 (go to question 7.9)

7.8   What are the three main persons or institutions that provide credit or loans to agricultural producers in this community?

a	b	c

National banks	1
Agricultural/development banks	2
Private banks	3
Agricultural credit unions or cooperatives	4
Private individuals	5
Export businesses	6
Packing businesses	7
Producer associations	8
Warehouses or middlemen	9
Other (specify)	10

7.9   Do the agricultural producers of this community receive loans or credits from individuals or institutions in other cities or regions?

Yes   [   ]   1
No   [   ]   2

7.10   What percentage of the agricultural producers in this community use loans or credits to support their activities?

_____

7.11   What are the two principal problems facing the agricultural producers of this community in terms of receiving loans and credits?

(a) _____

(b) _____

7.12   In the last three years, the harvests/yields have:

Increased   [   ]   1
Decreased   [   ]   2
Remained the same   [   ]   3

7.13   In the last three years, the sales of agricultural/livestock products in this community have:

Increased   [   ]   1
Decreased   [   ]   2
Remained the same   [   ]   3

8. COMMUNITY SUPPORT

8.1   Which of the following organizations exist in this community?

	Yes		No	
a. Community development committee	[ ]	1	[ ]	2
b. Cooperative (fishing, agriculture, crafts)	[ ]	1	[ ]	2
c. Parent-teacher association	[ ]	1	[ ]	2
d. Health committee	[ ]	1	[ ]	2
e. Youth group	[ ]	1	[ ]	2

	Yes	No
f. Sports group	[ ] 1	[ ] 2
g. Cultural group	[ ] 1	[ ] 2
h. Civic group	[ ] 1	[ ] 2
i. Other (specify)	[ ] 1	[ ] 2

8.2   Which persons or organizations help or support these community-based organizations?

	Yes	No
a. Local government	[ ] 1	[ ] 2
b. National government	[ ] 1	[ ] 2
c. Politicians	[ ] 1	[ ] 2
d. Religious organizations	[ ] 1	[ ] 2
e. School / teachers	[ ] 1	[ ] 2
f. Nongovernmental organizations	[ ] 1	[ ] 2
g. Business group	[ ] 1	[ ] 2
h. Service club	[ ] 1	[ ] 2
i. Prosperous citizens	[ ] 1	[ ] 2
j. The community as a whole	[ ] 1	[ ] 2

8.3   What buildings do people in this community regularly use for meetings and gatherings?

	Yes	No
a. Community center	[ ] 1	[ ] 2
b. Personal homes	[ ] 1	[ ] 2
c. Homes of political leaders	[ ] 1	[ ] 2
d. Homes of other local leaders	[ ] 1	[ ] 2
e. Churches or religious buildings	[ ] 1	[ ] 2
f. Health center / school	[ ] 1	[ ] 2
g. Government buildings	[ ] 1	[ ] 2
h. Business / commercial buildings	[ ] 1	[ ] 2
i. Other (specify)	[ ] 1	[ ] 2

8.4   Which members of the community participate most in solving the issues facing the community?

(a) By gender
Men	[ ]	1
Women	[ ]	2

Men and women equally   [   ]   3
Neither participate   [   ]   4

(b) By age
   Youth and adolescents   [   ]   1
   Adults   [   ]   2
   Older persons   [   ]   3
   Youth, adults, and elders
     equally   [   ]   4
   None participate   [   ]   5

(c) By employment status
   Workers   [   ]   1
   Unemployed or nonworkers [   ]   2
   Workers and nonworkers
     equally   [   ]   3
   Neither participate   [   ]   4

8.5   In the last three years, has the community organized to address a need or problem?

Yes   [   ]   1
No   [   ]   2 (go to question 8.8)

8.6   Around what issue(s) did the community organize?

(a) _____

(b) _____

8.7   Was/were the initiative(s) successful?

	Yes	No	Ongoing
a. Initiative #1	[ ] 1	[ ] 2	[ ] 3
b. Initiative #2	[ ] 1	[ ] 2	[ ] 3

8.8   What are the two main problems or needs that community members feel must be addressed or solved?

(a) _____

(b) _____

8.9 Are there any specific assistance programs to this community?

Yes   [ ]   1

No   [ ]   2 (go to question 8.11)

8.10 What are the two main programs and the institutions that support them?

(a) Program/institution _____

(b) Program/institution _____

8.11 Do any of the following problems exist in this community? If yes, who is the most affected or at-risk group (by age, gender, caste, ethnic group, etc.)?

	Yes		No		Most affected group
a. Burglaries	[ ]	1	[ ]	2	_____
b. Robberies	[ ]	1	[ ]	2	_____
c. Assaults	[ ]	1	[ ]	2	_____
d. Gangs	[ ]	1	[ ]	2	_____
e. Vandalism	[ ]	1	[ ]	2	_____
f. Violent disputes	[ ]	1	[ ]	2	_____
g. Alcohol abuse	[ ]	1	[ ]	2	_____
h. Substance (drug) abuse	[ ]	1	[ ]	2	_____
i. Teen pregnancy	[ ]	1	[ ]	2	_____
j. Domestic violence	[ ]	1	[ ]	2	_____
k. Child abuse	[ ]	1	[ ]	2	_____
l. Prostitution	[ ]	1	[ ]	2	_____
m. Other problems (specify)	[ ]	1	[ ]	2	_____

Annex 1C
Household Questionnaire

Length of interview

Time initiated: _____
Time terminated: _____

1. IDENTIFICATION OF SELECTED HOUSEHOLD:

1.1.   Province/state _____

1.2.   District   _____

1.3.   Subdistrict   _____

1.4.   Town/village   _____

1.5   Type of area: Urban   [   ]
                           Rural nonindigenous   [   ]
                           Indigenous   [   ]
                           Difficult access   [   ]

1.6   Location: Unit   _____
                           Number   _____

1.7   Address of selected household:
                           Community   _____
                           Street   _____
                           House number   _____
                           Other details _____

Interviewer: _____   Supervisor: _____

2. HOUSING CHARACTERISTICS AND HOUSEHOLD ROSTER

2.1   Type of house (*observation only*)

         Individual house   [   ]   1
         Open roof and patio   [   ]   2
         Apartment   [   ]   3
         Room within a larger house [   ]   4

Other (specify)   [   ]   5

2.2   What construction material is used for the majority of the exterior or walls of the house or building?

Cinderblock/brick/stone/
  concrete/cement   [   ]   1
Fiberglass   [   ]   2
Wood   [   ]   3
Adobe/wattle and daub   [   ]   4
Cane/straw/sticks   [   ]   5
No walls   [   ]   6
Other (specify)   [   ]   7

2.3   What is the construction material of most of the roof of this house?

Concrete/cement   [   ]   1
Tiles   [   ]   2
Metal (zinc, aluminum, etc.)   [   ]   3
Wood   [   ]   4
Straw or thatch   [   ]   5
Other (specify)   [   ]   6

2.4   What is the construction material of most of the floor of this house?

Concrete/cement   [   ]   1
Tiles, brick, granite   [   ]   2
Wood   [   ]   3
Vinyl   [   ]   4
Earth, sand   [   ]   5
Cane   [   ]   6
Other (specify)   [   ]   7

2.5   How many rooms are used by this household for sleeping only?

_____

2.6   What type of sanitary services does this household use?

Connected to sewage system   [   ]   1
Connected to septic tank   [   ]   2

Latrine   [   ]   3
None   [   ]   4
Other (specify)   [   ]   5

2.7   What is the primary source of water for this household?

Piped water system   [   ]   1
Private well   [   ]   2
Public well   [   ]   3
Open tap or faucet   [   ]   4
River or stream   [   ]   5
Other (specify)   [   ]   6

2.8   How does this household dispose of most of its garbage?

Public garbage service   [   ]   1
Private garbage service   [   ]   2
Throw in vacant lots   [   ]   3
Throw in river, stream, ocean   [   ]   4
Burn and/or bury   [   ]   5
Other (specify)   [   ]   6

2.9   What type of lighting does this household use?

Electricity (public source)   [   ]   1
Electricity (private source)   [   ]   2
Electricity (combination public
  and private)   [   ]   3
Only kerosene, gas, candles   [   ]   4
Other (specify)   [   ]   5

2.10   This home is

Owned and completely paid for[   ]   1
Owned with a mortgage   [   ]   2
Rented   [   ]   3
Given in exchange for services [   ]   4
Squatter   [   ]   5
Other (specify)   [   ]   6

NOTE: • *List all the people in the household first and then ask questions 2.12 to 2.20.*
• *The household is defined as all the people usually living together in this dwelling and sharing expenses.*

2.11 List names of all individuals in household. (*List household head first, use first names only.*)
2.12 What is " ____ "'s relationship to household head? (*Use code box on the next page.*)
2.13 Sex (male = 1, female =2)
2.14 How old is " ____ "? (*years*)
2.15 What is " ____ "'s marital status? (married = 1, common law = 2, divorced = 3 [go to 2.17],
   widow(er) = 4 [go to 2.17], never married = 5 [go to 2.17])
2.16 Is " ____ "'s spouse currently a member of the household? *If yes, use number of spouse. If no, write 99*
2.17 Occupation (*Use code box on the next page.*)
2.18 Currently employed? (yes = 1, no = 2)
2.19 Complete education level? (*Use code box on the next page.*)
2.20 How long have you lived in this community? (*years*)

	2.11	2.12	2.13	2.14	2.15	2.16	2.17	2.18	2.19	2.20
01										
02										
03										
04										
05										
06										
07										
08										
09										
10										

Code box for question 2.12

Head	01	Grandchild	08	Uncle/aunt	14
Wife/husband	02	Grandparent	09	Cousin	15
Son/daughter	03	Father-in-law/		Other relative	16
Father/mother	04	mother-in-law	10	Children from	
Sister/brother	05	Son-in-law/		another family	17
Stepson/		daughter-in-law	11	Other relative	18
stepdaughter	06	Sister-in-law/		Renter	19
Stepfather/		brother-in-law	12	Other nonrelative	20
stepmother	07	Nephew/niece	13		

Code box for question 2.17

Farmer	1	Private sector:	
Fisherman	2	Unskilled	6
Trade	3	Skilled	7
Manufacturing:		Public sector:	
Artisan	4	Unskilled	8
Industrial	5	Skilled	9
		Other	10

Code box for question 2.19

Illiterate, no schooling	1
Literate, no schooling	2
Primary incomplete	3
Primary complete	4
Secondary incomplete	5
Secondary complete	6
Vocational college	7
University	8
Other	9

3. GENOGRAM

(Using symbols below, record here family composition, household composition, organizational affiliation, and level of involvement. An example is on the next page.)

<u>Genogram symbols</u>

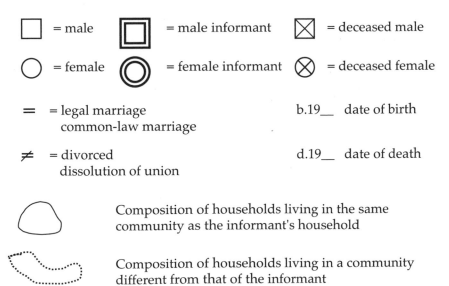

□ = male   ▣ = male informant   ⊠ = deceased male

○ = female   ◎ = female informant   ⊗ = deceased female

= = legal marriage
common-law marriage

b.19___ date of birth

≠ = divorced
dissolution of union

d.19___ date of death

Composition of households living in the same community as the informant's household

Composition of households living in a community different from that of the informant

Example

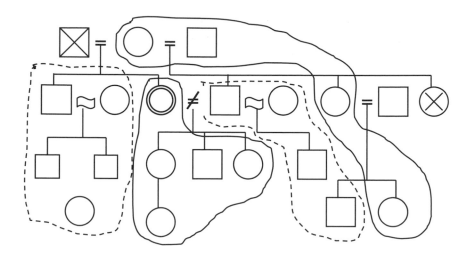

This example represents the situation of a divorced woman whose household includes her three children and granddaughter. In a household within the same community live her mother (a remarried widow); her stepfather; her half-sister, currently separated from her husband; and her niece. Another half-sister died some time ago. The respondent's former husband resides in another community. His household consists of his common-law wife, their son, and the respondent's nephew. The respondent's brother lives in common-law union with two sons and a child, a girl, who is not a blood relation.

4. STRUCTURAL SOCIAL CAPITAL

Now I would like to ask you some questions about how you feel about this village/neighborhood, and how you take part in the community activities. By community, I mean _____ [insert consensus definition from community profile].

4A.   Organizational Density and Characteristics

4A.1   Are you or is someone in your household a member of any groups, organizations, or associations? (*Probe: Who in the household belongs to which group? Are there any other groups or informal associations that you or someone in your household belongs to? Code below and record on genogram. If the household is not a member in any group, go to section 4B.*)

4A.2   Do you consider yourself/household member to be active in the group, such as by attending meetings or volunteering your time in other ways, or are you relatively inactive? Are you/household member a leader in the group?

Household member *(use roster code)*	Name of organization	Type of organization *(use codes below)*	Degree of participation *(use code below)*

Type of organization			
Farmers'/fishermen's group	1	NGO	10
Cooperative	2	Religious group	11
Traders' association/		Cultural association	12
business group	3	Political group	13
Professional association	4	Youth group	14
Trade union	5	Women's group	15
Credit/finance group	6	Parent group	16
Water/waste group	7	School committee	17
Neighborhood/village		Health committee	18
association	8	Sports group	19
Civic group	9	Other	20

Degree of participation	
Leader	1
Very active	2
Somewhat active	3
Not active	4

4A.3   Which of these groups is the most important to your household?
        (*List up to three by name and code type of organization.*)

Group 1: _____ [   ]

Group 2: _____ [   ]

Group 3: _____ [   ]

Now I'm going to ask you some questions about the members of these groups.

4A.4   Overall, are the same people members of these three different
        groups or is there little overlap in membership?

Little overlap	[ ]	1
Some overlap	[ ]	2
Much overlap	[ ]	3

			Group	
		1	2	3
4A.5	Are group members mostly of the same extended family? Yes 1 No 2			
4A.6	Are members mostly of the same religion? Yes 1 No 2			
4A.7	Are members mostly of the same gender? Yes 1 No 2			

		Group		
		1	2	3
4A.8	Are members mostly of the same political viewpoint or do they belong to the same political party? Yes 1 No 2			
4A.9	Do members mostly have the same occupation? Yes 1 No 2			
4A.10	Are members mostly from the same age group? Yes 1 No 2			
4A.11	Do members mostly have the same level of education? Yes 1 No 2			

4A.12   How does the group usually make decisions?

	Group	
1	2	3

The leader decides and informs
   the other group members.   1
The leader asks group members
   what they think and
   then decides.   2
The group members hold
   a discussion and decide
   together.   3
Other (specify)   4

4A.13   Overall, how effective is the group's leadership?

	Group	
1	2	3

Very effective	1
Somewhat effective	2
Not effective at all	3

4A.14   Do you think that by belonging to this group you have acquired new skills or learned something valuable?

	Group	
1	2	3

| Yes | 1 |
| No | 2 |

4B.   *Networks and Mutual Support Organizations*

Now I am going to ask you some questions about how the community functions and deals with problems.

4B.1   If the primary school of this village/neighborhood went without a teacher for a long time, say six months or more, which people in this village/neighborhood do you think would get together to take some action about it?

	Yes		No	
No one in the village/ neighborhood would get together (if yes, go to question 4B.3)	[ ]	1	[ ]	2
Local/municipal government	[ ]	1	[ ]	2
Village/neighborhood association	[ ]	1	[ ]	2
Parents of school children	[ ]	1	[ ]	2
The entire village/ neighborhood	[ ]	1	[ ]	2
Other (specify)	[ ]	1	[ ]	2

4B.2   Who would take the initiative (act as leader)?

_____

4B.3   If there were a problem that affected the entire village/neighbor-
        hood, for instance (RURAL: "crop disease"; URBAN: "violence"),
        who do you think would work together to deal with the situation?

	Yes		No	
Each person/household would deal with the problem individually (if yes, go to section 4C)	[ ]	1	[ ]	2
Neighbors among themselves	[ ]	1	[ ]	2
Local government/municipal political leaders	[ ]	1	[ ]	2
All community leaders acting together	[ ]	1	[ ]	2
The entire village/ neighborhood	[ ]	1	[ ]	2
Other (specify)	[ ]	1	[ ]	2

4B.4   Who would take the initiative (act as leader)?

_____

4C.   *Exclusion*

4C.1   Differences often exist between people living in the same vil-
        lage/neighborhood. To what extent do differences such as the
        following tend to divide people in your village/neighborhood?

	Not at all		Somewhat		Very much	
a. Differences in education	[ ]	1	[ ]	2	[ ]	3
b. Differences in wealth/ material possessions	[ ]	1	[ ]	2	[ ]	3
c. Differences in landholdings	[ ]	1	[ ]	2	[ ]	3
d. Differences in social status	[ ]	1	[ ]	2	[ ]	3
e. Differences between men and women	[ ]	1	[ ]	2	[ ]	3
f. Differences between younger and older generations	[ ]	1	[ ]	2	[ ]	3

g. Difference between long-
   time inhabitants and
   new settlers   [ ] 1   [ ] 2   [ ] 3
h. Difference in political party
   affiliations   [ ] 1   [ ] 2   [ ] 3
i. Differences in religious
   beliefs   [ ] 1   [ ] 2   [ ] 3
j. Differences in ethnic
   background   [ ] 1   [ ] 2   [ ] 3
k. Other differences (specify) [ ] 1   [ ] 2   [ ] 3

4C.2   Do these differences cause problems?

Yes   [ ] 1
No   [ ] 2 (go to question 4C.5)

4C.3   How are these problems usually handled?

	Yes	No
a. People work it out between themselves	[ ] 1	[ ] 2
b. Family/household members intervene	[ ] 1	[ ] 2
c. Neighbors intervene	[ ] 1	[ ] 2
d. Community leaders mediate	[ ] 1	[ ] 2
e. Religious leaders mediate	[ ] 1	[ ] 2
f. Judicial leaders mediate	[ ] 1	[ ] 2

4C.4   Do such problems ever lead to violence?

Yes   [ ] 1
No   [ ] 2

4C.5   Are there any services where you or members of your household
       are occasionally denied service or have only limited opportunity
       to use?

	Yes	No
a. Education/schools	[ ] 1	[ ] 2
b. Health services/clinics	[ ] 1	[ ] 2
c. Housing assistance	[ ] 1	[ ] 2
d. Job training/employment	[ ] 1	[ ] 2

e. Credit/finance	[ ]	1	[ ]	2
f. Transportation	[ ]	1	[ ]	2
g. Water distribution	[ ]	1	[ ]	2
h. Sanitation services	[ ]	1	[ ]	2
i. Agricultural extension	[ ]	1	[ ]	2
j. Justice/conflict resolution	[ ]	1	[ ]	2
k. Security/police services	[ ]	1	[ ]	2

4C.6   Do you think that there are other households in this community that have such access problems?

4C.7   If yes, what percentage of households is excluded?

Service	Others excluded?	Percentage excluded?
		<25%=1 25–50%=2 51–75%=3
	Yes = 1 No = 2	76–99%=4 100%=5
a. Education/schools	[ ]	[ ]
b. Health services/clinics	[ ]	[ ]
c. Housing assistance	[ ]	[ ]
d. Job training/employment	[ ]	[ ]
e. Credit/finance	[ ]	[ ]
f. Transportation	[ ]	[ ]
g. Water distribution	[ ]	[ ]
h. Sanitation services	[ ]	[ ]
i. Agricultural extension	[ ]	[ ]
j. Justice/conflict resolution	[ ]	[ ]
k. Security/policy services	[ ]	[ ]

4C.8   What are the reasons or criteria why some people are excluded from these services?

		Yes		No	
a. Income level	[ ]	1	[ ]	2
b. Occupation	[ ]	1	[ ]	2
c. Social status (class, caste)	[ ]	1	[ ]	2
d. Age	[ ]	1	[ ]	2
e. Gender	[ ]	1	[ ]	2
f. Race/ethnicity	[ ]	1	[ ]	2
g. Language	[ ]	1	[ ]	2
h. Religious beliefs	[ ]	1	[ ]	2
i. Political affiliation	[ ]	1	[ ]	2
j. Lack of education	[ ]	1	[ ]	2

4D.   Previous Collective Action

4D.1   In the past year, how often have members of this village/neighborhood gotten together and jointly petitioned government officials or political leaders with village development as their goal?

Never   [   ]   1 (go to question 4D.3)
Once   [   ]   2
A couple of times   [   ]   3
Frequently   [   ]   4

4D.2   Was this action/were any of these actions successful?

Yes, all were successful   [   ]   1
Some were successful and
  others not   [   ]   2
No, none were successful   [   ]   3

4D.3   How often in the past year have you joined together with others in the village/neighborhood to address a common issue?

Never   [   ]   1
Once   [   ]   2
A couple of times   [   ]   3
Frequently   [   ]   4

4D.4   In the last three years have you personally done any of the following things:

	Yes		No	
a. Voted in the elections	[ ]	1	[ ]	2
b. Actively participated in an association	[ ]	1	[ ]	2
c. Made a personal contact with an influential person	[ ]	1	[ ]	2
d. Made the media interested in a problem	[ ]	1	[ ]	2
e. Actively participated in an information campaign	[ ]	1	[ ]	2
f. Actively participated in an election campaign	[ ]	1	[ ]	2
g. Taken part in a protest march or demonstration	[ ]	1	[ ]	2
h. Contacted your elected representative	[ ]	1	[ ]	2
i. Taken part in a sit-in or disruption of government meetings/ offices	[ ]	1	[ ]	2
j. Talked with other people in your area about a problem	[ ]	1	[ ]	2
k. Notified the court or police about a problem	[ ]	1	[ ]	2
l. Made a monetary or in-kind donation	[ ]	1	[ ]	2
m. Volunteered for a charitable organization	[ ]	1	[ ]	2

4D.5   Have you been approached by someone personally during the last three years who asked you to do any of the following:

	Yes		No	
a. Vote in the elections	[ ]	1	[ ]	2
b. Actively participate in an association	[ ]	1	[ ]	2
c. Make a personal contact with an influential person	[ ]	1	[ ]	2
d. Make the media interested in a problem	[ ]	1	[ ]	2
e. Actively participate in an information campaign	[ ]	1	[ ]	2

f. Actively participate in
   an election campaign   [   ]   1   [   ]   2
g. Take part in a protest
   march or demonstration   [   ]   1   [   ]   2
h. Contact your elected
   representative   [   ]   1   [   ]   2
i. Take part in a sit-in or
   disruption of government
   meetings/offices   [   ]   1   [   ]   2
j. Talk with other people
   in your area about a
   problem   [   ]   1   [   ]   2
k. Notify the court or police
   about a problem   [   ]   1   [   ]   2
l. Make a monetary or
   in-kind donation   [   ]   1   [   ]   2
m. Volunteer for a charitable
   organization   [   ]   1   [   ]   2

4D.6   If some decision related to a development project needed to be
        made in this village/neighborhood, do you think the entire vil-
        lage/neighborhood would be called upon to decide or would the
        community leaders make the decision themselves?

        The community leaders would decide   [   ]   1
        The whole village/neighborhood would be called [   ]   2

4D.7   Overall, how would you rate the spirit of participation in this vil-
        lage/neighborhood?

        Very low   [   ]   1
        Low   [   ]   2
        Average   [   ]   3
        High   [   ]   4
        Very high   [   ]   5

4D.8   How much influence do you think people like yourself can have
        in making this village/neighborhood a better place to live?

        A lot   [   ]   1
        Some   [   ]   2
        Not very much   [   ]   3
        None   [   ]   4

5. Cognitive Social Capital

5A.   *Solidarity*

5A.1   Suppose someone in the village/neighborhood had something unfortunate happen to them, such as a father's sudden death. Who do you think they could turn to for help in this situation? *(Record first three mentioned.)*

a	b	c

No one would help	1
Family	2
Neighbors	3
Friends	4
Religious leader or group	5
Community leader	6
Business leader	7
Police	8
Family court judge	9
Patron/employer/benefactor	10
Political leader	11
Mutual support group to which s/he belongs	12
Assistance organization to which s/he does not belong	13
Other (specify)	14

5A.2   Suppose your neighbor suffered an economic loss, say (RURAL: "crop failure"; URBAN "job loss"). In that situation, who do you think would assist him/her financially? *(Record first three mentioned.)*

a	b	c

No one would help	1
Family	2
Neighbors	3
Friends	4
Religious leader or group	5
Community leader	6
Business leader	7
Police	8
Family court judge	9
Patron/employer/benefactor	10

Political leader   11
Mutual support group to which s/he belongs   12
Assistance organization to which s/he does not belong   13
Other (specify)   14

5B.   *Trust and Cooperation*

5B.1   Do you think that in this village/neighborhood people generally
        trust one another in matters of lending and borrowing?

        Do trust   [   ]   1
        Do not trust   [   ]   2

5B.2   Do you think over the last few years this level of trust has gotten
        better, gotten worse, or stayed about the same?

        Better   [   ]   1
        The same   [   ]   2
        Worse   [   ]   3

5B.3   Compared with other villages/neighborhoods, how much do
        people of this village/neighborhood trust each other in matters
        of lending and borrowing?

        Less than other villages/neighborhoods   [   ]   1
        The same as other villages/neighborhoods   [   ]   2
        More than other villages/neighborhoods   [   ]   3

5B.4   Suppose someone from the village/neighborhood had to go
        away for a while, along with their family. In whose charge could
        they leave (RURAL: "their fields"; URBAN: "their house")?
        (*Record first three mentioned.*)

a	b	c

        Other family member   1
        Neighbor   2
        Anyone from the village/neighborhood for this purpose   3
        Other (specify)   4
        No one   5

5B.5   Suppose a friend of yours in this village/neighborhood faced the following alternatives, which one would s/he prefer most?

RURAL:

Own and farm 10 hectares of land entirely by themselves   1
Own and farm 25 hectares of land jointly with
   one other person   2

URBAN:

Own a patio 10 m^2 alone   1
Own a patio 25 m^2 that is shared with one other family   2

5B.6   If you suddenly had to go away for a day or two, whom could you count on to take care of your children? (*Record first three mentioned.*)

a	b	c

Other family member   1
Neighbor   2
Anyone from the village/neighborhood for this purpose   3
Other (specify)   4
Don't have children   5

5B.7   Do you agree or disagree that people here look out mainly for the welfare of their own families and they are not much concerned with village/neighborhood welfare?

Strongly agree   [ ] 1
Agree   [ ] 2
Disagree   [ ] 3
Strongly disagree   [ ] 4

5B.8   If a community project does not directly benefit your neighbor but has benefits for others in the village/neighborhood, then do you think your neighbor would contribute time for this project?

Will not contribute time   [ ] 1
Will contribute time   [ ] 2

5B.9   If a community project does not directly benefit your neighbor
         but has benefits for others in the village/neighborhood, then do
         you think your neighbor would contribute money for this pro-
         ject?

         Will not contribute money   [   ]   1
         Will contribute money   [   ]   2

5B.10   Please tell me whether in general you agree or disagree with the
         following statements:

	Strongly agree	Agree	Disagree	Strongly disagree
a. Most people in this village/ neighborhood are basically honest and can be trusted.	[ ] 1	[ ] 2	[ ] 3	[ ] 4
b. People are always interested only in their own welfare.	[ ] 1	[ ] 2	[ ] 3	[ ] 4
c. Members of this village/neighbor- hood are more trustworthy than others.	[ ] 1	[ ] 2	[ ] 3	[ ] 4
d. In this village/ neighborhood, one has to be alert or someone is likely to take advantage of you.	[ ] 1	[ ] 2	[ ] 3	[ ] 4
e. If I have a problem, there is always someone to help me.	[ ] 1	[ ] 2	[ ] 3	[ ] 4
f. I do not pay attention to the opinions of others in the village/ neighborhood.	[ ] 1	[ ] 2	[ ] 3	[ ] 4
g. Most people in this village/neighborhood are willing to help if you need it.	[ ] 1	[ ] 2	[ ] 3	[ ] 4

h. This village/neigh-
   borhood has
   prospered in the
   last five years.   [ ] 1 [ ] 2 [ ] 3 [ ] 4
i. I feel accepted as
   a member of this
   village/
   neighborhood.   [ ] 1 [ ] 2 [ ] 3 [ ] 4
j. RURAL: If you lose
   a pig or a goat,
   someone in the
   village would help
   look for it or would
   return it to you.
   URBAN: If you
   drop your purse
   or wallet
   in the neighborhood,
   someone will see it
   and return it to you. [ ] 1 [ ] 2 [ ] 3 [ ] 4

5C.   *Conflict Resolution*

5C.1   In your opinion, is this village/neighborhood generally peaceful
       or conflictive?

       Peaceful   [ ] 1
       Conflictive   [ ] 2

5C.2   Compared with other villages/neighborhoods, is there more or
       less conflict in this village/neighborhood?

       More   [ ] 1
       The same   [ ] 2
       Less   [ ] 3

5C.3   Do people in this village/neighborhood contribute time and
       money toward common development goals?

       They contribute some or a lot. [ ]   1
       They contribute very little or
          nothing.   [ ] 2

5C.4   Compared with other villages/neighborhoods, to what extent do people of this village/neighborhood contribute time and money toward common development goals?

They contribute less than other villages/
  neighborhoods.   [   ]   1
They contribute about the same as
  other villages/neighborhoods.   [   ]   2
They contribute more than other
  villages/neighborhoods.   [   ]   3

5C.5   Are the relationships among people in this village/neighborhood generally harmonious or disagreeable?

Harmonious   [   ]   1
Disagreeable   [   ]   2

5C.6   Compared with other villages/neighborhoods, are the relationships among people in this village/neighborhood more harmonious, the same, or less harmonious than other villages/neighborhoods?

More harmonious   [   ]   1
The same   [   ]   2
Less harmonious   [   ]   3

5C.7   Suppose two people in this village/neighborhood had a fairly serious dispute with each other. Who do you think would primarily help resolve the dispute?

No one; people work it out
  between themselves   [   ]   1
Family/household members   [   ]   2
Neighbors   [   ]   3
Community leaders   [   ]   4
Religious leaders   [   ]   5
Judicial leaders   [   ]   6
Other (specify)   [   ]   7

Annex 1D
Organizational Profile Interview Guides

The overall objective of the institutional profile is to delineate the relationships and networks that exist among formal and informal institutions operating in the community, as a measure of structural social capital. Specifically, the profile assesses the organizations' origins and development (historical and community context, longevity, and sustainability); quality of membership (reasons people join, degree of inclusiveness of the organization); institutional capacity (quality of leadership, participation, organizational culture, and organizational capacity); and institutional linkages.

Between three and six institutions per community should be profiled. The organizations need to be identified through the community interviews and/or household survey as key organizations or those having the most impact or influence on community development.

For each organizational profiled, interviews need to be carried out with its leadership, members, and nonmembers. Individual interviews need to be conducted with up to three leaders per organization. The interviews should preferably be face-to-face, but a self-administered written questionnaire may be substituted. Focus group interviews should be carried out with members and nonmembers, with each group ideally having between 5 and 12 participants Depending on the size and diversity of the group's membership, anywhere from one to four focus groups should be conducted. Of the nonmembers, effort should be made to conduct two focus groups, one for nonmembers who want to be members and one for nonmembers with no interest in becoming a member.

Each focus group should have a moderator and two observers. The moderator's role is to facilitate the discussion, probe on key issues, elicit comments from all participants, and focus the discussion on the issues of interest without seeming to interrupt or ignore extraneous comments from participants. The observers' role is to take notes on the content of the discussion and process of group dynamics. Upon completion of the focus group interview, the moderator and observers should conduct a follow-up debriefing to refine the interview notes and discuss preliminary findings.

1. ORGANIZATIONAL IDENTITY

1.1   Name of organization ———————————————————

1.2   Type of organization ———————————————————

1.3   Membership   ———————————————————

1.4   Location (district, village, neighborhood) _____

1.5   Names of leaders _____

2. Leadership Interview Guide

2A.   *Origins and Development*

2A.1   How was your organization created? Who was most responsible
        for its creation (e.g., government mandate, community decision,
        suggestion of outside NGO)?

2A.2   What kinds of activities has the organization been involved in?

2A.3   In what ways has the organization changed its structures and
        purpose? What is the main purpose of your organization today?

2A.4   As the organization developed, what sort of help has it received
        from outside? Has it received advice and/or funding or other
        support from the government? What about from nongovernment
        sources? How did you get this support? Who initiated it? How
        was the support given? What benefits and limitations has the
        organization derived from this support?

2B.   *Membership*

2B.1   Can you tell us about the people involved in your organization?
        How do they become involved? Are all people in the community
        involved? If not, why are some members of the community not
        involved?

2B.2   Why do people join or are willing to serve (as officers/lead-
        ers/board members) in the organization? Is it hard to convince
        people to continue being active in the organization? What kinds
        of requests/demands do they make on the leadership and orga-
        nization?

2B.3   Are active members in this organization also members of other
        organizations in the community/region? Do people tend to be
        members of just one organization or join many simultaneously?
        Can you explain why?

2C.   *Institutional Capacity*

2C.1   How would you characterize the quality of *leadership* of this
        organization, in terms of...

        ...stability?

        ...number of leaders/availability?

        ...diversity/heterogeneity of leadership?

        ...quality and skills of leaders?

        ...relationship of leaders to staff and to the community?

2C.2   How would you characterize the quality of *participation* in this
        organization, in terms of...

        ...attendance at meetings, both internal to the organization and
        externally with other organizations?

        ...participation in decisionmaking within the organization?

        ...dissemination of relevant information prior to the decision?

        ...informal opportunities to discuss the decision?

        ...consultation processes with base organizations or with the
        community?

        ...broad debate, including opposition positions, and honesty?

        ...dissemination of the results of the decisionmaking process?

        ...the number of women, young people, poor people who work
        in the organization and who occupy positions of responsibility in
        the organization?

        ...whether any groups within the community feel excluded from
        the organization? What groups are they?

        ...the level of participation of more prosperous families (elites) in
        the organization?

...whether elites are sympathetic, supportive, interfering, adversarial, or negative influences?

2C.3   How would you characterize the *organizational culture* of this organization, in terms of...

...the existence and level of knowledge of the procedures and policies?

...whether the procedures and policies are carried out? Whether there are problems with nonattendance at meetings, theft of property or supplies?

...conflict resolution mechanisms, both within the community and within the organization?

...the nature of conflicts between the organization and community members?

2C.4   How would you characterize the *organizational capacity* of this organization, in terms of...

...carrying out specialized activities (e.g., credit, commercialization)?

...supervising and contracting consultants?

...preparing financial reports for banks, donors, and government?

...reacting to changing circumstances (e.g., price fluctuations, change in government)?

...developing specific plans for the future (instead of reacting to opportunities as they present themselves)?

...reflecting on and learning from previous experiences?

2D.   *Institutional Linkages*

2D.1   How would you characterize your organization's relationship with other community organizations? When do you feel the need to establish collaboration/links with them?

2D.2 Do you have links with organizations outside the village/neighborhood? With which ones? What is the nature of those links?

2D.3 Do you feel sufficiently informed about other organizations' programs and activities? What are your sources of information?

2D.4 Have you attempted to organize or work with other organizations to achieve a mutually beneficial goal? (*Ask for which activities.*) Is this a common strategy among organizations in this village/neighborhood? (*Probe as to reasons why or why not.*)

2D.5 Could you describe your relationship with the government? Have you had experience in trying to get government assistance? What was your experience? Which level of government do you find most cooperative (local, district, national)? Has the government made particular requests of your organization?

2D.6 Is your organization linked to any government program? Which government program(s) is your organization involved with? Why those particular programs? What sort of role does your organization play in the program? Are there certain characteristics of these programs that make it easier for your organization to work with the programs?

2D.7 Do you feel sufficiently informed about government programs and activities? What are your sources of information?

2D.8 Have you attempted to give inputs to the government? What were the circumstances? What have been the results? What kinds of challenges did you have to deal with? (*Probe for any role in planning, operation, and maintenance of government-sponsored services.*)

2D.9 Has your organization been invited to participate in any of the various government development planning processes? What do you think about these planning mechanisms?

2D.10 In general, how do you assess your organization's actual influence on government decisionmaking at the district level?

3. Members Interview Guide

3A.   Organizational History and Structure

3A.1   How did this group start?

3A.2   Who have been the leaders of this group? Who are the leaders now? How and why did the leadership change over time? What are the qualities of leadership?

3A.3   Why did you decide to join this group? What kinds of benefits do you get by being a member of this group?

3A.4   How are the leaders of this organization selected? How are decisions made? To what extent do you feel the organization represents your concerns to the outside world and to the government?

3A.5   Why are some people not members of this organization?

3A.6   How do you feel this organization complements, replaces, or competes with government institutions' activities in the community?

3A.7   How do you feel this organization complements, replaces, or competes with nongovernmental institutions' activities in the community?

3A.8   What would you do to make this organization more effective?

3B.   Institutional Capacity

3B.1   How would you characterize the quality of *leadership* of this organization, in terms of...

...stability?

...number of leaders/availability?

...diversity/heterogeneity of leadership?

...quality and skills of leaders?

...relationship of leaders to staff and to the community?

3B.2   How would you characterize the quality of *participation* in this organization, in terms of…

…attendance at meetings, both internal to the organization and externally with other organizations?

…participation in decisionmaking within the organization?

…dissemination of relevant information prior to the decision?

…informal opportunities to discuss the decision?

…consultation processes with base organizations or with the community?

…broad debate, including opposition positions, and honesty?

…dissemination of the results of the decisionmaking process?

…the number of women, young people, poor people who work in the organization and who occupy positions of responsibility in the organization?

…whether any groups within the community feel excluded from the organization? What groups are they?

…the level of participation of more prosperous families (elites) in the organization?

…whether elites are sympathetic, supportive, interfering, adversarial, or negative influences?

3B.3   How would you characterize the *organizational culture* of this organization, in terms of…

…the existence and level of knowledge of procedures and policies?

…whether the procedures and policies are carried out? Whether there are problems with nonattendance at meetings, theft of property or supplies?

…conflict resolution mechanisms, both within the community and within the organization?

...the nature of conflicts between the organization and community members?

3B.4   How would you characterize the *organizational capacity* of this organization, in terms of...

...carrying out specialized activities (e.g., credit, commercialization)?

...supervising and contracting consultants?

...preparing financial reports for banks, donors, and government?

...reacting to changing circumstances (e.g., price fluctuations, change in government)?

...developing specific plans for the future (instead of reacting to opportunities as they present themselves)?

...reflecting on and learning from previous experiences?

4. NONMEMBERS INTERVIEW GUIDE

4A.   Group #1: Nonmembers who want to be members

4A.1   In your opinion, do the benefits of this particular organization spread beyond its members?

4A.2   Why are some people not members of this organization? Why are you not a member of this organization?

4A.3   How far do you think this organization complements or competes with other community organizations?

4A.4   What is your view about how the organization deals with government? (For example, does kinship or party affiliation play a role in determining the relationship?)

4A.5   What is your view about how the organization deals with other organizations that work in the village/neighborhood?

4B.   Group #2: Nonmembers who do not want to be members

4B.1   In your opinion, do the benefits of this particular organization spread beyond its members?

4B.2   Why are some people not members of this organization? Why are you not a member of this organization?

4B.3   How far do you think this organization complements or competes with other community organizations?

4B.4   What is your view about how the organization deals with government? (For example, does kinship or party affiliation play a role in determining the relationship?)

4B.5   What is your view about how the organization deals with other organizations that work in the village/neighborhood?

Annex 1E
Organizational Profile Scoresheet

1. LEADERSHIP

1A. *Rotation*

1A.1   Does the organization's leadership change regularly?

Yes	[ ]	1
No	[ ]	2

1A.2   Is the amount of time the leaders remain in their position sufficient for acquiring experience and learning leadership functions?

Yes	[ ]	1
No	[ ]	2

1A.3   Is there the possibility of reelecting successful leaders?

Yes	[ ]	1
No	[ ]	2

1B. *Density/Availability*

1B.1   How many people within the organization have acquired the
capability and qualities to be effective leaders?

No one possesses these qualities	[ ]	1
Few (1 to 3)	[ ]	2
Some (4 to 6)	[ ]	3
Many (more than 6)	[ ]	4

1B.2   How many are put forward for leadership tasks?

Only a few are ready to be leaders.	[ ]	1
The group of candidates is limited but adequate.	[ ]	2
There is never a lack of candidates (candidates who are prepared, enthused, and available to assume a leadership role).	[ ]	3

1B.3   How amenable are former leaders to continued participation in the organization?

There are no previous leaders; the
   organization is new.   [ ]   1
Almost no participation by former leaders. [ ]   2
Some participation by former leaders.   [ ]   3
Active participation by former leaders.   [ ]   4

1C.   *Diversity/Heterogeneity*

1C.1   Do the leaders tend to come from a few groups or families that are always the same, or do the leaders represent a wider circle among the community?

From few groups   [ ]   1
From various groups within the
   community   [ ]   2
From almost all the groups within
   the community   [ ]   3

1C.2   What percentage of those that occupy leadership positions within the organization are women?

Less than 10%   [ ]   1
Between 10 % and 25%   [ ]   2
Between 26% and 50%   [ ]   3
More than 50%   [ ]   4

1D.   *Leadership Quality and Skills*

1D.1   In general, how would you characterize the quality of leadership in this organization in terms of...

	Excellent	Good	Adequate	Deficient
a. Education/training	[ ] 1	[ ] 2	[ ] 3	[ ] 4
b. Dynamism/vision?	[ ] 1	[ ] 2	[ ] 3	[ ] 4
c. Professionalism/ skills?	[ ] 1	[ ] 2	[ ] 3	[ ] 4
d. Honesty/ transparency?	[ ] 1	[ ] 2	[ ] 3	[ ] 4

1E.   Relationship between Leadership, Staff, and Constituency

1E.1   How would you characterize the relationship between the executive director and the management and technical staff?

Harmonious, without major problems [   ] 1
Coexisting, with occasional rivalries [   ] 2
Conflictive, with many problems [   ] 3
Dysfunctional, without communication
 or coordination [   ] 4

1E.2   What level of acceptance and legitimacy does the leadership have, especially among grassroots organizations whose communities are underrepresented?

The leaders are openly accepted and
 everyone recognizes their legitimacy
 to represent their interests. [   ] 1
The leaders are accepted by the
 majority of the community; the
 majority recognize their legitimacy. [   ] 2
The leaders are accepted by a minority
 of the community members; leaders
 have little legitimacy. [   ] 3
The leaders are not accepted and do
 not have legitimacy within the community. [   ] 4

2. PARTICIPATION

2A.   Frequency of Meetings

2A.1   Should the frequency with which the organization meets be greater, less, or remain the same?

Greater [   ] 1
Less [   ] 2
The same [   ] 3

2B.   Participation in Decisionmaking

2B.1   What have been the two most important decisions made in the past year?

Decision # 1: _____

Decision # 2: _____

2B.2   Thinking about these decisions, did any of the following take place?
(Code decision # 1 first, then continue with decision # 2.)

Topic	a. Prior dissemination of information	b. Opportunity for informal discussion	c. Consultation with grassroots	d. Widespread debate, opposing opinions, and frank discussion	e. Dissemination of results
	Yes = 1 No = 2	Yes = 1 No = 2	Yes = 1 No = 2	Yes = 1 No = 2	Yes = 1 No = 2
Decision # 1					
Decision # 2					

2C.   *Inclusiveness*

2C.1   In the last three meetings, what has been the level of participation of women, of youth, and of the poorest groups?

	Active	Moderate	Little/ None
a. Women	[ ] 1	[ ] 2	[ ] 3
b. Youth	[ ] 1	[ ] 2	[ ] 3
c. Poor	[ ] 1	[ ] 2	[ ] 3

2C.2   In comparison with earlier meetings, was this level of participation more, less, or the same?

	More	Less	Same
a. Women	[ ] 1	[ ] 2	[ ] 3
b. Youth	[ ] 1	[ ] 2	[ ] 3
c. Poor	[ ] 1	[ ] 2	[ ] 3

2C.3   To what degree does the organization truly represent its members?

Highly representative	[ ] 1
Somewhat representative	[ ] 2
Slightly representative	[ ] 3
Not representative at all	[ ] 4

2C.4   What percentage of the population in this community feels included as beneficiaries of the organization or feels its interests are represented by the organization?

Less than 25%	[ ] 1
Between 25 % and 50%	[ ] 2
Between 51% and 75%	[ ] 3
More than 75%	[ ] 4

2D.   *Participation by Elites*

2D.1   To what degree do the more prosperous families in the community (those with land, businesses, or professions) attend meetings, hold positions, or participate in activities of the organization?

Active	[ ] 1
Moderate	[ ] 2
Little/none	[ ] 3

2D.2   What is the relationship of the more prosperous families toward the organization itself?

They are a resource to be counted on, sympathetic and/or supportive.	[ ] 1
They could be a resource, demonstrating interest but currently are an interfering element.	[ ] 2

They could be a resource, but demonstrate no
interest and currently are indifferent.   [ ] 3
They cannot become a resource and represent an
adversarial or negative element.   [ ] 4

3. ORGANIZATIONAL CULTURE

3.1   How many members know the procedures, norms, and tasks of
        the organization?

        The majority of members   [ ] 1
        Some members   [ ] 2
        Few members   [ ] 3

3.2   How willing is the organization to confront problems with its
        members (if they were to happen) such as not attending meet-
        ings, avoiding work, or stealing property belonging to the orga-
        nization?

        The organization is very willing to confront
          damaging behavior on the part of its members.   [ ] 1
        The organization is sometimes willing to confront
          damaging behavior on the part of its members.   [ ] 2
        The organization has little capacity to confront
          damaging behavior on the part of its members.   [ ] 3

3.3   For serious cases, do guidelines or rules exist to sanction, fine, or
        expel the transgressor?

        Yes   [ ] 1
        No   [ ] 2

4. ORGANIZATIONAL CAPACITY AND SUSTAINABILITY

4A.   Specific Capacities

4A.1   What is the organization's capacity to...

	Excellent	Good	Adequate	Deficient
a. Carry out its specialized tasks (e.g., credit, training, com- mercialization)?	[ ] 1	[ ] 2	[ ] 3	[ ] 4

b. Supervise and contract
   specialized consultants
   or staff?   [ ] 1 [ ] 2 [ ] 3 [ ] 4
c. Prepare financial
   reports for banks,
   donors, or
   government?   [ ] 1 [ ] 2 [ ] 3 [ ] 4
d. Respond in a timely
   fashion to changes
   that affect the organization (e.g., price
   fluctuations, change
   of government)?   [ ] 1 [ ] 2 [ ] 3 [ ] 4
e. Develop specific
   plans for the future
   (instead of reacting
   to external oppor-
   tunities as they
   present themselves)? [ ] 1 [ ] 2 [ ] 3 [ ] 4
f. Reflect upon and
   learn from experience
   (build an institutional
   memory)?   [ ] 1 [ ] 2 [ ] 3 [ ] 4
g. Resolve problems or
   conflicts with other
   organizations or
   social actors?   [ ] 1 [ ] 2 [ ] 3 [ ] 4
h. Resolve problems
   or conflicts within
   the organization?   [ ] 1 [ ] 2 [ ] 3 [ ] 4

4B.   *Collective Action and Formulation of Demands*

4B.1   Does the organization have clearly defined processes for identi-
        fying the common needs and priorities of its members?

        Yes   [ ] 1
        No   [ ] 2

4B.2   In the last three years, have there been petitions or other formal expressions of demand by the membership?

Yes   [ ]   1
No   [ ]   2

4B.3   Have there been informal ways for members to express their demands?

Yes   [ ]   1
No   [ ]   2

4B.4   In what way has the organization addressed these demands?

Promotes demands of common interest   [ ]   1
Tries to identify common elements   [ ]   2
Tries to process them one by one   [ ]   3
There were no demands   [ ]   4

Annex 1F
Selection Criteria and Terms of Reference
For Interviewers (Panama Pilot Test)

Responsibilities

The objective of the study is to pilot test the research instruments that are part of the Social Capital Assessment Tool (SOCAT). Interviewers selected will have the following responsibilities:

- Be completely familiar with the content and application of the various data collection methods, including the community profile, the household questionnaire, and the organizational profile.
- Be able to answer any questions regarding the study, its objectives, and fieldwork activities.
- Select key informants to be interviewed according to the indicated sampling techniques.
- Obtain informed consent from all interview subjects prior to their participation in the study.
- Conduct interviews, whether group interviews, individual in-depth interviews, or individual surveys, using the indicated data collection instruments.
- Provide in timely fashion the primary source materials generated during the interviews, whether expanded observation notes, appropriately coded survey questionnaires, or other results of the qualitative interviews.
- Debrief field supervisors about the data collection process and the application of the instruments.

Skills

The interviewer must have certain qualities and skills to be able to undertake the diverse activities associated with the fieldwork. These include:

- Completion of secondary school education, preferably with some university-level studies in one of the social sciences.
- Previous experience conducting household surveys.
- Previous experience conducting focus group interviews and/or using participatory research techniques.
- Demonstrated ability to document, in detail and precisely, the main issues brought out in individual and group open-ended interviews.
- Ability to work in teams, coupled with demonstrated self-motivation.

- Availability to work six days a week, including Saturdays and Sundays, with long working hours.
- Availability to work in distant areas, in difficult terrain, under challenging conditions.

Selection Criteria

The final selection of the research team will be made at the conclusion of the training workshop. The workshop will present the study objectives, and the contents, justification, and application of the research instruments, and include practice applications of the instruments. The team of field supervisors will select the people for the position of interviewer. The selection criteria include demonstrated ability in the above-mentioned areas as well as:

- Diversity among team members that appropriately reflects the diversity of the research population in terms of gender, ethnicity, and social class.
- A complementary skill mix among team members regarding techniques for conducting qualitative individual and group interviews, conducting household surveys, drafting expanded field notes, transcribing field notes, and applying participatory research methods.

Annex 1G: Training Plan for Field Workers (Panama Pilot Test)

Day 1

8:00	Opening		
15"	Introduction to the workshop	*Lecture:* Review the workshop objectives, agenda, expectations.	*Handouts:* Pens, pads, notebooks, agenda, markers, masking tape
30"	Introduction of the workshop participants	*Group dynamic:* "Alliterative names" as an ice breaker: name, where from, previous research or field experience; name and alliterative adjective written on paper.	
45"	Introduction to the SOCAT study	*Lecture:* What is social capital? Overview, definitions, relation to other types of capital, relationship to economic development What is the SOCAT study? Objective, conceptual framework, structure of the tools, what the study is not. Who will participate? Criteria for selection of interviewers, review of terms of reference.	*Handouts:* Memos on social capital, SOCAT study, terms of reference for interviewers
9:30	Break		
9:45	Part I: Community profile		
15"	Overview presentation	*Lecture:* Objectives, structure, activities, materials.	*Handouts:* Community profile interview guide

30"	Qualitative participatory methodologies: In-depth interview techniques with groups	*Group discussion:* How to conduct a group interview; how to enter the community; role of the research team (facilitator and observers); using the interview guide; importance of transcripts.	
30"	Qualitative participatory methodologies: Community asset mapping	*Group discussion:* How to facilitate a participatory mapping of community assets; identification of the community's asset portfolio; the art of listening.	
30"	Qualitative participatory methodologies: Venn diagrams	*Group discussion:* How to facilitate a participatory Venn diagram; community assessment of the relative importance and accessibility of associations.	
20"	Qualitative participatory methodologies: Flowchart diagrams of organization networks	*Group discussion:* How to facilitate a participatory flowchart diagram; community assessment of the network relationships between and among associations; assessment of the quality of relationships (strong, weak, conflictive, etc.)	
10"	Review	*Lecture:* The final product of each community interview will be a folder containing the following: 1. Descriptive summary of the interview process (half page transcribed) 2. Expanded notes (integration of the	*Handout:* Examples of transcripts, maps, Venn diagrams and flowcharts

227

Time	Duration	Activity	Products / Notes
			observational and analytical notes of all research team members, transcribed)
			3. Methodological notes (transcribed)
			4. Community asset map(s) (on 8x11 paper)
			5. List of community needs assessment
			6. Complete list of community associations
			7. Venn diagram (on 8x11 paper)
			8. Organizational flowchart (on 8x11 paper)
			9. Raw field notes and other support materials
12:00		Lunch	
13:00	90"	Part I: Community profile (cont.) Review of the community interview guide, by sections: A. Definition of the community and identification of community assets B. Collective action and solidarity C. Community governance and decisionmaking D. Identification of local level institutions E. Relationship between the community and local level institutions F. Institutional networks and organizational density	*Group discussion:* Review the "why" of each question and its relationship to social capital measurement; interview products for each section include: A. Map drawing B. Group interview C. Group interview D. Drafting list of local-level institutions E. Drawing Venn diagram F. Drawing organizational flowchart

14:30	Break		
15:00	Part I: Community profile (cont.)		
90"	Application of the community interview guide	*Role play:* The objective of this exercise is to practice interview skills and evaluate participants' capabilities for conducting the community interviews. Assign the roles of facilitator, observers, and informants. Have the "research team" and the "community members" take 10 minutes to clarify their roles, strategies, responsibilities, etc.	Will need enough space to recreate a community interview plus all relevant materials ("research team" is responsible)
30"	Conclusion of the exercise	*Group discussion:* Comments regarding the role play; observations on the roles of facilitator, observer, participants; constructive criticism regarding ways to improve interview techniques, eliciting information, managing group dynamics.	
17:00	Finish		
	Homework assignments	Reading: • Community interview guide • Household questionnaire • Organization interview guide • Memoranda describing the SOCAT study • Terms of reference for interviewers	Hand out copies of all research instruments, support memoranda, and TORs

		Writing:
		• For all participants, draft in their own words an introduction to the study, appropriate for presentation to informants; should include references to the study objectives, the meaning of social capital, the use of participatory methods, and guarantee of confidentiality.
		• For those who played the role of observer, draft the expanded field notes.
		Practice:
		• Explain to someone not involved with the study the concept of social capital and its importance in the economic development of the community.
Day 2		
8:00	Review of previous day's work and homework assignments; questions and clarifications	*Group discussion:* Ask participants to recite their written explanations of the study and to make comments regarding accuracy of contents, style of delivery, clarity of language, etc.
9:00	Part II: Household survey	
15"	Overview	*Lecture:* Objectives, sampling and interview techniques, structure, materials.
75"	Review the first three sections	*Group discussion:*

	of the household survey questionnaire: 1. Identification of selected household 2. Housing characteristics and household roster 3. Genogram	Review the "why" of each question, its application and coding. For the genogram, show symbols used and draw a sample genogram.
10:30	Break	
90"	Application of the household questionnaire (first three sections).	*Role play:* In pairs, apply the first three sections of the questionnaire.
30"	Review of the exercise	*Group discussion:* In front of the class, have a third person describe a genogram from one of the interviews; question and answer period about interview techniques and coding; emphasize research objectives and relationship to social capital.
12:30	Lunch	
1:30	Part II: Household survey (cont.)	
120"	Review Section 4. Structural social capital	*Group discussion:* Review the "why" of each question, its application and coding.
3:30	Break	

231

3:45	Part II: Household survey (cont.)	
45"	Application of Section 4. Structural social capital	*Role play:* With the same partner, continue applying the household questionnaire through Section 4.
30"	Review of the exercise	*Group discussion:* Q&A; emphasize pilot research objectives.
17:00	Conclude	
	Homework assignment	Interview someone not involved in the study, applying the first four sections of the household questionnaire.
Day 3		
8:00 90"	Review of previous day's work and homework assignments; questions and clarifications	*Group discussion:* Have participants describe their experience with applying the questionnaire; discuss interview techniques, presentation and informed consent, areas of difficulty encountered and ways to solve them.
9:30	Break	
9:45	Part II: Household survey (cont.)	
60"	Review Section 5. Cognitive social capital	*Group discussion:* Review the "why" of each question, its application and coding.
60"	Application of Section 5. Cognitive social capital	*Role play:* With the same partner, continue applying

Time	Activity	Description	Notes
15"	Review of the exercise; conclusion of the presentation on the household survey	the household questionnaire through Section 5. *Group discussion:* Q&A; emphasize pilot research objectives.	
12:30	Lunch		
1:30 15"	Reintegration	*Group dynamic:* "When I think about 'social capital' I think of _____." Gauge whether participants are integrating social capital concepts; stimulate group.	
13:45	Review of Part I: Community profile		
120"	Application of the community interview guide	*Role play:* Practice interview skills and evaluate participants' capabilities for conducting the community interviews. Assign the roles of facilitator, observers, and informants. The "research team" and the "community members" should take 10 minutes to clarify their roles, strategies, responsibilities, etc. Choose a setting (i.e., urban, rural, indigenous) different from first community interview role play; all participants should have played an "observer" role at least once.	Will need enough space to recreate a community interview plus all relevant materials ("research team" is responsible)
15:45	Conclusion of the exercise	*Group discussion:* Comments regarding the role play; observations	

		on the roles of facilitator, observer, participants; constructive criticism regarding ways to improve interview techniques, eliciting information, managing group dynamics.
16:00	End	
	Homework assignment	Read: • Part III: Organizational Profile Write: • The "observers" from the community interview role play should write up their field notes.

Day 4

8:00	Review of previous day's work and homework assignments; questions and clarifications	*Group discussion:* Have participants describe their experience drafting field notes.
9:30	Break	
9:45	Part III: Organizational profile	
30"	Overview	*Lecture:* Objectives, sampling and interview techniques, structure, materials.
90"	Review of organizational interview guide; individual interviews with leadership	*Group discussion:* Review the "why" of each question, its application, and technique for drafting field notes. Review coding sheet that

Time	Activity	Description	Materials
11:45	Group interviews with members, group interviews with nonmembers	is filled in following interview.	
	Conclusion	*Group dynamic:* Write down words or phrases associated with "social capital."	
12:00	Lunch		
13:00	Part III: Organizational profile (cont.)		
120"	• Application of the organizational interview guide	*Field exercise:* Arrange previously with a local organization to conduct an individual interview with leaders and a group interview with members. Select an interviewer; all other participants are observers.	Provide interview guides, pads of paper, transportation to offices.
15:00	Break		
15:15	Part III: Organizational profile (cont.)		
45"	Follow-up to the field exercise	*Group discussion:* Review the details of the interview: technique, informed consent, findings. As a group, apply the closed coding form; Q&A; emphasize objectives and relationship to social capital.	
16:00	Logistics		
60"		*Group discussion:* • Final selection of interviewers • How field work will be managed	

Time	Activity
	• Team composition
	• Assignment of communities
	• Hand out materials (maps, instruments, paper, markers, etc.)
	• Contracts
	• Letters of introduction; identification cards
17:00	End of training

Annex 2

Does Social Capital Facilitate the Poor's Access to Credit?

Thierry van Bastelaer

In industrial economies households generally obtain credit against individual guarantees from commercial sources that reach loan decisions on the basis of readily available information on the borrower's credit risk. In most developing economies, however, poor households usually cannot provide these guarantees, especially not through mechanisms such as real estate–based collateral. This situation, combined with an overall lack of information about these potential borrowers' creditworthiness, virtually excludes this group of borrowers from formal credit markets.

However, several classes of institutional arrangements offer valid substitutes for individual collateral to poor households as well as low-cost alternatives to imperfect creditworthiness information to the lenders.[1] An increasing number of finance institutions provide credit to the poor on the basis of "social collateral," through which borrowers' reputations, or the social networks to which the borrowers belong, take the place of traditional physical or financial collateral. Since these arrangements build, to various degrees, on the extent and strength of personal relationships, they offer a fertile ground for analyzing the role of social capital in the provision of credit.[2] In addition, credit arrangements rely on several classes of social capital identified in the conceptual literature, such as horizontal, vertical, and ethnic-based relationships. Finally, the role of social connections in obtaining credit is also greatest for poor borrowers: as the financial needs of these borrowers increase, they become more attractive customers in the formal financial markets, and their reliance on immediate social networks for credit decreases.

This annex examines the empirical evidence documenting the relationship between social capital and the performance of credit delivery programs in the developing world. It suggests that although social ties facilitate the poor's access to credit and lower its cost, they do so in a more diverse and complex manner than the mainstream literature on development finance indicates. In addition to the horizontal networks of borrowers that are largely credited for the success of organizations like the Grameen Bank, credit delivery systems also rely heavily on vertical and hierarchical relationships between lenders and borrowers. This perspective helps to situate the relatively recent and innovative concept of microfinance within a continuum of institutional arrangements of credit for the poor.

The different types of credit arrangements targeted at the poor are discussed in this annex according to a roughly decreasing order of lender-borrower closeness and indigenous character of the lending methodology.[3] They are, respectively, rotating savings and credit associations (ROSCAs), local moneylenders, trade credit, and group-based microfinance programs. Some of these arrangements, especially the ROSCA and the group approach to lending, have generated more theoretical and empirical coverage than others—as well as more controversy—and this fact is reflected in the space devoted to both in the following discussion.

Rotating Savings and Credit Associations

Rotating savings and credit associations are a "response by a socially connected group to credit market exclusion" (Besley, Coate, and Loury 1993, p. 807) and a widespread way to crystallize social relations in an informal—yet often formally run—system of internal credit delivery.[4] Besson (1995) claims that the earliest identified ROSCAs go back more than 400 years, but Izumida (1992) describes the *kou* system, introduced in Japan in the 12th or 13th century, whose features are strikingly similar to that of the contemporary ROSCA.

A ROSCA is a group of men, women, or both who contribute to a collective fund that is at regular intervals distributed—in successive order, randomly, by bid at auction, or by collective decision—to one of the group's members. Besley, Coate, and Loury (1993, p. 807) point to a reason for the observed prevalence of random over bidding ROSCAs: "the [personal] gains from early default [in bidding ROSCAs] are greater, and individuals with the lowest disutility from social disapproval and sanctions have a stronger incentive to bid in order to obtain the pot early." In effect, all members of the group (except the last person in the rotation) receive an advance that they repay through their contribution to the fund for the duration of the cycle; the earlier an individual's position in the rotation, the larger the credit received, and the lower the risk faced (if a person fails to contribute after receiving the fund, only those members receiving credit later will be adversely affected). At the end of a cycle, that is, when each member has received the fund once, the ROSCA is dismantled or, more often, reconstituted with the same or similar membership. This creates the possibility that well-performing members of ordered ROSCAs can move up in the rotation, providing an incentive for a good payment record that spans several rotations, and—if new entrants are chosen carefully—potentially reinforcing the success of the association.

ROSCAs play an important role as a risk management tool; they can offer an insurance mechanism against income shocks, provided that these shocks are not correlated among participants. ROSCAs are an extension of traditional savings groups that, as documented by Begashaw (1978) and Maloney and Ahmed (1988), are constituted of individuals who regularly or irregularly deposit funds with an individual or a subset of the group. Funds are returned to individual savers at the end of a given period, and there is no systematic rotational distribution mechanism.

Van den Brink and Chavas (1997) in their study of a ROSCA system in a Cameroon village suggest that when properly run, this system is more efficient than all other credit arrangements in the region. It reaches 90 percent of all households, and handles thousands of transactions each year at a low transaction cost, accounting for about 11 percent of village income. Besley, Coate, and Loury (1993) have shown that in addition to providing an instrument with which to save for large or indivisible purchases, ROSCAs are an improvement over autarkic savings.

ROSCAs function as long as individuals value the benefits of membership in the association (or the absence of collective ostracism) more than the benefits of defaulting. As a result, all members generally contribute to the fund even after they have received the total group collection. The collective trust that enables this system to function can be present at the beginning of the first rotation, if the members are chosen on the basis of preexistent levels of trust among themselves. But, as Rutherford (2000) points out, the system can also create the levels of trust that make its operations possible, even if its members did not know each other at the beginning of the cycle. Rutherford describes the functioning of Bangladeshi ROSCAs, most of which are set up and run by small shopkeepers who recruit the members and arrange the rotational mechanism. Since most of the new members do not know each other, trust is nonexistent when the first rotation begins, and is built over time as participants learn to identify members who perform well and eliminate those who are unreliable. Rutherford writes (p. 41): "Trust is more of a verb than a noun [in Bangladesh]. Perfect strangers, coming together with the limited aim of running a ROSCA, can sometimes construct and practice trust more easily than people with histories of complex relationships with each other."[5]

Since all sources of the rotating funds are, by design, internally generated, one should expect that social factors would be a critical element of their performance. Although there are significant financial reasons to join a ROSCA, the main defining characteristic of a performing association lies in the reduction of the risk of opportunistic behavior that results from the peer pressure on all members to perform. Advancement toward the beginning of the rotation is a group-sanctioned recognition of the member's creditworthiness—due to his or her good payment record—while failure to contribute to the fund creates extraordinary pressures from other members for repayment. Outright default is seen by members as a direct threat to the survival of the ROSCA and is treated accordingly. The costs of default include social mechanisms that extend beyond the domain of the ROSCA into community sanctions such as peer pressure and social ostracism, which affect every aspect of that individual's social and economic life. Villagers claim that "not even death is an excuse" for default, indicating that obligations to the fund have a hereditary character. According to Van den Brink and Chavas (1997, p. 752), however, "while social pressure is certainly great, people do keep a sharp eye on the transactions costs involved in enforcing payment," as the costs of loan recovery eventually outweigh the benefits of enforced compliance.[6] Implicit in this cost assessment is the recognition that social relations can be damaged by enforcement of payment obligations and hence can adversely affect the social fabric that makes the ROSCA possible.

Although ROSCAs are financing instruments mostly used by the poor, others use them as well, in contrast to group-based microfinance organizations.[7] According to Adams and Canavesi de Sahonero (1989), the most likely ROSCA subscribers in developing countries can be found among white-collar workers in large cities.[8] Van den Brink and Chavas suggest, however, that in the case of Cameroon, the existence of looser social networks in urban settings results in enforcement mechanisms that rely less on community sanctions (such as loss of prestige) and more on forceful seizure of the delinquent member's property. Overall, though, the ROSCA appears to be a fairly inflexible system of credit delivery, whose survival relies almost entirely on the use of social pressures to preserve the personal resources of group members within the association.

Local Moneylenders

Loans from family and friends are perhaps the most common form of informal finance. These arrangements are characterized by uncollateralized loans that carry no or little interest, feature open-ended repayment arrangements, and have a strong focus on reciprocity. The traditional local moneylender can be seen as a commercialized variation on this widespread type of lending arrangement.

Moneylenders, typically landowners or traders, are often the only source of credit available to the poor in developing countries, especially in the rural areas of Asia.[9] Their loans are extended quickly, for short periods, and at interest rate levels that are high in comparison with other lenders, including group-based microfinance programs.

Like the other credit arrangements discussed here, moneylending is a method for dealing with imperfect information in segmented financial markets. Because of their long-term presence in the village and their networks of influence over many aspects of community life, moneylenders have a good knowledge of the creditworthiness of the borrowers and can design personalized interest rate structures accordingly. As Stiglitz (1990, p. 352) notes, "the local moneylenders have one important advantage over the formal [lending] institutions: they have more detailed knowledge of the borrowers. They therefore can separate out high-risk and low-risk borrowers and charge them appropriate interest rates." Most moneylenders are not primarily in the business of lending money: funds lent are often the means of obtaining returns on other transactions in which both lender and borrower are involved. Since these relationships are the very mechanism through which information about the borrower and his or her ability to repay is indicated to the lender, segmentation by borrower-lender clusters often arises. Timberg and Aiyar (1984) report that they asked an Indian moneylender how he decided to accept additional clients; he responded that he never had a new client. Onchan (1992) describes the arrangements within Thai villages, where half a dozen moneylenders routinely operate with little competition.

The lending relationships that moneylenders cultivate with the borrowers are of a long-term nature, and they are usually based on a pattern of personal interactions with the borrowers and their families. They directly draw on the traditional patron-client relationship or on a set of hierarchical social interactions reminiscent of the vertical dimensions of Coleman's (1988) definition of social capital. These relationships are by nature unequal, as the moneylender has several means—including harassment and force—to ensure repayment. Interest rates are often set in such a way that full repayment is unlikely and unexpected from the lender's side, and the loan is used as a way to secure asset transfers or long-term indenture relationships with borrowers and their families.

Trade Credit

Apart from self-finance, trade credit is, in many countries, the only source of operational funds for small and medium enterprises. Social relations are an important element of the traditional solutions to this single-source situation: trade credit among enterprises, or credit provided by shopkeepers to their customers. When information about borrowers is difficult to find, or when access to commercial banks or microcredit is unavailable, enterprises rely heavily on credit from their suppliers. Personal relationships between the purchaser and the supplier, as well as the links that result from a shared ethnic background, are critical elements of the existence of trade credit.

Stone, Levy, and Paredes (1992) describe an effective system of informal information gathering among microentrepreneurs in Brazil that, like the networks of diamond merchants in Europe, places a premium on untarnished reputation. Fafchamps (1996) compares the trade credit practices in three African countries. He finds that in countries where the manufacturing sector is relatively small (Ghana and Kenya, as opposed to Zimbabwe), credit information is available within Asian business groups, or as a result of repeated cash transactions. Using data from the World Bank's Regional Program for Enterprise Development, Biggs and Raturi (1998) empirically document how ethnic ties among Asian groups in Kenya significantly affect access to trade credit. They find that although borrowers' ethnicity is not an important determinant of access to commercial banks, more Asian- than African-owned firms give supplier credit, and that they prefer to do so within their own ethnic group, regardless of the length of the relationship between supplier and purchaser. Sanderatne (1992) reports that poor urban and rural households in Sri Lanka heavily rely on store credit, a variation on trade credit, to buy food and other provisions.

Group-Based Microfinance Programs

The peer monitoring, group lending, or "solidarity group" approach to credit delivery is based on the assumption that the poor represent a much lower credit risk than the formal financial sector generally assumes and that under specific circumstances they can be trusted to repay small uncollateralized loans. This approach uses a lending methodology that relies on traditional and personal interactions among borrowers. Group lending is the most visible—but by no means the earliest or most widespread—form of financial services for the poor, which are collectively labeled "microfinance."[10] Like the ROSCA, the group-lending technology has attracted the interest of practitioners as well as theoreticians.[11]

Although the group-based approach to lending to the poor saw a rapid expansion starting in the early 1970s, the concept is more than a century old. Woolcock (1998, p. 95) describes the conditions that led to the "first deliberate attempt to establish financial institutions with the poor in developing economies on the basis of their social, rather than their material, resources." He is referring to the "People's Banks," as the credit cooperatives that Frederick Raiffeisen created in mid-19th century Germany were collectively called. These cooperatives offer intriguing parallels with the goals, methods, and results of present-day group lending programs, as exemplified in some of the eligibility requirements for membership set forth by Raiffeisen: residence in small rural communities, trustworthiness as gauged by current members, and unlimited liability for loans of fellow members. Ghatak and Guinnane (1998) list two important differences between the People's Banks and Grameen-type models, both of which affect the role of social capital in explaining performance. The first difference is the source of funds: while some German cooperatives relied on external sources of funds for their on-lending operations, they mobilized a large part of their capital from local funds, cooperative assets, and member and nonmember deposits. The second difference relates to the duration of the group, which in the German model was a direct result of the long-term participation of members in the cooperative. In the Grameen approach, groups exist only for the duration of the extended loans, although in practice, groups that are constituted for new loans often share the same membership.[12]

The most visible and studied example of group-based lending is the Grameen Bank in Bangladesh, although many different variants of its approach have been implemented on other continents.[13] The bank was started in 1976 by Mohammad Yunus, a professor at the University of Chittagong, as a research project; by 1994 it had served half of all villages in Bangladesh. Of a total membership of more than 2 million, 94 percent are women. Small uncollateralized loans are repaid in weekly installments. Using the group-lending methodology and transparent loan decisions, the bank has consistently reported repayment rates in excess of 95 percent. (Note that microfinance specialists generally discount repayment rates as an indicator of performance of credit programs, focusing mostly on traditional financial indicators and, from the borrowers' side, the rate of return on investments they finance with the borrowed funds.) According to Khandker, Khalily, and Khan (1996), despite posting profits at the program level since 1986 (with the exception of 1992), the Grameen Bank is not yet fully independent of subsidies. Morduch (1998b) calculates that Grameen would have to raise the nominal rate on its loans from 20 percent a year to 33 percent to be able to function without subsidies. In addition, Grameen has benefited from a close relationship with the Bangladesh government—it was established by the Grameen Charter, a special decree of the Bangladesh (Central) Bank, and its board includes government officials.[14] This coproduction aspect of credit delivery systems is also described in Evans (1996). He reports on a Grameen replication model in Vietnam that apart from its high repayment rate, is characterized by the combination of preexisting relationships within the context of a close synergy with the municipal government.

Main Social Features of Group-Lending Programs and Supporting Evidence

This section describes the features of group-based lending programs that draw on social relations; it then examines the empirical role of these features in explaining the performance record of the programs and proposes additional explanations for their successes. Finally, it examines whether lending methodologies that draw on social capital–type factors reach the poorest members of their target membership.

FEATURE 1: *SELF-SELECTED, SMALL, AND HOMOGENEOUS BORROWERS' GROUPS IN DENSELY POPULATED AREAS ARE JOINTLY LIABLE FOR LOANS.*

The main constraint nonlocal lenders face in offering credit access to the poor resides in severe imperfect information problems, which Matin (1997) describes as hidden information, hidden action, and enforcement constraints.[15] The main innovation of group-based microfinance programs stems from the observation that potential customers of these programs have a comparative information advantage over the lender, which could be utilized to develop mutually advantageous financial services. As described by Matin (p. 262), joint liability

> is a contract in which the provision of the private good (for example, an individual's access to credit) is made conditional on the provision of the public good (group repayment). This is seen as an effective and less costly incentive making the borrowers use their knowledge about each other to screen the 'right' people (thereby smoothing the hidden information problem), engage in peer monitoring (thereby reducing the hidden action problem) and exert peer pressure (thereby alleviating the imperfect enforcement constraint).[16]

The combination of these three factors contributes to a cost of lending that, on average, is significantly lower than if the lender had to address each of them separately, allowing the lender to disburse larger amounts and to reach poorer people (through riskier loans) than if these factors were absent.[17]

Self-selection of group members is a major element of the group-based lending program process. Wenner (1995) finds in his study of credit groups of Costa Rica that groups that screened members according to reputation had a significantly lower delinquency level than those that did not. Similarly, Sharma and Zeller (1997) find in their empirical study of repayment performance of three group-based microfinance programs in

Bangladesh that default rates are lower for self-selected groups. In Burkina Faso, work by Kevane (1996) presents examples of ill-formed groups, several of which had been established by program officials and included members who had never met each other. Ghatak (1997) suggests that the ex ante threat of joint liability would lead to assortative matching. Hossain (1988), for example, reports that under the Grameen Bank scheme people are asked to choose as partners "like-minded people of similar economic standing who enjoy mutual trust and confidence." As a result "safe" borrowers face a lower effective interest rate compared with the risky borrowers. This, in turn, attracts "safe" borrowers back in the market, thereby improving the quality of the pool of borrowers. Self-management of groups is usually more successful than direct involvement by outsiders, although regular and sustained contact with NGO staff is a recognized element of high repayment rates, as detailed below.[18] Finally, the ability of groups to be constituted on the basis of earlier collective action (not necessarily credit-related) serves as a filtering device and increases the likelihood of good credit performance (Bratton 1986). The Bolivian BancoSol program includes groups that previously existed as ROSCAs, contributing to their high success rates as microfinance institutions.

The importance of *group size* in fostering program performance is subject to debate in the literature.[19] The Grameen Bank and most of its replications use groups of five, as a compromise between the search for economies of scale and easy enforcement of joint liability. BancoSol groups usually consist of five to seven members (Andersen and Nina 1998). Mosley and Dahal (1985) show that in a Grameen replication in Nepal, mutual trust was low in groups of more than 20 members.

Homogeneity of groups, mostly in terms of village location, gender, land-holding status, and income levels, has also been shown to be an important element of high repayment rates. While groups in Malawi often include kinship-related members (Schaefer-Kehnert 1983), Grameen does not allow members of the same family to be active in the same credit group. Using the example of Small Farmers' Development Program in Nepal, Devereux and Fishe (1993) suggest that the focus on group homogeneity helps reduce the potential for cross-subsidization between group members. They write (p. 106) that "[i]f groups are organized with non-homogeneous members, which might occur if some members misrepresent their economic status, then the potential for default or delinquency is high and the chance that the group will remain together over time is low." Conning (1996) adds that this homogeneity also relates to a relatively low covariance among the returns to borrowers' projects. [20]

The empirical evidence on the role of homogeneity in explaining group performance is mixed, however. The high level of racial and religious heterogeneity that characterizes the rural part of Arkansas where the Good Faith Fund attempted to replicate the Grameen model in 1988 is cited by Mondal and Tune (1993) as one of the reasons for the program's difficulties. Mosley (1996), however, reports the arrears rates reported by BancoSol in Bolivia between homogeneous and nonhomogeneous groups were not significantly different. He suggests that the likelihood of obtaining peer support is higher in a nonhomogeneous group. Sadoulet (1997) finds supports for this claim in a group-based microfinance program in Guatemala. He suggests that to the extent that participation in a group-lending scheme provides a forum for insurance arrangements, heterogeneity in risk can become an attractive element of the system. Similarly, a study by Zeller (1998, p. 618) of the determinants of repayment rates among 146 lending groups in Madagascar suggests that "heterogeneity in asset holdings among members, and related intragroup diversification in on- and off-farm enterprises, enables members to pool risks so as to better secure repayment of the loan."

The low level of *population density* in the Arkansas region studied by Mondal and Tune compounded the program's difficulties, as proximity among members facilitates mutual knowledge of creditworthiness and monitoring and the holding of regular meetings. In Bangladesh, Hossain (1988, p. 81) writes, "elements like taking the bank to the people and intensive interaction of bank staff with borrowers may not be appropriate and could become too costly for sparsely populated environments." Difficulties encountered by microfinance groups in setting up Grameen replications in the sparsely populated hills of Nepal help underscore the importance of high density for group lending program success.

Conning (1996) presents the theoretical argument that "social collateral" can replace individual collateral in group-based lending programs, but only under particular circumstances, and its varying presence helps explain the different success rates of lending programs. In Conning's words (p. 3),

> group borrowers must in effect meet collateral requirements not just as borrowers but also as monitors. For this reason, group loans will only be chosen over other sources of finance when group members have a decided cost advantage in monitoring and sanctioning each other relative to outside lenders and intermediaries. Borrowers will prefer to join groups where the returns to their projects are not too correlated for reasons quite apart from conventionally defined risk-sharing.

This approach highlights an important point about the cost of social capital creation in credit programs: group formation and participation are costly activities, and this fact affects the borrower's choice of credit source. Conning does not acknowledge that the borrower's choice is, in most instances, limited to traditional moneylenders or credit groups. The choice is itself simplified by two factors, the large interest rate differential in favor of the moneylender, and the observed segmentation of the credit market between moneylenders and credit groups on the basis of loan use.[21]

FEATURE 2: DENYING ACCESS TO FUTURE CREDIT TO ALL GROUP MEMBERS IN THE CASE OF DEFAULT BY ANY ONE MEMBER IS THE MOST EFFECTIVE AND LEAST COSTLY WAY OF ENFORCING JOINT LIABILITY.

Liability for loans depends on whether the loans are made to the group or directly to its members. Several studies suggest that regardless of the arrangement, *joint liability* has a positive impact on loan repayment rates. Hossain (1988) and Schaefer-Kehnert (1983) report repayment rates of 98.6 percent and 97.4 percent, respectively, in Bangladesh and Malawi, on loans made to individuals but guaranteed by the group. Tohtong (1988) reports similar rates for loans made by the Bank for Agriculture and Agricultural Cooperatives (BAAC) in Thailand under a similar arrangement. BAAC experienced less successful return rates with programs of joint liability on group loans. Bratton (1986) reports a different situation in Zimbabwe, where recovery rates were higher for group loans than for individual loans with joint liability (both were higher than the recovery rate on individual loans with individual liability), except in periods of bad harvests. According to Huppi and Feder (1990, p. 203), "if an individual repays while the majority of the group defaults, he or she would be made worse off by having paid their share and subsequently also being responsible for the share of delinquents." This observation reflects Conning's 1996 argument about the importance of low covariance among projects for repayment under joint liability. Joint liability on individual loans therefore appears in the literature as an attractive way to balance the contrary effects of peer pressure and free-riding by members. From the lenders' point of view, the most effective way to enforce joint liability would then be to deny access to future credit to all members of the group in case of default by any of its jointly liable members. This is known in the microfinance literature as the *contingent renewal principle*.

The next section examines the empirical validity of the two previously stated principles, and suggests that if social capital factors critically affect the efficacy of credit delivery programs for the poor, they do so through more channels than those described thus far.

The Mixed Evidence of the Role of Social Relations in Group-Lending Programs

The recent literature on microfinance has brought to light several findings that question or complement the role of the above two features of successful group lending in explaining claims of repayment rates above 95 percent.

It should first be mentioned, however, that there is considerable debate among practitioners about the computation and comparability of repayment rates. These rates can vary widely depending on a number of factors, particularly the proportion of the loan that needs to be reimbursed for the repayment record to remain immaculate, the length of eventual "grace periods," and the age of the groups included in the calculation. There is indeed some evidence that repayment rates decrease as the age of the borrowers' group increases, suggesting that as the end of the lending cycle nears and the marginal need for further credit decreases, individual interest in a good repayment record decreases and that group cohesion is insufficient to maintain collective repayment discipline. Hossain (1988) reports such a negative relationship between repayment performance and length of membership in several Grameen centers.

Although it is, in principle, the functional cornerstone of group-lending programs, the enforcement of *joint liability* is often limited by significant practical and political factors that do not, however, cause these programs to collapse. Several authors observe that while joint liability is widely discussed in weekly center meetings, it is not always enforced, making the threat of shared responsibility in many credit programs effectively noncredible.[22]

Jain (1996) studies the repayment history of two Grameen centers that had low repayment histories and were eventually closed, and reports that in no case were group members asked to repay the loans of defaulters, even at the cost of the closure of the center and the loss of credit access by all members in the center, including nondefaulters. Matin (1998) reports a general breakdown of joint liability in one of Grameen's oldest branches.[23] Montgomery (1996) reinforces this observation in a study of the repayment arrangements of the Bangladesh Rural Advancement Committee (BRAC): in 30 BRAC Village Organizations, made up of about 1,200 members, borrower groups did not resort to joint liability arrangements to maintain repayment discipline. Instead, defaulting borrowers relied on kin and close friends, rather than fellow borrowers, to meet weekly demands for repayment.

Failure to satisfy the demands of group-lending programs does, however, often lead to exclusion from the programs, and Montgomery provides anecdotal evidence that the poorest members face a larger risk of being subject to exclusion.[24] This finding suggests that instead of social capital being vested among peer borrowers, group-lending schemes rely heavily on traditional family and friend contacts, as mentioned previously, and that whatever social capital is developed within a Village Organization can play an exclusionary role against its poorest members.

Bennett, Goldberg, and Hunte (1996, p. 273) find that in two fledging group-based microfinance programs in Asia (RSDC in Nepal and SRSC in Pakistan), "many groups do not link access to new loans to past performance and very few actually assume credit risk for their fellow members." In another context, however, Ghatak and Guinnane (1998) provide specific examples of the actual enforcement record of German People's Banks. Since, as mentioned previously, operating funds for the cooperatives originated locally, the social pressure for repayment was significant and—although no comparative research is available—the anecdotal evidence suggests a stricter enforcement policy than observed in today's externally funded credit groups.

Several authors, including Armendáriz de Aghion and Morduch (1998), Ito (1998), and Rutherford (1996), argue that group-based microfinance programs, at least those they observed in Bangladesh, provide loans that help poor people better manage their other sources of income more often than they finance new investment projects. This observation—microfinance as an income-smoothing mechanism rather than an investment instrument—has the following implication for the role of social capital in credit provision. Almost all group-based microfinance programs are based on schedules of weekly collections of small amounts of principal and interest. Since these reimbursements usually start a few weeks after the first loan is given, only those borrowers who have access to sufficient liquidity to cover the first repayment will join the program. This suggests that these borrowers have a preexisting source of income, and that they are more interested in ensuring that income against risk by accumulating savings than they are in investing in a new business.[25] If this is the case, however, the microfinance program lends against the borrower's future income stream, rather than (or at least in addition to) the "social collateral" embodied in the joint liability clause.

In addition, the efficacy of the joint liability arrangement is sometimes affected by cultural or religious traits. The literature mentions several examples in Burkina Faso and Ireland where local norms of behavior are not naturally compatible with the importance of enforceability and credibility in financial transactions and with the concept of mutual penalties. Aryeetey (1996) suggests that in rural Africa, the pressure to repay a loan is directly linked to the fact that credit and debts are intensely private issues; pressure is therefore most effective because of the borrower's risk of being exposed as a debtor. Hence, under credit mechanisms that are communal and transparent, such as group lending, the shame of being exposed is diminished, along with the collective pressure to repay.

As a note of caution, it is important to recognize that empirical observations of credit programs are somewhat limited in pinpointing the actual role of joint liability in repayment records. When repayment is regular, it is by definition difficult to demonstrate this role. Moreover, the mixed evidence regarding actual enforcement of joint liability does not necessarily mean that the arrangement is ineffective.

Although the literature generally recognizes that *contingent renewal* is a much stronger incentive for repayment than joint liability, it has proven difficult to separate the efficacy of the two concepts. Indeed, if group members do not find threats of denial of future credit credible, joint liability loses most of its incentive power.[26] Weak enforcement of joint liability should therefore be observed concurrently with low occurrence of exclusion of defaulting members. Matin and Sinha (1998) found that in four Bangladeshi villages, very few microfinance customers thought that their chances of getting another loan depended on the performance of other members of their groups.

Matin (1998, p. 69) indicates that in his survey of Grameen,

> [t]here was a total of 81 groups [405 members] in the centres surveyed. Of these, there were only two groups where none of the members had any overdue loan at the time of survey. In about 35 percent of the groups, all the members had overdue loans. Despite this, borrowers [who had] outstanding loans, got a repeat loan from the bank.... [T]he bank sees [this] as an important way to contain the repayment crisis. As one bank staff put it, "You never solve a repayment crisis by withholding future access to loans. It is by ensuring future access that you might have a chance of solving it. If borrowers know that default does not carry any penalty and that they might not get further loans even if they cleared their loan, because of the group or because they have another overdue loan, they will simply not repay anything."

These observations reflect the fact that enforcing the termination threat is costly for the lender, as well as the borrower; renegotiation, delaying future loans, or manipulating their size are more likely outcomes in default situations. Enforcement of contingent renewal strategies on groups is also damaging to the credibility and political attractiveness of credit programs. Denial of future loans to the group if one individual defaults hurts the other members of the group who may be perfectly suitable clients, especially if the default results from an illness or a family crisis. In addition, strict enforcement affects a larger number of customers than in individual loan programs, since all group members' access to credit can be damaged by the actions of only one member. This is a real concern for group-based microfinance programs whose success is, in part, judged on the basis of large and growing memberships. These demands presumably affect the staff's handling of default cases.

To the extent that credit programs are run by NGOs characterized by a strong poverty alleviation goal (as is almost always the case), the potential effect of contingent renewal enforcement limits the lender's incentive to use this central element of repayment discipline as often as the risk of default would require it. The political cost of enforcing repayment by imposing sanctions on the poor also suggests why government-run group-based programs have a generally mixed performance record. Finally, rigorous enforcement of joint liability is not without social costs. The combination of these costs helps explain why group-based microfinance organizations are not always eager to enforce the two central elements of their methodology, joint liability and contingent renewal, suggesting that other social factors may be directly involved in explaining their continuing success.

Additional Social Elements of Group-Based Microfinance Programs

If, as the above evidence suggests, the two main features of group-based lending programs (joint liability and contingent renewal) are not always enforced, what compensating factors help explain their very high repayment rates? And do these factors feature social capital–type characteristics?

The first of the compensating factors involves the continuous relationship between program officers and the borrowers.[27] As a result of the weekly meetings between the loan officer and the borrowers, personal relationships between them develop. Woolcock (1999) observes that Grameen Bank loan officers are often called upon to assume the roles of marriage counselor, conflict negotiator, training officer, and civic leader. At the same time, the loan officer gradually acquires information about the borrowers' creditworthiness, which can be used in enforcing repayment schedules and other program decisions.

The second factor that helps explain why programs that do not strictly enforce their two main features remain successful relates to a—presumably unwitting—recreation of the traditional patron-client relationship (that is, vertical social capital) between loan officers and borrowers. Ito (1998, p. 9) writes that

fellow members of the same centre are loosely united with a sense of serving a common "patron" whose discretionary power to sanction loan applications serves them as the biggest incentive to act as they are expected to. In such a patron-client relationship, [Grameen] bank workers who are under tremendous pressure to maintain high repayment rates often pass this pressure on to bank members, who will then be forced into demonstrating their allegiance to their "patron" through exercising peer pressure on problematic members.[28]

Finally, Jain (1996, p. 83) suggests that the main function of Grameen groups and centers is to foster a culture wherein both the members and the loan officers follow the Grameen norms as a matter of routine or "cultural habit," as a result of "the repetition of identical behavior by all 30 members, week after week, 52 times a year." Similarly, the success of group-based microfinance organizations in instilling a common sense of duty and purpose among their staff (or "corporate culture") is another indication that social capital plays a distinct role in credit programs that target the poor, although not always and not necessarily—or directly— through its impact on peer pressure and joint liability schemes.

Credit for the Poorest?

Previous sections of this annex have presented evidence that social networks are important elements of most types of formal or informal programs that provide credit access to the poor. Regardless of the arrangements through which they combine borrowers and lenders, these networks achieve the enviable goal of closing a gap in the financial structure that commercial banks are unwilling or unable to fill. Some evidence suggests, however, that they have not been successful at completely closing this gap and that the poorest members of society often still do not have access to microfinance services.

If faced with an income-smoothing system, as described earlier, that requires regular repayments on a loan long before the investment creates a return, the most risk-averse—often the poorest—among the potential customers will not consider membership in a group-lending program. Hashemi (1997) reports the results of an exercise conducted in four villages where Grameen and the Bangladesh Rural Advancement Committee are active. This exercise was meant to determine why households targeted for membership in the programs chose not to join. Forty-nine percent of the nonparticipating respondents cited concern about not being able to repay the loan and being burdened with another debt as the major reason for not joining. Very poor village members who do apply for membership have little chance of being accepted as part of a joint liability group under a situation where entrepreneurial ability matters less than preexisting income in the screening process (Ito 1998). In addition, the costs faced by the lender when trying to overcome the poorest's aversion to repayment risk often require subsidization, an option that is increasingly unattractive to microfinance organizations and donors (Morduch 1998a). Finally, and as mentioned previously, screening processes tend to be more rigorous in indigenous credit programs that depend exclusively on local sources of funds (such as ROSCAs), and hence the poorest are even less likely to have access to credit under such programs.

Conclusion

An important determinant of the role of social ties that emerges from the literature is the existence and durability of credit systems characterized by the closeness of the borrowers to the source of funds (and, in a related fashion, the endogeneity of the lending methodology). When the credit provider is closely related to the borrower (and, presumably, the arrangement between them is of their own design), the role of interpersonal ties is a central element in ensuring repayment. When, conversely, there is no a priori relationship between the borrower(s) and the lender (and, as is often the case, the lending arrangements are extraneously proposed by the lender to the borrower), social factors are less likely to be central elements in explaining credit discipline, and their mobilization requires significantly more effort.[29] This gradation helps explain why ROSCAs, which are based on indigenous structures and are internally funded, rely on social pressure among the lenders-borrowers to guarantee financial discipline to a much larger extent than group-based lending programs. The 19th century German credit cooperatives represent a middle ground between these two situations: although they used joint liability mechanisms to ensure repayment, most of their operating funds were provided locally. Not surprisingly, their repayment records—at least based on the available anecdotal evidence—were very high.

The literature also suggests that the use of existing social ties improves access to credit for the poor, but that it does so through various channels whose relative importance is subject to significant debate. This finding is especially true in view of the large variations in geographical, economic, social, and political settings in which these lending programs operate. There is little doubt that social connections among borrowers in group-lending schemes allow for significant economies in screening, mutual monitoring, and enforcement. The importance of these connections in ensuring repayment through peer pressure, however, is the source of much controversy in the literature. Indeed, joint liability and contingent renewal, the two main instruments of peer pressure for repayment, are often imperfectly enforced by lenders, hence damaging the credibility of the system with the borrowers. Yet this breakdown in one of the main tenets of the group-based approach does not necessarily result in the institutional weaknesses or failings that should be expected to follow.

The imperfect correlation between enforcement and program success suggests that in addition to the well-documented interborrower relations, other factors help account for high repayment rates; in particular the quality of the relationship between the borrowers and the lender organization's staff plays a role that has been underrepresented in the literature. A critical element of program success is the existence of trust between borrowers and lenders, which is in large part created and maintained by the predictable and transparent application of the lender's rules. Implicit or unconscious reliance on traditional patron-client relationships between loan agents and borrowers reinforces adherence to the program's rules, even if they are not consistently enforced. In addition, the "corporate culture" among the staff of the lender organization also appears to be a critical element of program performance. The capacity of microfinance organizations to instill high levels of trust and mutual support among their field workers is one of the main characteristics of their operations, and that in turn reflects their ability to draw successfully on the diverse social elements of their environment in developing successful programs of credit delivery for the poor. Such programs, however, have not been fully successful at harnessing these social elements to ensure that the poorest members of the communities in which they operate are given equal access to credit.

Notes

1. Stiglitz and Weiss's (1981) paper on incomplete information equilibrium in credit markets has served as the theoretical background for many empirical inquiries into credit market interactions. Stiglitz (1990, p. 238) writes: "Unless new institutions find substitutes for the mechanisms used by the moneylenders to overcome the problems of screening, incentives and enforcement, the moneylenders' power is unlikely to be broken by the entry of institutional credit."

2. In a number of developing countries, access to commercial credit (or favorable lending terms) can often be secured through personal relationships between borrowers and bank managers. Although these relationships testify to personal relations that are, at times, sufficiently strong to result in extralegal transactions, they will not be covered in this annex, which focuses on finance that targets the poor.

3. This classification was inspired in part by Michael Woolcock's doctoral dissertation (1998).

4. The concept of ROSCA is known as *pasanaku* in Bolivia, *njangeh* in Cameroon, *susu* in Ghana, *chit fund* in India, *arisan* in Indonesia, *partners* in Jamaica, *kye* in Korea, *tontine* in Senegal, and *cheetu* in Sri Lanka. Under their different formats,

ROSCAs have been extensively studied by anthropologists, economists, and sociologists.

5. This observation highlights one of the persistent riddles in the literature on social capital: is trust a left- or right-hand side variable? Collier (1998, p. 7) presents an attractive solution to the puzzle: "[trust] is an intermediate variable, produced by S[ocial] I[nteraction] and producing a reduction in transactions costs, but its durability gives it the property of capital."

6. Van den Brink and Chavas (1997) also describe a "trouble bank" from which ROSCA members can borrow to cover their contribution to the fund. Similar emergency funds for Indonesian ROSCAs are described by Hospes (1992). Other means of avoiding default include adjusting the order of rotation so that high-risk members are moved toward the end of the cycle, or taking one high-risk member's desired commodity and keeping it as collateral until the end of the rotation.

7. Because of a programmatic focus on poverty alleviation and correspondingly strict targeting principles, most group-based microfinance organizations exclusively serve the poor's financial needs.

8. Adams (1992) mentions a ROSCA operating in 1987 among employees, all holders of doctoral degrees, of the International Monetary Fund.

9. For descriptions of moneylending practices in Africa, see Adegboye (1969) and Udry (1990).

10. "Microfinance" is a more recent concept than "microcredit." It was developed in the early 1990s to include both the borrowing (microcredit) and deposit-taking (microsavings) aspects of financial services for the poor.

A number of microfinance programs, such as Bank Rakyat Indonesia (BRI) and Badan Kredit Kecamatan (BKK) in Indonesia, are based on individual-liability loans. They feature repayment rates comparable to those of group-lending systems, suggesting that more is at play in explaining high repayment performance than social networks among borrowers. These programs build on preexisting relationships within communities, by using the testimony of a respected community figure as collateral on the borrower's loan. The three largest microfinance programs in Indonesia, BRI, BKK, and Badan Kredit Desa (BKD), built their successful lending programs on this type of social collateral (Robinson 1992, 1994). This arrangement is apparently specific to Indonesia, according to Armendáriz de Aghion and Morduch (1998, pp. 5–6), who attribute it to a "long history of strong but decentralized village government structures on which programs like the BKD can piggy-back—and replication has not been attempted elsewhere."

11. For theoretical approaches to the role of groups in addressing imperfect information and transaction costs in credit delivery, see, for example, Banerjee, Besley, and Guinnane (1994); Besley and Coate (1995); Conning (1997); Devereux and Fishe (1993); Madajewicz (1997); Stiglitz (1990); Stiglitz and Weiss (1981); and Varian (1990).

12. For more information on the German precursor of the approach to banking for the poor, see Tilly (1989).

13. According to Pitt and Khandker (1995), group-based lending programs have shown promising results in Bangladesh, Cameroon, Malawi, Malaysia, and Korea. The methodology has proven less successful in Egypt, India, Kenya, Lesotho, and Venezuela. Group-lending methodologies have also been introduced in poor areas of industrial countries, where they have met with mixed success.

Severens and Kays (1997) have identified 328 microenterprise lending programs in 47 states in the United States in 1995. Eighty-five percent of these programs were less than 10 years old, but in that relatively short period of time, they had collectively lent $126 million to 171,555 people. According to Light and Pham (1998), about 20 percent of these programs in the United States use a group-lending methodology; others are based on individual loans. Among the former group, the relatively short track record of the Women's Self-Employment Project in Chicago is more promising than that of most other group-based credit programs in the United States, whose performance has been much less effective than that of the model in Bangladesh. Balkin (1993, pp. 253–54) suggests that the poor in the United States "are relatively impoverished in social capital"; Solomon (1991) notes that in the United States, the loan discipline exerted over members does not match that exhibited by Grameen.

14. While this has been presented as an example of successful public-private collaboration in the provision of credit to the poor, the inability of other microfinance organizations in Bangladesh to claim a similar status under the Grameen Charter has led some to suggest that the benefits from this coproduction scheme do not extend to all microfinance providers.

15. "Hidden action" refers to the use that the borrower makes of the loan and to the accuracy of the reporting of income from the loan-financed activity.

16. The importance of the screening-out process in the success of the group-lending approach cannot be overstated. By increasing their attention to the screening process, members decrease the need for peer monitoring and pressure at a later stage.

17. See Andersen and Nina (1998) for a theoretical demonstration of how limited joint liability group-lending reduces interest rates for clients who are not able to offer collateral.

18. These observations mirror the findings of Narayan (1995), Ostrom (1995), and Uphoff (1992) that voluntary organizations with roots in the community are more effective than externally imposed groups.

19. See examples for the Dominican Republic in Adams and Romero (1981) and Devereux and Fishe (1993); for Ghana in Owusu and Tetteh (1982); and for Zimbabwe in Bratton (1986).

20. The importance of group homogeneity, already mentioned in the section on ROSCAs, presents an intriguing counterpart to a conclusion of Grootaert's (1999) study of the determinants of household expenditures in Indonesia. According to this study, internal heterogeneity of associations—in terms of gender and educa-

tional background—improves their members' access to credit. Moreover, *within* credit groups, heterogeneity is associated with higher individual probabilities to access credit and with higher amounts received. Grootaert's data do not indicate whether such heterogeneity also affects repayment rates.

21. The overall lack of competition between established moneylenders and microfinance NGOs can be explained partly by a de facto segmentation of the market between investment and consumption financing needs, the former usually being met by NGOs and the latter by moneylenders. The relative stability of this cohabitation is exemplified by the general lack of convergence of interest rates charged by moneylenders and NGOs.

22. Inversely, weak enforcement of the contingent renewal rule adversely affects members' investment in joint liability avoidance strategies.

23. Matin (1998, p. 75) writes that "to the extent that the effectiveness of peer pressure decreases as the proportion of irregular borrowers increases, the bank will focus effort in containing irregularities by encouraging individual liability (even partial) and thereby rewarding the relatively regular borrowers. This implies that the potency of enforcing joint liability in triggering peer pressure is highest when it may be least required (i.e., when most borrowers are regular repayers) and fails when required the most."

24. BRAC's own reports indicate that the annual dropout rate from its credit program was 16 percent in 1992 and 10 percent in 1993, although it is difficult to estimate the proportion of these rates that results from exclusionary peer pressure.

25. In effect, they are borrowing against future savings, which likens them to ROSCA members. This observation, made by Rutherford (1996), is consistent with the previous mention of the earlier incarnation of some BancoSol groups as ROSCAs. Ito (1998) points out that Grameen-type loans are not intrinsically conducive to the start-up of new businesses. The small size of the loan, the weekly repayment schedule and meeting obligation, and the inflexible reimbursement schedule represent significant constraints to the development of business projects that are generally risky and do not usually produce quick returns.

26. Similarly, and as Huppi and Feder (1990) point out, contingent renewal has a positive effect on repayments only as long as borrowers believe that the majority of their peers will also repay and that the lender is in a position to provide continued access to credit in the future to "good" clients.

27. As Kähkönen suggests in her review of the literature on social capital and water delivery in annex 3, vertical relationships between providers and users are as important to the success of delivery programs as relationships within user associations.

28. The combination of an individual relationship (which itself leads to less imperfect creditworthiness information) with a patron-client style of dependence presents an interesting parallel between microfinance programs and traditional moneylending activities.

29. The mobilization of savings both from members and the general public by credit organizations blurs the line between these two extreme situations. As a larger part of the organization's capital comes from its members, and less from donors, the role of social ties in enforcing repayment discipline would be expected to increase. It would be interesting to conduct research linking the share of internally generated loanable funds to the enforcement of joint liability arrangements and repayment performance.

References

Adams, Dale W. 1992. "Taking a Fresh Look at Informal Finance." In Dale W. Adams and Delbert Fitchett, eds., *Informal Finance in Low-Income Countries*. Boulder, Colo.: Westview Press.

Adams, Dale W., and M. L. Canavesi de Sahonero. 1989. "Rotating Savings and Credit Associations in Bolivia." *Savings and Development* 13: 219–36.

Adams, Dale W., and A. A. P. Romero. 1981. "Group Lending to the Rural Poor in the Dominican Republic: A Stunted Innovation." *Canadian Journal of Agricultural Economics* 29: 217–24.

Adegboye, R. O. 1969. "Procuring Loans by Pledging Cocoa Trees." *Journal of the Geographical Association of Nigeria* 12: 63–76.

Andersen, Lykke E., and Osvaldo Nina. 1998. "Micro-Credit and Group Lending: The Collateral Effect." Working Paper 1998–18. University of Aarhus, Department of Economics, Denmark.

Armendáriz de Aghion, Beatriz, and Jonathan Morduch. 1998. "Microfinance beyond Group Lending." Princeton University, Department of Economics, Princeton, N.J. Processed.

Aryeetey, Ernest. 1996. "Rural Finance in Africa: Institutional Development and Access for the Poor." Paper presented to the Annual World Bank Conference on Development Economics, April 25–26, Washington, D.C. Processed.

Balkin, Steven. 1993. "A Grameen Bank Replication: The Full Circle Fund of the Women's Self-Employment Project in Chicago." In Abu Wahid, ed., *The Grameen Bank: Poverty Relief in Bangladesh*. Boulder, Colo.: Westview Press.

Banerjee, Abhijit V., Timothy Besley, and Timothy W. Guinnane. 1994. "Thy Neighbor's Keeper: The Design of a Credit Cooperative with a Theory and a Test." *Quarterly Journal of Economics* 109 (2): 491–515.

Begashaw, G. 1978. "The Economic Role of Traditional Savings and Credit Institutions in Ethiopia." *Savings and Development* 4: 249–62.

Bennett, Lynn, Mike Goldberg, and Pamela Hunte. 1996. "Ownership and Sustainability: Lessons on Group-Based Financial Services from South Asia." *Journal of International Development* 8 (2): 271–88.

Besley, Timothy, and Stephen Coate. 1995. "Group Lending, Repayment Incentives, and Social Collateral." *Journal of Development Economics* 46 (1): 1–18.

Besley, Timothy, Stephen Coate, and Glenn C. Loury. 1993. "The Economics of Rotating Savings and Credit Associations." *American Economic Review* 83 (4): 792–810.

Besson, Jean. 1995. "Women's Use of ROSCAs in the Caribbean: Reassessing the Literature." In Shirley Ardener and Sandra Burman, eds., *Money-Go-Rounds: The Importance of Rotating Savings and Credit Associations for Women*. Washington, D.C.: Berg.

Biggs, Tyler, and Mayank Raturi. 1998. "Ethnic Ties and Access to Credit: Evidence from the Manufacturing Sector in Kenya." World Bank, Africa Region, Washington, D.C. Processed.

Bratton, Michael. 1986. "Financing Smallholder Production: A Comparison of Individual and Group Credit Schemes in Zimbabwe." *Public Administration and Development* 6 (2): 115–32.

Coleman, James. 1988. "Social Capital in the Creation of Human Capital." *American Journal of Sociology* 94 (Supplement): S95–S120.

Collier, Paul. 1998. "Social Capital and Poverty." Social Capital Initiative Working Paper 4. World Bank, Social Development Department, Washington, D.C.

Conning, Jonathan. 1996. "Financial Contracting and Intermediary Structures in a Rural Credit Market in Chile: A Theoretical and Empirical Analysis." Ph.D. diss. Yale University, Department of Economics, New Haven, Conn. Processed.

————. 1997. "Peer-Monitoring, Joint-Liability, and the Creation of Social Collateral." Williams College, Department of Economics, Williamstown, Mass. Processed.

Devereux, John, and Raymond P. H. Fishe. 1993. "An Economic Analysis of Group-Lending Programs in Developing Countries." *Developing Economies* 31 (1): 102–21.

Evans, Peter. 1996. "Government Action, Social Capital, and Development: Reviewing the Evidence on Synergy." *World Development* 24 (6): 1119–32.

Fafchamps, Marcel. 1996. "Market Emergence, Trust, and Regulation." Stanford University, Department of Economics, Stanford, Calif. Processed.

Ghatak, Maitreesh. 1997. "Joint Liability Group-Lending Contracts and the Peer Selection Effects." University of Chicago, Department of Economics, Chicago. Processed.

Ghatak, Maitreesh, and Timothy W. Guinnane. 1998. "The Economics of Lending with Joint Liability: A Review of Theory and Practice." Yale University, Department of Economics, New Haven, Conn. Processed.

Grootaert, Christiaan. 1999. "Social Capital, Household Welfare, and Poverty in Indonesia." Local Level Institutions Working Paper 6. World Bank, Social Development Department, Washington, D.C.

Hashemi, Syed Mesbahuddin. 1997. "Those Left Behind: A Note on Targeting the Hardcore Poor." In Geoffrey Wood and Iffath A. Sharif, eds., *Who Needs Credit: Poverty and Finance in Bangladesh.* London: Zed Books.

Hospes, Otto. 1992. "Evolving Forms of Informal Finance in an Indonesian Town." In Dale W. Adams and Delbert Fitchett, eds., *Informal Finance in Low-Income Countries.* Boulder, Colo.: Westview Press.

Hossain, Mahabub. 1988. *Credit for the Alleviation of Rural Poverty: The Grameen Bank in Bangladesh.* Washington, D.C.: International Food Policy Research Institute.

Huppi, Monika, and Gershon Feder. 1990. "The Role of Groups and Credit Cooperatives in Rural Lending." *World Bank Research Observer* 5 (2): 187–204.

Ito, Sanae. 1998. "The Grameen Bank and Peer Monitoring: A Sociological Perspective." Working Paper 3. University of Sussex, Institute of Development Studies, Brighton, U.K.

Izumida, Yoichi. 1992. "The Kou in Japan: A Precursor of Modern Finance." In Dale W. Adams and Delbert Fitchett, eds., *Informal Finance in Low-Income Countries*. Boulder, Colo.: Westview Press.

Jain, Pankaj S. 1996. "Managing Credit for the Rural Poor: Lessons from the Grameen Bank." *World Development* 24 (1): 79–89.

Kevane, Michael. 1996. "Qualitative Impact of Study of 'Credit with Education' in Burkina Faso." Freedom for Hunger Research Paper 3. Santa Clara University, Department of Economics, Davis, Calif.

Khandker, Shahidur R., M. A. Baqui Khalily, and Zahed H. Khan. 1996. "Grameen Bank—Performance and Sustainability." Discussion Paper 306. World Bank, Washington, D.C.

Light, Ivan, and Michelle Pham. 1998. "Microcredit and Informal Credit in the United States: New Strategies for Economic Development." University of California, Department of Sociology, Los Angeles.

Madajewicz, Malgosia. 1997. "Capital for the Poor: The Role of Monitoring." Harvard University, Department of Economics, Cambridge, Mass. Processed.

Maloney, Charles, and A. Ahmed. 1988. *Rural Savings and Credit in Bangladesh*. Dhaka: University Press.

Matin, Imran. 1997. "The Renegotiation of Joint Liability: Notes from Madhupur." In Geoffrey Wood and Iffath A. Sharif, eds., *Who Needs Credit: Poverty and Finance in Bangladesh*. London: Zed Books.

———. 1998. "Rapid Credit Deepening and the Joint Liability Credit Contract: A Study of Grameen Bank Borrowers in Madhupur." Ph.D. diss. University of Sussex, Institute of Development Studies, Brighton, U.K. Processed.

Matin, Imran, and Saurabh Sinha. 1998. "Informal Credit Transactions of Microcredit Borrowers in Rural Bangladesh." *IDS Bulletin* 29 (4): 66–80.

Mondal, Wali, and Annie Tune. 1993. "Replicating the Grameen Bank in North America: The Good Faith Fund Experience." In Abu Wahid, ed., *The Grameen Bank: Poverty Relief in Bangladesh*. Boulder, Colo.: Westview Press.

Montgomery, Richard. 1996. "Disciplining or Protecting the Poor? Avoiding the Social Costs of Peer Pressure in Micro-Credit Schemes." *Journal of International Development* 8 (20): 289–305.

Morduch, Jonathan. 1998a. *The Microfinance Promise*. Stanford, Calif.: Stanford University Press.

———. 1998b. *The Grameen Bank: A Financial Reckoning*. Princeton, N.J.: Princeton University Press.

Mosley, Paul. 1996. "Metamorphosis from NGO to Commercial Bank: The Case of BancoSol in Bolivia." In David Hulme and Paul Mosley, eds., *Finance Against Poverty*, vol. 2. London: Routledge.

Mosley, Paul, and Rudra Prasad Dahal. 1985. "Lending to the Poorest: Early Lessons from the Small Farmers' Development Programme, Nepal." *Development Policy Review* 3 (2): 193–207.

Narayan, Deepa. 1995. "Designing Community-Based Development." Environment Department Paper 7. World Bank, Washington, D.C.

Onchan, Tongroj. 1992. "Informal Rural Finance in Thailand." In Dale W. Adams and Delbert Fitchett, eds., *Informal Finance in Low-Income Countries*. Boulder, Colo.: Westview Press.

Ostrom, Elinor. 1995. "Incentives, Rules of the Game, and Development." In M. Bruno and Boris Pleskovic, eds., *Annual World Bank Conference on Development Economics 1995*. Washington, D.C.: World Bank.

Owusu, K. O., and W. Tetteh. 1982. "An Experiment in Agricultural Credit: The Small Farmer Group-Lending Programme in Ghana (1969–1980)." *Savings and Development* 6 (1): 67–85.

Pitt, Mark M., and Shahidur R. Khandker. 1995. "The Impact of Group-Based Credit Programs on Poor Households in Bangladesh: Does the Gender of Participants Matter?" Department of Economics Working Paper 95–39. Brown University, Providence, R.I.

Robinson, Marguerite S. 1992. "Rural Financial Intermediation: Lessons from Indonesia, Part I: The Bank Rakyat Indonesia: Rural Banking

1970–1991." HIID Development Discussion Paper 434. Harvard Institute for International Development, Cambridge, Mass.

————. 1994. "Savings Mobilization and Microenterprise Finance: The Indonesian Experience." In Maria Otero and Elisabeth Rhyne, eds., *The New World of Microenterprise Finance: Building Healthy Financial Institutions for the Poor*. West Hartford, Conn.: Kumarian Press.

Rutherford, Stuart. 1996. "A Critical Typology of Financial Services for the Poor." ACTIONAID Working Paper 1. ACTIONAID, London.

————. 2000. *The Poor and Their Money*. Delhi: Oxford University Press.

Sadoulet, Loïc. 1997. "The Role of Insurance in Group Lending." Princeton University, Department of Economics, Princeton, N.J. Processed.

Sanderatne, Nimal. 1992. "Informal Finance in Sri Lanka." In Dale W. Adams and Delbert Fitchett, eds., *Informal Finance in Low-Income Countries*. Boulder, Colo.: Westview Press.

Schaefer-Kehnert, Walter. 1983. "Success with Group Lending in Malawi." In J. D. Von Pischke, Dale W. Adams, and Gordon Donald, eds., *Rural Financial Markets in Developing Countries*. Washington, D.C.: World Bank.

Severens, C. Alexander, and Amy J. Kays. 1997. *1996 Directory of U.S. Microenterprise Programs*. Washington, D.C.: Aspen Institute.

Sharma, Manahar, and Manfred Zeller. 1997. "Repayment Performance in Group-Based Credit Programs in Bangladesh: An Empirical Analysis." *World Development* 25 (10): 1731–42.

Solomon, Lewis. 1991. *Microenterprise: Human Reconstruction in America's Inner Cities*. Internet: http://www.dlcppi.org/texts/social/microent.txt.

Stiglitz, Joseph E. 1990. "Peer Monitoring and Credit Markets." *World Bank Economic Review* 4 (3): 351–66.

Stiglitz, Joseph E., and Andrew Weiss. 1981. "Credit Rationing in Markets with Imperfect Information." *American Economic Review* 71 (3): 393–410.

Stone, Andrew, Brian Levy, and Ricardo Paredes. 1992. "Public Institutions and Private Transactions: The Legal and Regulatory Environment for Business Transactions in Brazil and Chile." Policy Research Working Paper 891. World Bank, Washington, D.C.

Tilly, Richard. 1989. "Banking Institutions in Historical and Comparative Perspective: Germany, Great Britain, and the United States in the Nineteenth and Early Twentieth Century." *Journal of Institutional and Theoretical Economics* 145: 189–209.

Timberg, Thomas A., and C. V. Aiyar. 1984. "Informal Credit Markets in India." *Economic Development and Cultural Change* 33: 43–59.

Tohtong, C. 1988. "Joint-Liability Groups for Small-Farmer Credit: The BAAC Experience in Thailand." *Rural Development in Practice* 1 (1): 4–7.

Udry, Christopher. 1990. "Credit Markets in Northern Nigeria: Credit as Insurance in a Rural Economy." *World Bank Economic Review* 4 (3): 251–70.

Uphoff, Norman. 1992. *Learning from Gal Oya: Possibilities for Participatory Development and Post-Newtonian Social Science.* Ithaca, N.Y.: Cornell University Press.

Van den Brink, Rogier, and Jean-Paul Chavas. 1997. "The Microeconomics of an Indigenous African Institution: The Rotating Savings and Credit Association." *Economic Development and Cultural Change* 45: 745–72.

Varian, Hal R. 1990. "Monitoring Agents with Other Agents." *Journal of Institutional and Theoretical Economics* 146 (1): 153–74.

Wenner, Mark D. 1995. "Group Credit: A Means to Improve Information Transfer and Loan Repayment Performance." *Journal of Development Studies* 32 (20): 263–81.

Woolcock, Michael. 1998. "Social Theory, Development Policy, and Poverty Alleviation: A Comparative Historical Analysis of Group-Based Banking in Developing Economies." Ph.D. Diss. Brown University, Department of Sociology, Providence, R.I. Processed.

———. 1999. "Learning from Failures in Microfinance: What Unsuccessful Cases Tell Us about How Group-Based Programs Work." *American Journal of Economics and Sociology* 58 (1): 17-42.

Zeller, Manfred. 1998. "Determinants of Repayment Performance in Credit Groups: The Role of Program Design, Intragroup Risk Pooling, and Social Cohesion." *Economic Development and Cultural Change* 46 (3): 599–620.

Annex 3
Does Social Capital Matter in the Delivery of Water and Sanitation?

Satu Kähkönen

Failure of the state and the private sector to provide adequate levels of water and sanitation services in many developing countries has in the past two decades led to the adoption of a community-based approach to water and sanitation delivery. This approach calls for cooperation between the government and community in the delivery of water and sanitation. By emphasizing demand-led design of services and community management of water and sanitation systems, this approach represents a dramatic shift from the traditional top-down, state-centered approach to water and sanitation management.[1] The community-based approach is argued to have three benefits: it provides a means to tailor the water and sanitation systems to communities' needs and preferences by involving users in the system design; it enables the use of local resources (such as labor and materials) by involving users in construction and system management, thereby alleviating fiscal pressures on government; and it increases transparency and accountability in resource use by increasing the flow of information and interaction between system users and the government (Isham and Kähkönen 1998a, Korten 1986).

Community management of water and sanitation systems requires a group effort. Community members are expected to act collectively and design, construct, operate, and maintain the systems together. For this purpose, they are expected to build up a network or an association of users that coordinates and regulates the actions of different community members for system management. Community members are thus made to work together and rely on one another for the provision of water and sanitation.

How effectively the community acts as a group and provides the services has been argued to depend, among other things, on certain aspects of the social structure of the community, in particular, the social and economic homogeneity of users, and the existence of other social networks, associations, and trust between households. The cooperation, networks, and associations established among users and other stakeholders for water and sanitation delivery and the above-mentioned elements of the social structure that affect the relations among people are referred to as social capital in this annex.[2]

The objective of this annex is to explore the role of social capital in community-based rural water and urban sanitation delivery. This is done by reviewing the existing empirical literature on the impact of social capital on irrigation management, rural drinking water delivery, and urban sanitation. The annex reviews the performance of efforts that rely on the cooperation of users to deliver water and sanitation and the factors that influence that cooperation.

Irrigation and drinking water delivery are traditionally dealt with separately because of the different nature of these goods and their different economic and social contexts. Both irrigation and access to safe drinking water have an impact on welfare, but through different routes: irrigation is a critical input in agricultural production affecting welfare through increased yields, while access to safe drinking water affects welfare primarily by reducing water-borne diseases and infections. At the same time, there are similarities between irrigation and rural drinking water delivery, as manifested by the application of the community-based approach to the delivery of both services.

The review of existing literature indicates that the community-based approach that empowers users to collectively design and manage water and sanitation systems has a lot of promise. The systems built following that approach generally perform better than systems built and managed by government alone. However, cooperation and collective action among users is not always forthcoming. Several factors have been shown to influence the success of communal cooperation. One of these factors is social capital in the community—for instance, in the form of other community groups, networks, and associations, and mutual trust among users. Social and economic homogeneity of users also has been shown to have a positive impact on user cooperation. In these instances, people tend to know one another, be accustomed to working together, and share social norms, all of which makes collective action easier. Social capital alone, however, does not ensure that the water system performs well. A host of other factors, such as actions of the government, appropriateness of technology used, technical skills of users, access to spare parts, and legal recognition of user groups, have been shown to have a critical bearing on the performance of collective effort.

This annex contains three self-contained sections that can be read independently: (1) a review of the empirical evidence on the influence of social capital on irrigation management, (2) a description of the impact of social capital on rural drinking water delivery, and (3) a discussion of the influence of social capital on urban sanitation.

Social Capital and Irrigation Management

The performance of many large-scale, government-managed irrigation systems has fallen short of expectations; the provision of irrigation water has been inadequate and its allocation unsatisfactory. Faulty design and construction, ineffective operation, and insufficient maintenance have led to poor performance of systems (Ascher and Healy 1990; Chambers 1988; Ostrom, Schroeder, and Wynne 1993; Subramanian, Jagannathan, and Meinzen-Dick 1997).

The nature of irrigation services complicates their management and often leads to conflicts in water allocation and inadequate system operation and maintenance. First, irrigation services are rival: the use of water by one farmer reduces the amount available to others, since the flow of water available at any one time in an irrigation system is limited. This implies that it is essential to have a fair and transparent system to allocate water among irrigators to avoid conflicts. Second, irrigation services are nonexcludable. Once the irrigation system has been constructed, its large size and other factors make it costly to exclude farmers from using it and from drawing more water than the allotted amount.[3] Thus, even if an allocation system were in place, illegal water drawing could distort it. Indeed, to increase their access to water, especially in large-scale government projects, farmers commonly construct illegal outlets, break padlocks, draw off water at night, and bribe officials to issue more water (Chambers 1980). The combination of these two characteristics—rivalry and nonexcludability—leads to Hardin's (1968) "tragedy of commons" in irrigation: inefficient use of irrigation water and lack of maintenance of the irrigation system; irrigators compete for water but have no incentives to contribute to maintenance, since they cannot easily be excluded from the use of the system even if they are not contributing.

As a response to poor performance of large-scale, government-managed irrigation systems, donors and national governments have begun to advocate community management of irrigation systems at the watercourse level. While community management of small-scale irrigation systems has been prevalent for decades, involvement of users in the management of large-scale systems has been rare. This change in approach has meant shifting the emphasis in irrigation projects from the engineering designs to the organization of farmers in order to make the most effective use of irrigation systems (Ostrom 1992).

Involving farmers in system management is viewed as a way to ensure their cooperation, improve the provision and allocation of irrigation water, and maintain the system. System users are considered to be in a better position than government officials to craft and enforce a fair water allocation system and create mechanisms to curb illegal use, given the existing social networks and connections among them. The Asian Development Bank (1973, p. 50), for example, writes:

> The success of an irrigation project depends largely on the active participation and cooperation of individual farmers. Therefore, a group such as a farmers' association should be organized, preferably at the farmers' initiative or if necessary, with initial government assistance, to help in attaining the objectives of the irrigation project. Irrigation technicians alone cannot satisfactorily operate and maintain the system.

Empirical evidence indicates that community management indeed improves the performance of irrigation systems and that community-managed systems tend to work better than government-managed schemes. For example, Lam (1998) reports that in Nepal, an average community-managed irrigation system is better maintained, delivers water more effectively, and ensures higher agricultural productivity than an average government-managed system. According to Cernea (1987), the establishment of farmer organizations in the San Lorenzo irrigation project in Peru has helped improve the maintenance of the system and increase agricultural productivity. In the Mexico Third Irrigation Project, farmers who are members of local irrigation groups have experienced a threefold increase in average farm income (Cernea 1987). Uphoff (2000) reports that the introduction of farmer organizations for decisionmaking, resource mobilization, management, communication, and conflict resolution has turned the Gal Oya irrigation system, once known to be the most deteriorated and disorganized irrigation system in Sri Lanka, into one of the most efficient and most cooperatively managed systems. Community management of irrigation has increased the production of rice per unit of irrigation water by about 300 percent. According to Uphoff, at least two-thirds of this increase results from the creation of new roles and social relationships and from the activation of certain norms and attitudes among irrigators.

Although promising, community management is not a panacea. Community management of irrigation requires collective action of irrigators, which is not automatic. Farmers who use the system need to act as a group, make decisions about the water allocation, and organize the operation and maintenance of the system. Typically, irrigators in each community form an irrigation association to manage the system.[4] However, since irrigation services are rival and nonexcludable, each irrigator still has an incentive to free-ride on others' efforts, if given a chance. Irrigators will act as a group and hold to their commitments only if they are provided selective incentives, that is, rewards for action or punishment for inaction (Olson 1965). The experience with community-managed irrigation projects confirms that organizing farmers is often a challenge; many irrigation projects have failed in that effort (Lam 1998, Ostrom 1992).

Factors for Success

Under what circumstances is collective action among irrigators likely to be successful—what are the needed selective incentives? A large body of literature on community-managed irrigation attempts to answer this question.

Some elements of the social structure—in particular, social and economic heterogeneity and mutual trust among irrigators—have been argued to influence the emergence and sustenance of collective action, affecting, among other things, compliance with the operational rules. Freeman and Lowdermilk (1985, p.111), for example, state:

> Compliance with organizational rules for allocation, maintenance, construction, and conflict resolution always occurs within a nested set of other social relationships—kinship, political, religious, educational, work, and recreational networks. Compliance with the rules of the local irrigation command organization will be judged not only according to the expectations of local irrigators, but also according to different sets of rules formulated for behavior in these other networks.

Although they may be established for other purposes, social networks can facilitate cooperation in irrigation. In communities with a set of dense social networks, people tend to know one another and to be accustomed to working together. This may make the organization of farmers for irrigation easier. Also, the social pressure exerted through these networks may help to deter free-riding.

These factors, along with several others either internal or external to the community, have been identified as influencing the success of collective action in irrigation. They are listed in table A3.1 and discussed at greater length below.

SIZE OF THE IRRIGATION SYSTEM. The size of the irrigation system—measured by the system area or the number of users—is commonly held to influence the success of collective action among farmers. In his theory of collective action, Olson (1965) suggests that the larger the group, the less likely it will succeed in acting collectively. As the size of the group

Table A3.1 Community-Managed Irrigation: Selected Factors Influencing Performance of Community Management

Factor	Evidence
Size of irrigation system	Dayton-Johnson (1998), Lam (1998), Tang (1992)
Operational rules of irrigation associations	Maass and Anderson (1986), Ostrom (1992)
Social homogeneity of irrigators	Fresson (1979); Lam (1998); Lowdermilk, Early, and Freeman (1978); Lynch (1988); Merrey and Wolf (1986); Tang (1992)
Economic homogeneity of irrigators	Bardhan (1995), Dayton-Johnson (1998), Lam (1998), Tang (1992)
Mutual trust among irrigators	Lam (1998)
Legal recognition of irrigation associations	Ostrom (1992); Subramanian, Jagannathan, and Meinzen-Dick (1997)
Coordination with government	Chambers (1988), Freeman and Lowdermilk (1985), Hunt (1989), Lam (1998), Wade (1994)
Water scarcity	Uphoff, Wickramasinghe, and Wijayaratna (1990); Wade (1994)

increases, the net benefits from collective action for an individual decrease as the costs of coordinating and organizing activities increase. However, Hardin (1982) and Sandler (1992) point out that the group size affects simultaneously different contexts in which individuals organize for collective action. How group size affects collective action in a particular situation is not necessarily negative but depends on the sum of these effects.

Not surprisingly, empirical evidence on the impact of system size on the performance of community-managed irrigation systems is mixed. While some studies suggest that the performance does not depend on the size of the irrigation system, others indicate the opposite.

The results of Lam (1998) and Tang (1992), for example, indicate that the size of an irrigation system is not associated with system performance. Lam explored the performance of irrigation systems in Nepal using data from 89 case studies. He converted the qualitative information in these cases into quantitative data by using a standard set of structured coding forms and then analyzed the data econometrically. He shows that the size of irrigation systems, whether measured by the system area, number of irrigators, or total length of canals, does not have a statistically significant effect on the physical condition of the system and water delivery. Tang obtains similar results. He systematically analyzed 47 case studies on community-managed irrigation systems around the world. Like Lam, he converted the qualitative information in the case studies into quantitative data by using a standard set of structured coding forms, then entered the results into a database for analysis. He finds that the size of the irrigation system, number of irrigators, and the size of the irrigated area do not have a significant relationship to the system maintenance and irrigators' compliance with rules. Similar evidence on the impact of group size has been obtained in areas other than irrigation (Esman and Uphoff 1984).

Dayton-Johnson (1998), by contrast, suggests that the size of the irrigation association—that is, the number of irrigators—influences indirectly the collective effort to manage the irrigation system by affecting the operational rules of the group. The operational rules then influence the performance of the system. His empirical analysis is based on data collected from 54 community-managed irrigation systems in the Mexican state of Guanajuato.

OPERATIONAL RULES. For the collective action of farmers to be sustainable, it is critical that these groups craft operational rules that govern the use, operation, and maintenance of the irrigation system and thus the interaction among irrigators (Ostrom 1992).[5] These rules affect the day-to-day decisions made by users about access to and allocation of water (how, when, where, and who can withdraw water); each irrigator's maintenance responsibilities (how, when, where, and who maintains the system); monitoring arrangements (who monitors the actions of irrigators, and how); and sanctions against misconduct (what rewards or sanctions will be assigned to those who obey or disobey the rules). By providing order to the operation and management of the system, these rules promote stability and help farmers plan their activities.

Irrigation associations typically draw up the operational rules. The rules may differ to some extent from season to season as the availability of water varies. A set of rules crafted during the wet season may work well when water is abundant, but not work at all during the dry season when water is scarce. In southeastern Spain, for example, irrigators have established different rules for allocating water in three different conditions of water availability: abundance, seasonal low, and extraordinary drought (Maass and Anderson 1986).

SOCIAL AND ECONOMIC HOMOGENEITY OF IRRIGATORS. Previous studies on irrigation have indicated that social and economic homogeneity of irrigators can also affect the emergence and sustenance of collective action (Singleton and Taylor 1992). Social homogeneity refers to whether irrigators are from the same village, ethnic group, kinship, caste, or religion, while economic homogeneity refers to the landholding size or income of irrigators.

It is argued that homogeneity influences the outcome of collective action by increasing the number of social ties and norms that irrigators can draw upon in building cooperation (Subramanian, Jagannathan, and Meinzen-Dick 1997). In general, the more socially or economically heterogeneous a group is, the less likely it is to organize for collective action. Heterogeneity is seen to increase potential factionalism within a group, which can be manifested in disputes or in one faction's dominance of the organization.

Social homogeneity of irrigators. A number of case studies provide anecdotal and qualitative evidence on the impact of social homogeneity of irrigators—with respect to caste, kinship, ethnic and cultural background—on the effectiveness of collective action.[6] In addition, a couple of studies provide quantitative evidence on the topic.

- *Caste.* Fresson (1979), who studied the functioning of irrigation associations in Senegal, shows that in some cases heterogeneity of irrigators with respect to caste contributes to disputes. She argues that while the large number of irrigators makes group organization difficult, the size of the group is less important than the homogeneity of its members for effective collective action. Fresson's argument is based on qualitative data on caste and disputes, collected through interviews from four irrigation communities in Senegal. She reports that although the irrigators in these communities were heterogeneous with respect to caste, no one caste monopolized the irrigation associations; in each community the association was representative of the whole community. However, in two of the four communities, caste played a role in disputes about water distribution. The dominant castes in these communities tried to monopolize the use of irrigation water, which resulted in violent confrontations.

- *Kinship and cultural norms.* Lowdermilk, Early, and Freeman's (1978) study provides qualitative support for the argument that the homogeneity of irrigators with respect to kinship is likely to ease collective action. They studied irrigation associations in Pakistan, where collective action is typically organized within kinship groups known as *biradaris.* The researchers report that irrigation associations in polarized communities are less effective than associations in more homogeneous settlements.

  The potential conflicts among kinship groups are reinforced in some Pakistani communities—in particular, in the northern part of the country—by the cultural concept of *izzat,* which means honor. One can acquire *izzat* only at someone else's expense, which implies that the success of one person is a threat to all the others (Merrey and Wolf 1986). This concept of honor can hinder the cooperation among irrigators as Merrey and Wolf (1986, p. 39) describe:

> Men oppose or support decisions and programs based on their perceptions of their competitors' position. For example, even though all farmers suffered the exactions of a corrupt tubewell operator, they did nothing because, informants explained, if one man or group proposed petitioning for his removal, others would oppose. This would be done not out of love for the tubewell operator but to prevent others from gaining some advantage from the issue or to pursue some long-standing grudge.

- *Ethnic and cultural background.* Lam (1998) and Lynch (1988) provide anecdotal evidence on the negative influence of ethnic and cultural heterogeneity on collective action for irrigation. According to Lam, Nepalese farmers of the same ethnic background are often unwilling to work with farmers of different ethnic backgrounds. In particular, this is common among ethnic groups with a high level of solidarity. Lynch reports that in the La Huyalla irrigation system in Peru, because of their different background and habits, immigrants caused a major disruption to the management of the local irrigation system. The fact that they lacked experience or a tradition of working in a group further hindered their assimilation into the local group.

  People with different ethnic or cultural backgrounds may sometimes have difficulties communicating with one another and acting collectively. As Denzau and North (1993) point out, since people have limited cognitive capabilities, they adopt a variety of conceptual orientations to make sense of the world. These include values, norms, experiences, and perceptions of the world that have been taught and ingrained in a community where one has grown up. Hence, people who have grown up in different communities may have different values, norms, and perceptions of the world, which may in some cases hinder communication and collective action among them.
- *Social factions.* Tang (1992) shows that in some situations, social and cultural factions can inhibit coordination among irrigators by raising the cost of organizing collective action. Unlike the previously cited studies, Tang attempts to provide more systematic evidence on the impact of social factors on collective action by systematically analyzing 47 case studies on community-managed irrigation systems. One of the issues he studied was whether there were any ethnic, cultural, clan, racial, caste, or other social differences among the irrigators that may have affected their capacity to communicate with one another effec-

tively, and how the irrigation systems had performed in these communities. Of the 47 cases analyzed, seven were reported to have factions among irrigators that had inhibited communication. In two of these seven cases, the irrigation system performed satisfactorily—that is, the system was reportedly well maintained and irrigators complied with the operational rules, but in the other five cases, the irrigation system performed poorly.[7] Tang's results, however, have to be treated cautiously because of his very small sample size.

Economic Homogeneity of Irrigators. Empirical evidence suggests that economic inequality of irrigators has a negative effect on collective action. Lam's (1998) analysis indicates that in Nepalese communities where wealth distribution among irrigators is highly uneven, irrigation systems tend to be associated with lower levels of performance. In these communities, rich farmers are frequently unwilling to cooperate with poor farmers. Rich farmers often find themselves able to provide and maintain systems without any contribution from their less wealthy neighbors. As a result, although a certain level of collective action may be organized and provided by rich farmers, such a level is likely to be less than optimal.

Tang (1992) obtains similar results, finding that "a low variance of the average annual family income among irrigators tends to be associated with a high degree of rule conformance and good maintenance." Dayton-Johnson (1998) also finds that economic inequality, measured by differences in landholding size, has a negative impact on collective action of irrigators in Mexico. Bardhan (1995) reviews case studies of community-managed irrigation systems in Asia and reports that case studies from the Indian states of Gujarat and Tamil Nadu suggest that the egalitarian nature of the community and/or small differences in farm sizes are conducive to the formation of irrigation groups.

MUTUAL TRUST AMONG IRRIGATORS. Lam's 1998 study also indicates that a high level of mutual trust among irrigators is associated with a high level of irrigation system performance: mutual trust enhances system performance by counteracting irrigators' incentives to free-ride and ignore the operational rules. Lam uses the degree to which oral promises are kept among irrigators as an indicator of trust: high credence given to oral promises indicates a high level of trust. The performance of the irrigation system is in turn measured by its physical condition, water delivery, and agricultural productivity of the community.

LEGAL RECOGNITION OF IRRIGATION ASSOCIATIONS. The social structure of the community is not the only factor influencing the emergence and sustenance of collective action. For example, for community management of irrigation to work at all, it is obvious that the policy environment needs to be conducive to community management, and farmers need to have a legal right to organize (Ostrom 1992; Subramanian, Jagannathan, and Meinzen-Dick 1997). However, as Ostrom (1992) points out, as long as the irrigation system is in an isolated location and is used primarily for subsistence agriculture, legal rights are not crucial. But in densely populated areas, where farmers grow cash crops, conflicts about water allocation are likely to escalate, and legal rights will gain importance.

If an irrigation association is not recognized as a legitimate form of organization, the leaders of the association cannot represent the interests of their members before administrative and judicial bodies. Also, the police or formal courts may not enforce any decisions made by the group, and it is difficult to hold group officials and members accountable for their actions. Legal recognition thus increases the credibility of the association not only in the eyes of outsiders, but also in the eyes of the irrigators.

COORDINATION WITH GOVERNMENT IRRIGATION BUREAUCRACY. The coordination of activities between the irrigation association at the watercourse level and the government bureaucracy at the higher levels of the irrigation system also critically influences system performance. Irrigation associations at the watercourse level do not operate in isolation; they are typically part of a larger irrigation scheme. They maintain the system and control the allocation of irrigation water within the community, while the government irrigation bureaucracy above the watercourse level is responsible for integrating the community's needs into the overall irrigation plan and ensuring that the promised water is actually delivered to the community. Farmers and government officials are thus engaged in a shared project aimed at ensuring that enough water reaches the community at the right time.

The functioning of the partnership between the irrigation association and government officials requires careful communication and coordination across different organizational levels. Freeman and Lowdermilk (1985) emphasize that this partnership requires disciplined organizations at both ends. In particular, clear understanding of the division of labor and good working relationships between officials and farmers are needed at the handover points (Wade 1994, Chambers 1988, Hunt 1989). Farmers need to be able to trust the government irrigation bureaucracy, and government officials in turn need to respect farmers' views and control of the system at the community level.

Lam's 1996 study of Taiwanese irrigation systems provides an example of a strong working relationship and good coordination between farmers and government officials. According to Lam, there are two key elements to the good relationship in Taiwan. First, government officials frequently reside in local communities where they work. They therefore automatically become part of these communities, and any wrongdoing on their part that harms the community could put them under much social pressure or ostracism. Second, officials tend to serve in particular stations for long periods of time. Because they know that they have to deal with the same group of farmers for a long time, investing time and effort into developing a good relationship with farmers makes strategic sense for these officials. The networks of trust and collaboration that are created this way span the public-private boundary and bind the state and civil society together.

WATER SCARCITY. Previous empirical studies indicate that farmers are more likely to act collectively in irrigation projects when they face sufficient water scarcity so that they are motivated to invest in organizing themselves, and when they are assured that organization could make a substantial difference in their yields. Wade (1994) studies the conditions for collective action in irrigation in the Indian state of Karnataka, collecting qualitative data from 41 villages. He finds that water scarcity and the resulting risk of crop loss lead some villages to overcome the obstacles to collective action and set up an irrigation association to manage the irrigation system. According to Wade, villages at the tail end of the irrigation system, where the water is most scarce, are most likely to have farmers acting collectively. In those instances, the potential net benefits from collective action are clear and substantial.

Uphoff, Wickramasinghe, and Wijayaratna (1990) further refine these results and show that farmers are willing to manage and maintain irrigation systems collectively where the water supply is relatively scarce rather than absolutely scarce or abundant. Their results are based on quantitative analysis of survey data gathered from 500 farmers in the Gal Oya irrigation scheme in Sri Lanka. According to Uphoff, Wickramasinghe, and Wijayaratna, there is an inverted-U relationship between water scarcity and returns to organization. Specifically, where water is abundant—typically at the head end of the irrigation system—access to water is not a problem, and thus net benefits from collective action are minimal. Where water is absolutely scarce—typically at the tail-end of the system—even collective action of farmers cannot alleviate the water shortage, and hence the net benefits from organization are low. In the middle range of the irrigation system, by contrast, water is relatively scarce, and potential net benefits from collective action are high.

Summary

Available case study and quantitative evidence indicates that community management built on social networks, norms, and interaction among irrigators often improves the performance of irrigation systems. However, collective action and cooperation among irrigators are not always forthcoming and are determined by social capital and other factors.

Different dimensions of social capital have been shown to affect the effectiveness of collective action and collective decisionmaking at the community level. Empirical evidence indicates that economic and social homogeneity of irrigators with respect to caste, kinship, and ethnic and cultural background aids collective action. This is achieved through increasing the number of norms and social ties that irrigators can draw upon in building cooperation. Also, mutual trust among irrigators is shown to promote collective action by counteracting irrigators' incentives to free-ride and ignore the operational rules.

However, whether or not collective action can be expected to emerge at all depends heavily on factors other than the social structure. For example, the relative degree of water scarcity in a community is shown to affect the returns to, and thus the emergence of, collective action: households in communities with relatively scarce water supply have the highest expected returns and thus the strongest incentives to act collectively, while households in communities with absolutely scarce or abundant water supply have very low expected returns to collective action and thus weak incentives to cooperate.

Since irrigation associations are typically part of a larger irrigation scheme—they manage the system within the community, while the government is handling the system above the watercourse level—actions of the government also influence the performance of community management and irrigation systems. Coordination of activities between the government and community is critical. A clear understanding of the division of labor and good working relationships between officials and farmers are needed at the handover points for the system to work properly.

Social Capital and Rural Drinking Water Delivery

The delivery of rural drinking water is another aspect of rural water services where donors have begun to advocate a community-based approach. In rural drinking water delivery, this approach adopts a demand-responsive focus on what users want and what they can afford (Briscoe and Ferranti 1988). Failure of governments to provide adequate levels of safe drinking water to rural villages and to maintain the existing water systems—partly due to limited funds, imperfect information about demand, and poor governance—has led to this changed thinking about water delivery.[8] The community-based approach to rural water delivery is based on the premise that water is an economic good that has a value and that it should be managed at the lowest appropriate level with users involved in the planning and implementation of projects (Garn 1998, Sara and Katz 1998). This approach recognizes that knowledge, skills, and time of villagers can be productively harnessed to expand the pool of resources available for water delivery, and thereby also help to ensure that the services provided match the demand.

Community-based drinking water delivery typically calls for a joint effort by community members and government in service design and construction (Watson and Jagannathan 1995). Community members are expected to participate in the design process; in particular, to choose collectively the type and level of service based on their willingness to pay. In addition, communities are typically asked to contribute cash or labor to construction and to take care of the operation and maintenance of the system collectively. Community members are also expected to form a water user group to coordinate the management of the system in the community.

Narayan (1995) shows that user participation in rural water projects indeed contributes significantly to project effectiveness. She analyzed data from 121 case studies of rural water supply projects in different developing countries. Like Tang (1992) and Lam (1998), Narayan converted the qualitative information in these case studies into quantitative data using structured coding forms, and then carried out empirical analysis of the data. She used several different measures of participation, differentiating between options where water users were merely provided information about the project and where users were empowered to make decisions. The measures also reflected whether the users participated in all stages of the project (design, construction, operation, and maintenance). Narayan's analysis indicates that user participation significantly increases the overall economic benefits from water systems, the percentages of target population reached by water systems, and the environmental benefits from these systems. While Narayan (1995) does not establish causality from participation to water system performance, work by Isham, Narayan, and Pritchett (1995) presents evidence on the causal link.

Sara and Katz (1998) obtain similar results: sustainability of water systems is higher in communities where a demand-responsive approach is employed and water users participate in system design than in those communities that do not follow a demand-responsive approach. Specifically, Sara and Katz find that the sustainability of water services is higher in communities where household members make informed choices about whether to build a system, the type of system to be built, and the level of service to be provided. These results are based on an econometric analysis of quantitative data from six community-based rural water projects in Benin, Bolivia, Honduras, Indonesia, Pakistan, and Uganda. In total, 125 rural communities in these countries were included in the study. Quantitative data were collected through household and water committee surveys, and technical assessments of water systems. These data were supplemented by qualitative data gathered during the surveys.

However, the performance of rural water projects that use the community-based approach varies a great deal. Water systems perform well in some communities but have failed in others. One reason for the varied performance is that users and government officials do not always cooperate in different stages of the project as expected. Government officials do not always involve users in the system design, even when required to, or pay attention to the user demand and preferences for the system. They may also fail to monitor the construction of the system. Since contributing to system management has a cost, users also often fail to participate in the design process, contribute labor or cash to construction, or carry out the assigned operation and maintenance tasks without additional incentives, even if they had initially agreed to do so. As in the case of irrigation, each water user has an incentive to free-ride on others' efforts and not to do his or her share of system management. In other words, users often fail to build a functioning network that provides benefits to all participants. The desire to have a working water system is not always enough to sustain the group effort.

Factors for Success

In the existing literature on community-based rural water delivery, several factors have been identified that influence the incentives of users to act collectively and the effectiveness of this collective action as reflected by the performance of water systems. Table A3.2 summarizes selected factors that have been shown to influence the performance of community management.

The list in table A3.2 is by no means exhaustive. Since this paper focuses on social capital, other factors have been aggregated into a few categories such as "coordination with government." Not surprisingly, many of the factors listed in the table are the same as those that influence the performance of community-managed irrigation systems. Each of the above-mentioned factors is discussed in more detail below.

SOCIAL HOMOGENEITY OF WATER USERS. Watson and others (1997) present isolated case study evidence on how social heterogeneity of water users may hinder collective action. They tell a story of a village in Pakistan made up of two social groups: people displaced by the construction of a major dam, and immigrants from the Indian portion of Kashmir. In 1980 the government and villagers jointly constructed the village water system. A water committee consisting of representatives from both groups

Table A3.2 Community-Based Rural Drinking Water Delivery: Selected Factors Influencing Performance of Community Management

Factor	Evidence
Social homogeneity of water users	Watson and others (1997)
Operational rules of water user groups	Isham and Kähkönen (1998b), Sara and Katz (1998)
Prior organization of water users	Narayan (1995)
Participation of users in other community groups	Isham and Kähkönen (1998b)
Coordination with government	Isham and Kähkönen (1998b), Sara and Katz (1998)
Legal recognition of water user groups	Watson and others (1997)
Skills and knowledge of users	Isham and Kähkönen (1998b), Rondinelli (1991), Sara and Katz (1998)
Appropriate technology and access to spare parts	Rondinelli (1991)

was formed to manage the system. Management of the system through this committee, however, failed. In a few years, the social and political conflicts between the two groups had reached such a level that the water committee dissolved, and management of the system had to be handed back to the government.

OPERATIONAL RULES OF WATER USER GROUPS. As in the case of irrigation, the existence and effectiveness of rules that govern the operation, use, and maintenance of a water system within a community influence the effectiveness of collective action by guiding interaction among users. In particular, rules about decisionmaking, monitoring, and sanctions are seen as critical for the effectiveness of community management. These rules, if properly implemented and enforced, provide households with an incentive to participate in the design process, contribute the required inputs to construction, and operate and maintain the system together with other community members.

Isham and Kähkönen (1998a,b) show that operational rules about community participation in the design process and the existence of arrangements for monitoring household contributions to the management of the system are, in particular, positively associated with the success of collective action and performance of the water system. Isham and Kähkönen studied the performance of three community-based rural water projects in Sri Lanka and India and collected quantitative and qualitative data on the performance and impact of water systems from 50 Sri Lankan and Indian communities served by these projects. The data reveal that in communities where household contributions to construction, operation, and maintenance of the system are monitored, community management is more successful and systems perform better than in those communities where contributions are not monitored. Also, the results indicate that when users participate in designing the system and make the final decision about the type of a system to build, they are more satisfied with the system, which leads to better performance. The results of Sara and Katz (1998) complement these findings. Their analysis indicates that it is important to craft rules that allow *all* users to participate in decisionmaking. They find that unless *all* water users are given a chance to express their preferences about the system directly, community representatives often fail to consider the demands of certain segments of the population, such as women or the poor.

PRIOR ORGANIZATION OF WATER USERS. Narayan (1995) shows econometrically that the extent to which water users are organized prior to the project is positively associated with user participation in system management. If users are already organized, there is a social basis for cooperation; users already know each other through existing networks and have a tradition of working together. In other words, preexisting social capital promotes collective action.

PARTICIPATION OF USERS IN OTHER COMMUNITY GROUPS. Isham and Kähkönen (1998b) provide further and more extensive empirical evidence on the importance of preexisting social capital in the form of other community groups for the success of collective action and performance of water systems. Such preexisting social capital promotes the participation of water users in system management by reducing the cost of collective action. During the design phase, the collective demand for the type of system and level of service is more likely to be expressed in communities where community members are accustomed to working together, where leaders are accountable, and where all stakeholders have a voice. During the construction and the operation and maintenance phases, water user groups are more likely to function well in communities that already have cohesive community groups and a tradition of civic activities. Communities that have strong social ties often work well together because they share values about mutual assistance. In tightly networked communities, the formal and informal social ties among people may constrain free-riding and provide incentives for water users to hold to their commitments. For example, when a user does something that violates the community norms, that person may be punished through gossip and ostracism.

Isham and Kähkönen use three different indicators of social capital to test these conjectures. The first indicator is the number of community groups or associations that a household belongs to. The second one is an index that captures the characteristics of these community groups, including the heterogeneity of group members by religion, gender, and occupation; decisionmaking mechanisms within the group; and members' assessment of the effectiveness of group functioning. In an attempt to capture the quantity and quality of community groups, a third indicator, a "social capital index," combines the number of groups and their characteristics.[9] The analysis reveals that all three indicators of social capital are positively associated with users' participation in the design process and construction monitoring. In other words, the greater the number of community groups that households belong to and the more heterogeneous and well-functioning these groups are, the more likely the water users are to hold to their commitments, all of which results in better water system performance.

This last result regarding the group heterogeneity may at first seem inconsistent with the literature that emphasizes the importance of group homogeneity. However, this is not necessarily the case.[10] The very existence of community groups with a heterogeneous membership indicates that there are unlikely to be any major social factions in the community that could hinder collective action. Water users of different genders, religions, occupations, and backgrounds are accustomed to working together—social heterogeneity does not hinder communication. Unfortunately, Isham and Kähkönen do not test separately the impact of community heterogeneity on household participation in system management.

COORDINATION WITH GOVERNMENT. Coordination of activities within the community is not enough to ensure effective community management of rural drinking water systems; coordination of activities between government agencies and water user groups at the community level is also needed. For the approach to work, both parties, not only the community, have to cooperate and honor their commitments to carry out their assigned tasks.[11] Above all, to ensure that the system matches the demand, the government must involve community members in system design, construction, and management as designed and then coordinate the tasks between the government and community.

However, that does not always happen. Sara and Katz (1998) find that government agencies are often unresponsive to communities' needs and do not carry out their assigned tasks properly. In several of the six projects Sara and Katz studied, private contractors were used for construction. Hiring and monitoring the work of these contractors was the responsibility of the government, but in some countries, lack of accountability meant that government officials failed to monitor the work, which led to substandard construction quality and delays in implementation. Communities in turn had no way to ensure that contractors or government agencies honored the choices the communities had made, or to hold the project staff accountable for a poorly constructed or incomplete system. This eroded community members' trust in government, hampered further collaboration, and diminished users' incentives to manage the system.

Brown and Pollard (1998), who studied the sustainability of water systems in Indonesia, find that in several cases, users were excluded from the design phase. Further, even when government officials involved community members in system design, the final design decision often ignored the expressed preferences of users.

How effectively, if at all, the government carries out its tasks depends on the structure and operational rules within the government (Isham and Kähkönen 1998a,b). These rules govern the behavior of government officials by providing them with incentives to perform their assigned tasks. They include, for example, rules about monitoring and sanctions. Isham and Kähkönen provide some qualitative case study evidence on the importance of these rules but no quantitative evidence on the kinds of rules that are most critical for system performance.

LEGAL RECOGNITION OF WATER USER GROUPS. As in the case of irrigation, water user groups need to be recognized as legal entities by the government to be fully effective. For example, in Bolivia, water user groups that had existed for over a year became effective organizations only after the government had recognized them legally. Among other things, the legalization permitted them to open bank accounts. Only at that point did community members trust the organizations enough to make their required financial contributions for the system's management (Watson and others 1997). In other words, without government backing, water user groups sometimes have difficulties enforcing the operational rules; the threat of sanctions is not credible. If the group, however, is recognized as a legal entity, police and other judicial bodies can be used to enforce its decisions if and when needed. This threat of governmental coercion promotes compliance with the rules as well as accountability among group leaders.

SKILLS AND KNOWLEDGE OF USERS. In addition to all the factors mentioned above, the effectiveness of community management depends critically on the skills of community members for operating and maintaining the water system. Even a community with a high demand for water and willingness to manage the system may lack the capacity to operate and maintain the system on its own. In Tanzania, for example, community management failed in many villages because the users did not know how to maintain and repair the systems—no operation and maintenance manuals or training in basic system maintenance and repair was provided to them (Rondinelli 1991).

Sara and Katz (1998) show quantitatively that training of household members and water committees in system operation and maintenance improves system sustainability by building the capacity and commitment to maintain it. Hygiene education is also positively associated with the willingness to maintain the system, according to Sara and Katz (1998). People in rural communities often do not recognize that some of their diseases are caused by water they consume. Educating users about the health benefits of safe water handling, hygiene practices, and protection of the water source may affect how people value their water source and increase their willingness to maintain the system. Isham and Kähkönen (1998b) show that hygiene training also enhances the health impact of rural water projects.

APPROPRIATE TECHNOLOGY AND ACCESS TO SPARE PARTS. Even the best-organized and trained community management efforts will fail if the project does not have the appropriate technology. One of the lessons from water supply projects during the 1960s and 1970s was that community management in developing countries was difficult or impossible with the pumps and equipment imported from industrial countries (Rondinelli 1991). Most of these pumps were made of materials that broke down easily in the climates and under the conditions of use in developing countries. Spare parts were difficult to obtain in a timely manner, and replacements were costly. Hence, using appropriate technology and developing a reliable system for obtaining spare parts are essential conditions for successful community management.

Summary

The empirical evidence indicates that the community-based approach can enhance the performance of rural drinking water systems. However, the success of collective action among community members is not automatic.

How effectively, if at all, community members work together to manage the system depends partly on existing social capital in the community. The empirical evidence suggests that the existence of other, non-water-related networks and associations in a community aids collective action for water delivery. In those instances, households are accustomed to working together, and formal and informal ties among people constrain free-riding and provide incentives for households to participate in system management as designed. Evidence also indicates that the existence of social capital in this form aids the crafting and enforcement of operational rules that govern the use, operation, and maintenance of the water system in the community.

Social capital may promote collective action and coordination within the community, but it does not ensure that the water system performs well. Social capital is only one of several factors that influence the effectiveness of community management and performance of water systems. For example, community-based water services are typically joint efforts of the government and community and may perform poorly if the government fails to fulfill its obligations or if the coordination between communal and governmental ranks is poor. Collective action is fruitless if users do not possess the skills to operate and maintain the system. Finally, all actions may be perfectly coordinated and users possess the needed skills to manage the system, but without appropriate technology and access to spare parts, even the best-organized and -trained community management efforts will fail.

Social Capital and Urban Sanitation

Inadequate sanitation is one of the major environmental health problems facing poor urban residents of developing countries. Despite heavy investments in the sector in the 1980s, the number of urban people without access to sanitation increased by about 70 million during that decade (Serageldin 1995). In total, about 37 percent of the urban population in developing countries still lacks access to adequate sanitation (Wright 1997). The majority of these people are poor and live in squatter settlements, illegal subdivisions, and working-class neighborhoods. Government agencies that work in urban water and sanitation tend to concentrate their activities in large cities and focus primarily on middle- and upper-income neighborhoods, leaving the poor neighborhoods unserved (Watson and Jagannathan 1995). As a result, the poor resort to disposing wastes in gullies along footpaths or digging pit latrines that quickly fill and contaminate the groundwater. These practices obviously pose a major public health hazard.

One reason that poor neighborhoods often do not have public sanitation is that conventional urban sanitation systems with high design standards are prohibitively expensive and technically difficult to install in most poor neighborhoods. These neighborhoods are commonly located on the worst urban land far away from sewer trunk lines, and they have narrow streets and irregular layouts. All these factors, by raising the cost of construction, dampen government's interest in making work in poor neighborhoods a priority. Conventional systems that were built in poor neighborhoods often suffered from a number of problems, including low connection rates, poor construction work, poor operation and maintenance, and poor financial sustainability (Watson 1995).

However, in some countries, low-cost urban sanitation systems that require users to participate in system management have been introduced in the past two decades. In these countries, the number of housing units connected to the low-cost sanitation systems has been growing steadily throughout the 1980s (Watson 1995). The best known of these systems are the condominial system in Brazil and the Orangi Pilot Project in Pakistan.

In the early 1980s, Brazilian engineers developed a condominial system—a low-cost waterborne sanitation system—that addresses many of the technical and financial barriers to urban sanitation in poor neighborhoods. It is called a condominial system because it resembles a system that might be designed for a co-owned apartment building. Mejia (1996, p. 32) describes the underlying rationale of the system as follows:

> At...bottom...was the understanding that the water company could not deal directly with each family in a "helter-skelter" community.... Instead, families had to band together to negotiate and commit to operate and maintain the service to a group of some twenty to fifty *barracos* (homes). This way of generating and supporting communal inter-dependence helped work out affordable solutions: people could afford what they wanted and the water company would recover its capital and operating costs.

Brazil's condominial system differs from the conventional sanitation system in two ways: it uses innovative, low-cost engineering designs; and it requires residents to participate in managing the system. The low-cost designs, while making the systems affordable to the poor, demand more maintenance, which is one reason user participation is required.

Instead of designing sanitation systems with cast-iron pipes sunk deep under urban streets at high per-household cost, condominial systems typically use feeder lines with much smaller pipes that can run through urban blocks either in the backyards, front yards, or sidewalks of those being served. By placing these lines away from heavy traffic, the cost of constructing the feeder section is 50 to 80 percent lower than that of con-ventional designs (Watson 1995). The feeder lines are then connected to larger trunk lines that are constructed under urban streets according to the regular engineering standards and that lead to treatment plants (Ostrom 1996).

The project staff involves residents in the project from the beginning, organizing a series of neighborhood meetings where an overview of the process and the benefits and costs of a condominial system are present-ed. In these meetings, the choices that residents will have to make and the implications these decisions will have on the cost and maintenance of the system are discussed in detail. In general, residents are expected to main-tain the feeder lines as a group, while the government takes care of the trunk line and treatment facilities.

The project goes forward only if residents as a group decide they want it. This ensures that the system matches user demand and that the connec-tion rate is high. If they agree to have a system, residents collectively need to decide about the location and layout of feeder lines at the block level; dif-ferent layouts have a different cost per household. All residents together need to decide whether they will dig the feeder lines themselves or hire a private contractor for the work. Finally, before construction begins, all res-idents need to sign a formal petition requesting a condominial system and committing themselves to the payment of the agreed-upon connection fee and tariff, and to the operations and maintenance of the system.

Usually, the first few blocks that construct a condominial system serve as demonstration projects in the neighborhood; other blocks can see the results in practice and compare the functioning of different layouts. Typically, once the first few blocks have been completed, the construction of systems rapidly spreads to other blocks.

The Orangi Pilot Project in Karachi has supported similar efforts with low-cost (shallow and small-bore) sewers and community involvement in system management. The project has empowered the users to plan, construct, and maintain their own latrines (Wright 1997).

Overall, the results of condominial systems in Brazil and Pakistan have been impressive in terms of improved sanitation coverage. More than 75,000 condominial connections were built in Brazil in 1980–90, serv-ing about 370,000 residents (Watson 1995). The Orangi Pilot Project had a substantial demonstration effect: although it helped only about 15 per-cent of Karachi residents to build condominial sewers, another 25 percent later built sewers on their own, simply copying what they had learned from their neighbors (Watson 1995). Not surprisingly, other developing countries have also adopted condominial systems. Similar systems have been constructed, for example, in Kenya, Indonesia, and Paraguay (Watson and Jagannathan 1995).

The performance of these condominial systems has been mixed, however. Studies point to difficulties in all stages of design, construction, and maintenance. They are plagued by difficulties similar to those affecting community-managed irrigation and drinking water projects, namely, sustenance of collective action among residents, actions or inaction of the public agency, and coordination of activities between residents and the public agency (Ostrom 1996, Watson 1995).

Cooperation among residents is a major problem in many condominial systems and, as a result, collective maintenance of feeder lines often fails (Watson 1995). In condominial systems, each household is responsible for removing any blockages in the feeder line on its own property. However, in collective lines, the responsibilities of each household can sometimes be opaque. Since blockage removal is a dirty and unpleasant task, each resident has an incentive not to do the work but wait for others to act.

Maintenance of feeder lines may also falter where residents lack the skills to maintain the system or where the neighborhood has a high turnover rate of residents. According to Watson (1995), maintenance training is not typically provided in all neighborhoods as part of the project. Further, in neighborhoods where resident turnover is high, new residents are not always aware of the network's existence, or they may not be advised properly about their responsibilities for its operation and maintenance. Also, in transitional neighborhoods, shared communal norms and networks that could aid collective action among residents are likely to be weak or missing.

Government officials often shirk their duties as well. They do not always involve residents in the planning. As with conventional systems, routine maintenance of trunk lines is often inadequate (Watson 1995). This may lead to a complete blockage of feeder lines, as flow velocities in upstream sections slowly decrease and suspended solids settle and build up. However, the most common cause of poor performance of condominial systems is the substandard quality of construction. The reason for the poor quality is rarely a design flaw, but rather insufficient supervision during construction and a failure to remedy the problem once it is detected.

In sum, the community-based approach that uses low-cost technologies for urban sanitation has produced impressive results. However, as in the case of irrigation and rural drinking water delivery, ensuring cooperation among residents is a major challenge. The same factors that influence collective action in rural water delivery are likely to affect the outcome of collective action in urban sanitation, although no studies on these topics seem to have been conducted yet.

Conclusions

This annex has analyzed the role of social capital in community-based irrigation, rural drinking water, and urban sanitation delivery by reviewing the literature on the topic. Existing empirical evidence indicates that community management that builds on social networks, norms, and interaction among users often improves the performance of water and sanitation systems. Several factors, including social capital, have been shown to influence the effectiveness of community management.

How effectively users manage the system as a group has been shown to depend partly on social capital in the community. While the establishment of a functioning user group for water and sanitation management creates social capital, the organization of that group is aided by preexisting social networks, norms, trust, and interaction among neighbors. Specifically, the empirical evidence indicates that the existence of other networks and associations in a community (that is, groups unrelated to water and sanitation) as well as mutual trust among users aid collective action. In those instances, users are accustomed to working together, and the resulting formal and informal ties among people constrain free-riding and provide incentives for users to participate in system management. In addition, economic and social homogeneity of irrigators with respect to caste, kinship, and ethnic and cultural background promotes collective action by increasing the number of norms and social ties that users can draw upon in building cooperation. Evidence indicates that existence of social capital in this form aids the crafting and enforcement of operational rules that govern the use, operation, and maintenance of the water or sanitation system in a community.

Social capital may promote collective action and coordination within the community, but social capital alone by no means ensures that the water or sanitation system performs well. Other factors also influence the effectiveness of community management. Whether collective action of users can be expected to emerge at all depends heavily on factors other than the social structure of the community. For example, the relative degree of water scarcity in a community is shown to affect the expected net returns to, and thus the emergence of, collective action. Since community-based water and sanitation delivery is typically a joint effort of the government and community, with both parties contributing complementary inputs into the process, the system's performance depends also on actions of the government and coordination of communal and governmental tasks. Further, community management can only work if users possess the skills and knowledge to operate and maintain the system. Finally, the importance of using appropriate technology and having access to spare parts must be recognized.

Notes

1. Since water and sanitation systems have certain technological and economic characteristics that lead to their underprovision in markets, they have traditionally been viewed as a government responsibility. For a discussion on the evolution of approaches to water and sanitation delivery over time, see Black (1998).

2. There are several definitions and interpretations of social capital in the literature. See, for example, Coleman (1988), Grootaert (1998a), and Putnam (1993).

3. Irrigation services are common pool goods, rival, and nonexcludable (Ostrom 1992). Based on the presence or absence of rivalry and excludability, goods and services can be classified into four categories: private, public, toll, and common pool goods. See Ostrom, Gardner, and Walker (1994) and Picciotto (1997) for a more detailed discussion.

4. These groups are sometimes called councils, committees, or water user groups. In this annex, the term "irrigation associations" is used to refer to user groups at the watercourse level.

5. Ostrom (1990, 1992) differentiates between operational, collective-choice, and constitutional choice rules. For simplicity, they are combined here into one category.

6. Since some of the results are also based on very small samples, they need to be treated with caution.

7. Interestingly, all five cases of poor system performance were from India or Pakistan. This may be due to the fact that almost all complex irrigation systems in the sample were from these countries. However, it may also reflect the fact that in many parts of these countries, farmers are divided into various caste or kinship groups (Tang 1992). Although these divisions may not prohibit cooperation among farmers, they may make communication among farmers difficult and thereby raise the cost of collective action.

8. Briscoe and Garn (1995) and Garn (1998) review the poor performance of the traditional top-down approach and the economic underpinnings of the community-based approach.

9. The indicator was based on the "Putnam index" in Narayan and Pritchett (1997).

10. The empirical evidence on the impact of social heterogeneity on group functioning in general is also mixed. See, for example, Grootaert (1998b).

11. Government provides technical knowledge and partial funding, while users provide labor and other production inputs.

References

Ascher, William, and Robert Healy. 1990. *Natural Resource Policy Making in Developing Countries*. Durham, N.C.: Duke University Press.

Asian Development Bank. 1973. *Proceedings of Regional Workshop on Irrigation Water Management*. Manila: Asian Development Bank.

Bardhan, Pranab. 1995. "Rational Fools and Cooperation in a Poor Hydraulic Economy." In Kaushik Basu, Prasanta Pattanaik, and Kotaro Suzumura, eds., *Choice, Welfare, and Development: A Festschrift in Honour of Amartya K. Sen*. Oxford, U.K.: Oxford University Press.

Black, Maggie. 1998. "Learning What Works: A 20 Year Retrospective View on International Water and Sanitation Cooperation." World Bank, UNDP-World Bank Water and Sanitation Program, Washington, D.C. Processed.

Briscoe, John, and David Ferranti. 1988. "Water for Rural Communities: Helping People Help Themselves." Report 11204. World Bank, Water Supply and Sanitation Sector, Washington, D.C.

Briscoe, John, and Harvey Garn. 1995. "Financing Water Supply and Sanitation under Agenda 21." *Natural Resources Forum* 19 (1): 59–70.

Brown, Gillian, and Richard Pollard. 1998. "Responding to Demand: Two Approaches from Indonesia." World Bank, Water Supply and Sanitation Sector, Washington, D.C. Processed.

Cernea, Michael. 1987. "Farmer Organization and Institution Building for Sustainable Development." *Regional Development Dialogue* 8 (2): 1–24.

Chambers, Robert. 1980. "Basic Concepts in the Organization of Irrigation." In E. Walter Coward, ed., *Irrigation and Agricultural Development in Asia: Perspectives from Social Sciences*. Ithaca, N.Y.: Cornell University Press.

———. 1988. *Managing Canal Irrigation: Practical Analysis from South Asia*. Cambridge, U.K.: Cambridge University Press.

Coleman, James. 1988. "Social Capital in the Creation of Human Capital." *American Journal of Sociology* 94 (Supplement): S95–S120.

Dayton-Johnson, Jeff. 1998. "Rules, Inequality, and Collective Action in Poor Hydraulic Economies: A Model with Evidence from Mexico." University of California, Department of Economics, Berkeley, Calif. Processed.

Denzau, Arthur, and Douglass North. 1993. "Shared Mental Models: Ideologies and Institutions." Working Paper. Washington University, Center for the Study of Political Economy, St. Louis, Mo.

Esman, Milton, and Norman Uphoff. 1984. *Local Organizations: Intermediaries in Rural Development.* Ithaca, N.Y.: Cornell University Press.

Freeman, David, and Max Lowdermilk. 1985. "Middle-Level Organizational Linkages in Irrigation Projects." In Michael Cernea, ed., *Putting People First: Sociological Variables in Rural Development.* Oxford, U.K.: Oxford University Press.

Fresson, Silvianne. 1979. "Public Participation in Village-Level Irrigation Perimeters in the Matam Region of Senegal." In D. Miller, ed., *Self-Help and Popular Participation in Rural Water Systems.* Paris: Organisation for Economic Co-operation and Development, Development Center.

Garn, Harvey. 1998. "Managing Water as an Economic Good." In *Proceedings of the Community Water Supply and Sanitation Conference*, pp. 7-10. Washington, D.C.: World Bank.

Grootaert, Christiaan. 1998a. "Social Capital: The Missing Link?" Social Capital Initiative Working Paper 3. World Bank, Social Development Department, Washington, D.C.

————. 1998b. "Social Capital, Household Welfare, and Poverty in Indonesia." Local Level Institutions Working Paper 6. World Bank, Social Development Department, Washington, D.C.

Hardin, Garrett. 1968. "The Tragedy of Commons." *Science* 162: 1243–48.

Hardin, Russell. 1982. *Collective Action.* Baltimore, Md.: Johns Hopkins University Press.

Hunt, Robert. 1989. "Appropriate Social Organization? Water User Associations in Bureaucratic Canal Irrigation Systems." *Human Organization* 48 (1): 79–90.

Isham, Jonathan, Deepa Narayan, and Lant Pritchett. 1995. "Does Participation Improve Performance? Establishing Causality with Subjective Data." *World Bank Economic Review* 9 (2): 175–200.

Isham, Jonathan, and Satu Kähkönen. 1998a. "Improving the Delivery of Water and Sanitation: A Model of Coproduction of Infrastructure Services." IRIS (Center for Institutional Reform and the Informal Sector) Working Paper 210. University of Maryland, College Park, Md.

————. 1998b. "The Institutional Determinants of the Impact of Community-Based Water Services: Evidence from Sri Lanka and India." Background paper for the Operations Evaluation Department, World Bank, Washington, D.C. Processed.

Korten, David. 1986. *Community Management: Asian Experience and Perspectives.* West Hartford, Conn.: Kumarian Press.

Lam, Wai Fung. 1996. "Institutional Design of Public Agencies and Coproduction: A Study of Irrigation Associations in Taiwan." *World Development* 24 (6): 1039–54.

————. 1998. *Governing Irrigation Systems in Nepal: Institutions, Infrastructure, and Collective Action.* San Francisco: ICS Press.

Lowdermilk, Max, A. C. Early, and D. M. Freeman. 1978. "Irrigation Water Management in Pakistan: Constraints and Farmer Responses." Technical Report No. 4, Vol. 4. Water Center of Colorado State University, Fort Collins, Colo.

Lynch, Barbara D. 1988. "Local Resource Mobilization and Peruvian Government Intervention in Small Highland Irrigation Systems." Cornell University, Department of City and Regional Planning, Ithaca, N.Y. Processed.

Maass, Arthur, and Raymond L. Anderson. 1986. *...and the Desert Shall Rejoice: Conflict, Growth and Justice in Arid Environments.* Malabar, Fla.: Robert E. Krieger.

Mejia, Abel. 1996. "Brazil: Municipalities and Low-Income Sanitation." In *The World Bank Participation Sourcebook.* Washington, D.C.

Merrey, Douglas, and James M. Wolf. 1986. "Irrigation Management in Pakistan: Four Papers." Research Paper 4. International Irrigation Management Institute, Colombo, Sri Lanka.

Narayan, Deepa. 1995. "The Contribution of People's Participation: Evidence from 121 Rural Water Supply Projects." Environmentally Sustainable Development Occasional Paper Series 1. World Bank, Washington, D.C.

Narayan, Deepa, and Lant Pritchett. 1997. "Cents and Sociability: Income and Social Capital in Rural Tanzania." Policy Research Paper 1796. World Bank, Washington, D.C.

Olson, Mancur. 1965. *The Logic of Collective Action: Public Goods and the Theory of Groups.* Cambridge, Mass.: Harvard University Press.

Ostrom, Elinor. 1990. *Governing the Commons: The Evolution of Institutions for Collective Action.* New York: Cambridge University Press.

————. 1992. *Crafting Institutions for Self-Governing Irrigation Systems.* San Francisco: ICS Press.

————. 1996. "Crossing the Great Divide: Coproduction, Synergy, and Development." *World Development* 24 (6): 1073–87.

Ostrom, Elinor, Roy Gardner, and James Walker. 1994. *Rules, Games, and Common-Pool Resources.* Ann Arbor: University of Michigan Press.

Ostrom, Elinor, Larry Schroeder, and Susan Wynne. 1993. *Institutional Incentives and Sustainable Development: Infrastructure Policies in Perspective.* Boulder, Colo.: Westview Press.

Picciotto, Robert. 1997. "Putting Institutional Economics to Work: From Participation to Governance." In Christopher Clague, ed., *Institutions and Economic Development: Growth and Governance in Less-Developed and Post-Socialist Countries."* Baltimore, Md.: Johns Hopkins University Press.

Putnam, Robert D. 1993. "The Prosperous Community—Social Capital and Public Life." *The American Prospect* 13: 35–42.

Rondinelli, Dennis. 1991. "Decentralizing Water Supply Services in Developing Countries: Factors Affecting the Success of Community Management." *Public Administration and Development* 11: 415–30.

Sara, Jennifer, and Travis Katz. 1998. "Making Rural Water Sustainable: Report on the Impact of Project Rules." World Bank, UNDP-World Bank Water and Sanitation Program, Washington, D.C.

Sandler, Todd. 1992. *Collective Action.* Ann Arbor: University of Michigan Press.

Serageldin, Ismail. 1995. *Toward Sustainable Management of Water Resources.* Washington, D.C.: World Bank.

Singleton, Sara, and Michael Taylor. 1992. "Common Property, Collective Action, and Community." *Journal of Theoretical Politics* 4 (3): 309–24.

Subramanian, Ashok, Vijay Jagannathan, and Ruth Meinzen-Dick. 1997. "User Organizations for Sustainable Water Services." Technical Paper 354. World Bank, Washington, D.C.

Tang, Shui Yan. 1992. *Institutions and Collective Action: Self-Governance in Irrigation.* San Francisco: ICS Press.

Uphoff, Norman. 2000. "Understanding Social Capital: Learning from the Analysis and Experience of Participation." In Partha Dasgupta and Ismail Serageldin, eds., *Social Capital: A Multifaceted Perspective.* Washington, D.C.: World Bank.

Uphoff, Norman, M. L. Wickramasinghe, and C. M. Wijayaratna. 1990. "Optimum Participation in Irrigation Management: Issues and Evidence from Sri Lanka." *Human Organization* 49 (1): 26–40.

Wade, Robert. 1994. *Village Republics: Economic Conditions for Collective Action in South India.* San Francisco: ICS Press.

Watson, Gabrielle. 1995. "Good Sewers Cheap? Agency-Customer Interaction in Low-Cost Urban Sanitation in Brazil." In *Water and Sanitation Currents.* UNDP-World Bank Water and Sanitation Program, World Bank, Washington, D.C.

Watson, Gabrielle, and Vijay Jagannathan. 1995. "Participation in Water and Sanitation." Participation Series Paper 2. World Bank, Environment Department, Washington, D.C.

Watson, Gabrielle, Vijay Jagannathan, Richard Gelting, and Hugo Beteta. 1997. "Water and Sanitation Associations: Review and Best Practices." In Ashok Subramanian, Vijay Jagannathan, and Ruth Meinzen-Dick, "User Organizations for Sustainable Water Services." Technical paper 354. World Bank, Washington, D.C.

Wright, Albert. 1997. "Toward a Strategic Sanitation Approach: Improving the Sustainability of Urban Sanitation in Developing Countries." World Bank, UNDP-World Bank Sanitation Program, Washington, D.C. Processed.

Index